D1598804

"Sarah Birnbach's lovely memoir is a thoughtful meditation on sacrifice, memory, gender roles, and of course—grief."
—**A.J. Jacobs, author of** *The Year of Living Biblically*

"*A Daughter's Kaddish* is a heartwarming, sometimes heart-wrenching, and always honest story of Sarah Birnbach's sacred year of mourning after her beloved father's death. By melding her personal memoir with a thoughtful Jewish ritual narrative, Birnbach highlights her burgeoning identity and commitment as an observant Conservative Jew, a feminist, and a devoted member of her twice-daily minyan at her own shul. This book stands as a beautiful tribute to her father; his memory will survive as a blessing forever upon all who read it."
—**Rabbi Mindy Avra Portnoy, rabbi emerita, Temple Sinai, Washington, DC, and author of** *A Tale of Two Seders*

"In her debut memoir, Sarah Birnbach tells the story of her transformative, eleven-month journey to redeem her father's soul. By committing to the twice-daily recitation of the Kaddish, she develops deep relationships with fellow mourners near and far and with God. Birnbach's love letter to her father is a meditation on grief and the power of a spiritual practice to transcend our most painful losses."
—**Michelle Brafman, author of** *Washing the Dead*

"Sarah Birnbach has made a major contribution to the literature of bereavement. She weaves together her personal story, grief, and spiritual development into a work that will move readers of diverse backgrounds and experiences."
—**Kate Thompson, author of** *Therapeutic Journal Writing*

"A brave and beautifully crafted memoir of love, loss, and enduring faith, rich with emotionally resonant stories. As we follow Birnbach's spiritual transformation, we come to a deeper understanding of unconditional love in action and the power of devotion. *A Daughter's Kaddish* is enlightening, enlivening, and profoundly inspiring."
—**Kathleen Adams, LPC, founder/director, Center for Journal Therapy, and coauthor of** *Your Brain on Ink*

"Her father told her not to do it. She should leave Kaddish to someone else. But Sarah Birnbach fights back and embraces a custom that has been for so long the province of men. As we see on these pages, she—and we, her readers—are the richer for it. And we can only imagine that her father is smiling down on her with joy."
—**Ari L. Goldman, author of** *Living a Year of Kaddish*

"Sarah Birnbach tells an inspiring story of faith and determination in *A Daughter's Kaddish*, a modern take on an ancient ritual."
—**Arch Campbell, former news anchor, NBC**

"A beautifully written book, *A Daughter's Kaddish* takes us on a woman's journey to say the Mourner's Kaddish, an untraditional path of grieving that tests her in many ways. At the heart of this book is a daughter's love and devotion and a path to healing the past."
—**Linda Joy Myers, president, National Association of Memoir Writers, and author of** *Song of the Plains*

"Heartwarming and heartbreaking. . . . Reading Birnbach's words deepened my thought process about my own beliefs and helped me better understand my own familial relationships. . . . Our stories matter and can matter to others. An all-around, enjoyably insightful read."
—**Jeanne Baker Guy, award-winning author of** *You'll Never Find Us: A Memoir*

A Daughter's Kaddish

A Daughter's Kaddish

My Year of Grief, Devotion, and Healing

SARAH BIRNBACH

WONDERWELL

Library of Congress Control Number: 2022906264

ISBN 978-1-63756-022-8 (hardcover)
ISBN 978-1-63756-023-5 (EPUB)

Editor: Allison Serrell
Cover and interior design: Morgan Krehbiel
Cover photo: Courtesy of the author
Photos on page 128: Taken by the author's mother, Nettie Birnbach
Photos on page 129: Top photo by Vinell Studios, center photo by L'Image Studio,
    bottom photo by Sandy Kavalier
Photos on page 130: Top photo by the author, bottom photo by unknown photographer
Photos on page 131: Bottom left photo by the author's niece Bronwyn Smith;
    all other photos by unknown photographer
Photo on page 235: Courtesy of Mount Ararat Cemetery
Author photo on page 285: Helen Don Photography

"My Father's Blessing" first appeared in *Talking Writing*, Winter 2018
"Bigger Isn't Always Better" first appeared in *JOFA Journal* (Jewish Orthodox Feminist
    Alliance), Spring 2019

Published by Wonderwell in Los Angeles, CA
www.wonderwell.press

WONDERWELL

Distributed in the US by Publishers Group West and
in Canada by Publishers Group Canada

Printed and bound in Canada

Dedicated to
Moshe Israel ben Yosef Tzvi v Roisa
Of Blessed Memory

May his memory be a blessing for life in the world to come

And to all who enabled me
to honor him as he wanted
in the spirit of our faith

And to my granddaughter, Dahlia, who carries his
Hebrew name so that his memory may live on.

CONTENTS

TIMELINE

Month	Hebrew Calendar 5760 to 5761	Secular Calendar 2000 to 2001
Day of death	20 Elul, 5760	20 September, 2000
Burial	22 Elul, 5760	22 September, 2000
Shiva	23 Elul to 28 Elul, 5760	23 to 28 September, 2000
Rosh Hashanah	1 and 2 Tishri, 5761	30 September and 1 October, 2000
Yom Kippur	10 Tishri, 5761	9 October, 2000
Sukkot	15 Tishri to 22 Tishri, 5761	14 to 20 October, 2000
Passover	15 Nisan to 22 Nisan, 5761	8 to 15 April, 2001
Final Kaddish	20 Av, 5761	9 August, 2001
Yahrzeit	20 Elul, 5761	8 September, 2001

NOTE: All Jewish holidays are celebrated according to the Jewish calendar, which is a lunisolar calendar. The months correspond to the cycles of the moon, while the years correspond to the cycles of the sun. The Gregorian calendar is a purely solar calendar. This explains why holidays are marked on the same day each year on the Jewish calendar, while the day on the Gregorian calendar differs from year to year. All Jewish holidays begin at sundown on the evening before the date shown.

MOURNER'S KADDISH

Mourners and those observing Yahrzeit:
Yitgadal v'yitkadash sh'mei raba, b'alma di v'ra, ki-r'utei,
v'yamlikh malkhutei b'hayeikhon u-v'yomeikhon
u-v'hayei d'khol beit Yisra-el,
ba'agala u-vi-z'man kariv, v'imru amen.

Congregation and mourners:
Y'hei sh'mei raba m'varakh l'alam u-l'almei almaya.

Mourners:
Yitbarakh v'yishtabah v'yitpa-ar v'yitromam v'yitnasei
v'yit-hadar v'yit-aleh v'yit-halal sh'mei d'Kudsha, b'rikh hu
*l'ela min kol birkhata v'shirata
*Between Rosh Hashanah and Yom Kippur:
l'ela l'ela mi-kol birkhata v'shirata
tushb'hata v'nehamata da'amiran b'alma, v'imru amen.

Y'hei sh'lama raba min sh'maya
v'hayim aleinu v'al kol Yisra-el, v'imru amen.

Oseh shalom bi-m'romav, hu ya'aseh shalom
aleinu v'al kol Yisra-el, v'imru amen.

May God's name be exalted and hallowed throughout the world that He created, as is God's wish. May God's sovereignty soon be accepted, during our life and the life of all Israel. And let us say: Amen.

May God's great name be praised throughout all time.

Glorified and celebrated, lauded and worshiped, exalted and honored, extolled and acclaimed may the Holy One be, praised beyond all song and psalm, beyond all tributes that mortals can utter. And let us say: Amen.

Let there be abundant peace from heaven, with life's goodness for us and for all Israel. And let us say: Amen.

May the One who brings peace to His universe bring peace to us and to all Israel. And let us say: Amen.

AUTHOR'S NOTE

Each letter in the Hebrew alphabet has a numerical value. The letters Het (ח), with a value of eight, and Yud (י), with a value of ten, combine to make eighteen. Het-Yud spells the word *Chai*, which means "life" or "living." Multiples of eighteen are therefore considered a good omen for life.

According to Jack Riemer in *Jewish Reflections on Death*, ". . . a Jewish book on death has to be addressed to life, for we do not study death in order to become morbid or depressed, but to learn from facing death something about how to live."[i]

In the months following my father's death, as I pursued a ritual of mourning traditionally reserved for males, I learned much about how to live after loss. The thirty-six chapters of this memoir—twice Chai—represent two lives.

The root of the word *memoir* is "memory." The most reliable memoirs are those derived from journal entries, which enable us to attest to the accuracy of the experiences. This memoir was created through such a process.

This is a work of nonfiction. As with all memoirs, this work is seen through a specific lens—mine. I have told everything as accurately as I can and in the most generous way I know how.

Introduction

I stared into the dark, shadowy hole, at the plain pine box that contained my once vibrant and vivacious father. The American flag that had been draped over his coffin was folded into the familiar triangle, then handed to my mother with a stiff, outstretched arm and lackluster words: "On behalf of the country he served and the President of the United States, I present you with this flag."

My mother, frozen in place, stared expressionless into the distance and clung to the flag, which my father had requested to symbolize his pride in his military service with the Allied Forces during World War II, and to honor that part of his life he had devoted to this country, which he loved.

In that hole lay the man who carried me when I couldn't walk, following a serious blood clot in my leg as a nineteen-year-old; the man who always boasted that he made "the best eggs this side of the Rockies," masking nonexistent culinary skills; the man who taught me to love the beach and the ocean before I was old enough to walk, and who showed me how to ride the waves before the invention of boogie boards.

Once the eulogies were finished, it was time for the gut-wrenching ritual of shoveling dirt onto the coffin. Mom went first; then it was my turn. As I pitched dirt onto my father's coffin, every muscle in my body felt twisted as in the jaws of a vise. My salty tears watered the grave.

My sisters, Lois and Jane, followed by Dad's older brother, Dad's six grandchildren, other family members, and then friends, ambled slowly and quietly, one by one, to the mound of soil, took the shovel, and thrust the dirt onto my father's coffin. The custom of family and friends filling the grave, instead of paid strangers, represents the last act of *kevod ha'met*—the Hebrew term meaning "respect for the dead." Helping to fill the grave means you have left nothing undone. Each person replaced the shovel into the dirt mound rather than passing it to the next person, to avoid transmitting death's sorrow and delay leaving the deceased.

Witnessing a grave being filled in this way is believed to give mourners closure. Each shovelful of dirt that hits the coffin is supposed to signal the finality of death, ridding mourners of any illusion that the deceased still lives. This process is intended to honor the deceased and help healing begin.

Not for me. Each jarring *thunk* of dirt that hit Dad's coffin felt like a punch to my ribcage.

My father hated being in dirt. He had lived in foxholes for months on end as a front-line soldier during World War II. "Living in a foxhole is the worst kind of living," he once told me.

I wanted to yell, "Stop! Don't put dirt on him! How can you all suffocate him like this if you love him?"

Instead, I stood transfixed, feeling the weight of that earth as if it were pressing on my own chest and cutting off my oxygen supply. I stared at the half-hidden casket, recalling the advice my father had given me for selecting it: "Even though your mother is a nurse and has seen many deaths, I'm afraid she'll be in no state to handle the arrangements for my funeral. I trust you to handle the details."

I was surprised that my father hadn't prepaid for his funeral. He always planned ahead, ensuring his legal documents (wills, trusts, and advance directives) were complete and current and leaving notes about what to do upon his death. I assumed that he didn't want the funeral home to have a penny of his money one minute before it was neces-sary—so typical of him. I shook my head and muffled a chuckle think-ing of his fiscal prudence.

"Choosing a coffin makes the death seem more real," Dad had cautioned me.

"Most funeral homes have a well-lit room where they display expensive and elaborate caskets. You'll see fancy bronze and stainless-steel coffins with beautiful brushed finishes, and mahogany and cherry coffins with satin linings and shiny brass handles. They'll look magnificent. Walk right past them. The plain pine boxes are always kept in the back corner, without any lights illuminating them. But that's the one I want—the plain pine box with a Star of David on top. After seeing all the enticing coffins, that one will look dusty, maybe even a little depressing. Don't second-guess yourself. Don't worry about it or feel bad. *That's* the one I want."

Judaism holds that every human being is created equal, and that we are all equal in death. So that the poor aren't ashamed if they can't afford an expensive casket, traditional Jews are buried in plain pine boxes, held together with wooden pegs rather than metal screws or nails—wood that decomposes naturally, so the body can return to the earth. Selecting the simplest coffin reflects the value of democracy in death and cuts down on unnecessary expense.

At the funeral home, I had walked like a woman with a mission to the far, dimly lit corner of the casket room, propelled by love.

"My father wants this one," I said with conviction, pointing to the plain pine box. "With the Star of David on top." My mask of confidence hid the ripping of my heart.

Despite its bright lights and shiny metals, the casket room was the saddest place in the funeral home. I didn't linger.

Eyeing the casket, now nearly buried under russet-colored soil, I knew my father would be proud of me. I had fulfilled his wishes, as he knew I would. But not without fistfuls of tear-soaked tissues.

—

Only fifteen minutes earlier, my family had gathered in the dismal receiving hall with its worn, brown furnishings at Mount Ararat Cemetery in Farmingdale, New York. My nineteen-year-old daughter, Rachel, and seventeen-year-old son, David, stood looking ill at ease as they greeted arriving friends and relatives. Next to them were Lois's two daughters and Jane's two daughters—my nieces—ranging in age from seven to twenty-two years. As the only grandson, David had a special place in our family, and in my father's heart.

Given that my parents were married for fifty-four years, they could never understand, nor could I explain, how the marriages of all three of their daughters had ended in divorce.

Dad's longtime rabbi, A. David Arzt, had quietly shepherded me, my mother, and my two younger sisters into a far corner of the room. He looked much older than I recalled, with silver hair and deep lines etched into his face. I had last seen him twenty-two years earlier at my grandmother's funeral.

He and my father shared an enduring and close bond, cemented when my father had attended twice-daily services in the rabbi's synagogue for eleven months after my grandfather died. Eight years later, when my grandmother died in our home, Rabbi Arzt had arrived within minutes. My father never forgot the rabbi's responsiveness and kindness that night. This was typical of him—he had a long memory for anyone's benevolence. And here was the rabbi again, consoling us and grieving with us as if he were part of our family.

The rabbi pulled four black ribbons from his pocket. Called *keriah*, the ribbons are a modern substitute for the biblical custom of tearing one's clothing as an expression of grief. One by one, he tore them lengthwise. The *fsht fsht* sound of the cotton fabric ripping symbolized our hearts breaking, and the severing of the relationship between Dad and each of us. With each slit, I flinched, the sound as penetrating as fingernails scratching a blackboard.

Moving from oldest to youngest, the rabbi pinned the first torn ribbon onto my mother's dress, then fastened the next one to my navy

4

suit jacket, just over my heart. I laid my right hand over it, touching the grief that lived there—a symbol that I was now and forever a mourner. Through wet eyes, I watched him move on to my two sisters.

Lois, two and a half years my junior, had married a Christian man, joined his church, and relinquished Judaism. I remembered the many years that my father refused to speak to her because she had married outside our faith, which broke my heart, and I was grateful that their fissure had healed long before Dad died. Now she stepped forward without hesitation, allowing the rabbi to pin the ribbon to her dress.

"This is for Dad," she said, facing me.

Then Jane accepted her ribbon. Five years younger than me, she had always claimed to have the closest relationship with Dad because they were both the youngest of three same-gender siblings.

My sisters and I were as different as our fingerprints. Someone once characterized the way we dressed as "Sarah is conservative banker, Lois is *Little House on the Prairie*, and Jane is ritz and glitz." While it wasn't totally accurate, it came very close. At fifty-one, forty-nine, and forty-six years old, each of us was an accomplished professional; I was a human resource consultant and entrepreneur, Lois was a teacher of challenged adolescents, and Jane was a fundraising executive for non-profit organizations. But in that moment, my sisters and I—each with slight touches of silver dotting our brunette hair—stood side by side, united in our grief for our father.

When the time arrived to begin the service, my mother, my sisters, and I lined up behind the hearse for the walk to Dad's gravesite. Fulfilling this traditional *mitzvah* (commandment) of *halvayat hamet*, "escorting the deceased," is considered an act of utmost respect and piety.

My mother's voice pierced the air. "You will conduct yourselves with dignity. There will be *no* crying," she commanded us.

Lacking the emotional energy to protest, I stared into the back of the black Cadillac, straining to see through the dark windows to the coffin carrying the parent who had praised me, supported my dreams, raised my confidence, brought joy to my life, and buffered me from my autocratic and cantankerous mother. Gone was my bulwark.

What's in store for me now, Daddy? Who's going to make me giggle? Who's going to listen to my troubles and offer sage wisdom? Who's going to convince me that I have the strength and fortitude to handle anything life hurls at me? Who's going to reassure me that everything will be okay, now that it isn't?

Trudging behind the hearse, my surroundings blurred, my body moved as if laden with giant rocks. I would behave with dignity, but I would not restrain my grief. My beloved father was dead.

———

Standing around the open grave with the heat of the sun on our heads, we were thirty-some people bonded by our love for this man, who cherished his life and everyone in it. This simple graveside service delivered exactly the burial he had wanted. If he were alive, enjoying the gentle breeze under the cloudless sky and appreciating the 70-degree day, he would have said, "What a perfect day to be on the golf course."

Two days earlier, I had watched him take his last breath, knowing that his greatest wish—to live his life to the fullest and then die peacefully, without compromising the quality of his remaining days—had come true. Death had freed him from the anticipated, protracted life-draining battle with terminal lymphoma, which had stricken him seven years earlier. No one would ever poke or prod him again, draw blood or insert more tubes, as they had during the nine torturous days he had lain in a drug-induced coma in the North Ridge Medical Center. No one would ever again handle him like an inanimate object. His suffering was over; God had shown compassion to a kindhearted man. I was thankful . . . but I felt no relief. Just numb. Empty.

I would never again hear his voice singing Barbra Streisand songs painfully off-key, or hear his exuberant laugh, or feel his arms hug me; nor would I dance with him, as I had at all of our family's joyous events, or see his eyes light up when he let my children drive his prized golf cart, or smell the musky fragrance of the Old Spice aftershave he wore. I would never again hear his three-note lyrical whistle whenever he met me at an airport or searched for me in a crowd.

I faded in and out of the proceedings, listening but not hearing, looking but not seeing. Finally, the *thunk thunk* sounds ended. The rabbi sprinkled some dirt from Israel onto Dad's coffin so that his first vision in the world to come would be soil of the Holy Land. Then, enunciating each syllable clearly, he led us in the Mourner's Kaddish—the traditional Jewish prayer believed to elevate the souls of the dead and guide them through God's judgment stage. For the first time, I recited the words that would soon become as familiar to me as the Pledge of Allegiance.

"Yitgadal v'yitkadash sh'mei raba . . ."

Glorified and sanctified be God's great name . . .

Friends and extended family members formed the traditional two rows for us to walk through—reminders that we were surrounded by supportive others. Walking slowly from my father's grave between the walls of human comfort, I began an eleven-month journey that meant structuring my life around reciting the Mourner's Kaddish in synagogue every day, twice a day, no matter what. I became an *avelah* (female mourner), undertaking the traditional male role of praying to elevate my father's soul to *Gan Eden* (the Garden of Eden; paradise in the afterlife), with no idea of the challenges awaiting me.

CHAPTER 1

The Promise

In 1970, I anticipated celebrating my twenty-first birthday with a joyful coming-of-age celebration. Instead, my family was plunged into grief by my paternal grandfather's sudden fatal heart attack. He was buried the day before my birthday, making any festivities inappropriate according to Jewish custom.

An Austrian immigrant, my grandfather was a hard man to warm up to; a gambler, a smoker, and an authoritarian, he fit today's stereotype of a workaholic to a tee. Because my father worked with him six days a week in the family furniture store, my sisters and I saw my grandfather only on obligatory holidays like Father's Day, Passover, and Thanksgiving. His death was the first I had experienced.

My father, his two brothers, and my grandmother were observing the seven-day *shiva* (post-burial) period in my aunt and uncle's home in Queens, New York. Sitting on the white plastic-covered sofa in the living room, I thought it ironic that the living were grieving for the dead in a room called the "living room" that, until now, had always been an unused space, barren of life or activity.

My father rose from the low stool where he would sit in mourning for the next six days—a traditional symbol of having been brought low by grief. His six-foot frame was diminished, bent in sorrow. Weariness had replaced the usual sparkle in his brown eyes, and a scruffy stubble layered a five o'clock shadow across his face.

"I want to talk to you," he said as he dropped stiffly into the seat next to me.

"Dad?" I was alarmed by his inflection, which didn't sound like the start of a birthday greeting.

"When I die, I want you to hire a man to say the Mourner's Kaddish for me," he proclaimed with no hint of emotion.

I winced. Why was he talking about dying? I didn't want to think about his death. Unable to formulate a response, I remained quiet, focusing on his mournful eyes.

"You can pay someone to say it for me for the full eleven months. You won't have to worry about the money," he added, as if this might be some kind of reassurance. "Just take it from my estate."

This is crazy talk, I thought. *Is he really worried about money?*

He continued. "You can find the *shammos,* the man who oversees the services in any synagogue, or you can go to an old-age home to find a man to say the prayer for me twice daily."

I was bewildered. My father was an energetic, active forty-six-year-old man in excellent physical health. And hiring some stranger felt wrong, almost repulsive. But I was like a soldier ambushed in a surprise attack. I swallowed my uneasiness and did my best to keep my voice from shaking.

"Okay, Dad. I promise."

What else could I say to my grieving father, who now saw his own mortality more clearly? My father had never asked me for anything. How could I deny him this one request?

"Thank you. Good. No more worrying. End of discussion."

With that, he got up from the sofa, shuffled in his stockinged feet back to his low seat, and left me sitting stunned, relieved the morbid conversation was over.

Thinking my father invincible—and the idea of his dying incomprehensible—I got up and headed toward the kitchen, drawn by the aroma of freshly brewed coffee and the scent of the freshly baked pastries we had received.

Before I got very far, I heard my father, his two brothers, and seven other men convene for the evening prayers. I turned to see them swaying back and forth, their indecipherable words droning like the buzzing of bees. I had never seen anyone pray at home, and I eyed the scene as if the men were actors on a television screen. Watching my father cry—something I'd never witnessed—made me weep, too.

And then came the words, enunciated more clearly than any others: *"Yitgadal v'yitkadash sh'mei raba . . ."*

Glorified and sanctified be God's great name . . .

The first words of the Mourner's Kaddish.

I stared at this unfamiliar scene until the prayers ended, when I turned again toward the kitchen to join my cousins in lighter conversations. I put the promise I had made to my father out of my mind, where it stayed for more than two decades.

———

The Mourner's Kaddish, a declaration of faith and a sanctification of God's name, has become the hallmark of bereavement for Jews around the globe. A ten-person quorum (*minyan*) is required to recite the Mourner's Kaddish,[ii] fulfilling God's commandment (Leviticus 22:32) that an "assembly" must be present when He is sanctified. Chanting the prayer is a public act.

The Kaddish prayer, which mentions neither death nor mourning, serves two purposes: to bring merit to the souls of the dead by elevating them through God's judgment stage, and to provide fellowship to the bereaved in a time of profound loneliness. This community helps the mourner's spirit move from despair to hope, from isolation to companionship, and from the departed to the living.

Traditional Jews, including my father, believe that after death, the redemption of their souls depends on having the Mourner's Kaddish recited twice daily in synagogue, in the presence of a minyan, for eleven months. Doing this is one way to fulfill the Fifth Commandment—

"Honor thy father and mother"—and shows God that the soul of the departed deserves a place in Gan Eden. It is considered the ultimate sign of love and respect.

My father undertook this obligation with devotion, honoring the soul of his Orthodox father. Later, he did the same for his mother. He then devoted ten years to organizing a regular minyan to support grieving members of his own congregation.

This obligation is traditionally fulfilled by sons. The problem for my father: he had only daughters. In fact, after the birth of my two younger sisters, he would often repeat the baseball idiom, "Three strikes . . . I'm out!"

My dad, who adopted the patriarchal values of his own father, believed that women could not say Kaddish because they were not counted as part of the minyan. In earlier centuries, Jewish women were "exempted" from the rituals, prayer services, and religious obligations that are strictly dictated by the clock, as the demands of children and domestic chores—women's primary responsibilities—limited her availability. The traditional practice in a household with no sons was to "hire a Kaddish"—a male to chant the Mourner's Kaddish for the prescribed eleven months.

———

Under the circumstances, my father's request to hire a Kaddish made sense. At the time of my grandfather's death, I'd had no formal Jewish education. When my dad had considered enrolling my sisters and me in religious school as youngsters, my grandfather, Orthodox in his judgments about the role of women, opposed the idea. Jewish education for girls in the early 1950s was an anomaly among Orthodox Jews.

"Girls don't need a religious education," my grandfather had declared. "Their job is to make a Jewish home and raise the children. Send your daughters to ballet class instead." And that is exactly what my father did.

My dad wasn't the kind of man to oppose his father, nor was my grandfather the type of man to be opposed. Even though my grandfather had given up many of his Orthodox practices when he assimilated into American society, and had abandoned Sabbath observance when he opened a furniture store—"Saturday is the busiest day in retail," he always said—he remained resolute about the place of women in Judaism.

Although my parents belonged to a Conservative synagogue, we never talked about what it meant to be Jewish. Our home was devoid of most Jewish rituals. My mother's lack of religious practice and synagogue attendance sent the unspoken message to my sisters and me that religious observances were superfluous.

Until my grandfather's death, my father went to synagogue only on Rosh Hashanah and Yom Kippur—the High Holy Days—echoing his father's assimilation. On those once-a-year holidays, wearing a new dress and patent leather Mary Janes with lace-trimmed white ankle socks, I sat next to him for hours when he would otherwise have been at work. Those days felt so special that I didn't notice the lack of connection they had to our daily lives.

In 1970, when my grandfather died and I made my promise, an American woman still could not get a credit card in her own name (even if she was married); she could be fired from her job if she became pregnant; she was excluded from most Ivy League colleges; and she could not even run in the Boston Marathon. Since women were excluded from these aspects of secular life as well, was it any wonder that my father asked me to hire a man?

I don't imagine it ever occurred to my dad that any of his three daughters would embrace Judaism or go to any length to say Kaddish for him, the man we loved so dearly.

CHAPTER 2

Through the Generations

Both of my grandfathers left home at an early age. In 1901, my paternal grandfather, George, left his Orthodox home in Galicia (a region in the former Austrian Empire spanning modern-day Poland and Ukraine) at age fifteen. He spent the next three years working his way across Europe, trying to earn enough money for steerage passage to the United States. After passing through Ellis Island, he settled in New York City and became a merchandise peddler, selling wares he carried from door to door. He soon developed a steady clientele. When his route became too large for him to carry all the merchandise needed by his customers, he befriended Lena Bornstein, a widowed storekeeper whose husband had died after the couple emigrated from Russia. She allowed him to store his merchandise in her notions shop so he could drop off and pick up needed bundles as he traversed his circuit.

Lena had six grown daughters that she wanted wed, and she persuaded George to date one of her girls. He took a liking to Rose, and on June 25, 1916, the couple married.

In 1928, George returned to Europe to visit his family. His father was displeased that George had abandoned Orthodox Judaism, cut his *payot* (side curls), and assimilated into American culture. When he left to return to America, George could not have imagined that he would never see any member of his immediate family again. In 1939, my grandfather got word from a family friend that his parents had been shot in a street of their town by Nazi officers. All six of his siblings were killed during the Holocaust; only the three children of his baby brother escaped Nazi Germany and survived the war.

My maternal grandfather, Fred Sodikow, fled Mogilev (in the Russian Empire) at the time of the pogroms against the Jews, leaving behind a wife and two children. He arrived in the United States in 1913 with only one small suitcase. He was twenty-one years old. Once here, he found work as a tailor and met and married my grandmother, Sarah, also an immigrant from Russia.

According to Jewish law, if my grandfather had not obtained a *get* (a Jewish divorce) from his first wife, my mother would have been considered an illegitimate child in our religion, as Jewish law would not have recognized my grandfather's second marriage to Sarah. My mother carried the doubt about her birthright until after my grandfather's death in 1962. When going through his papers, she found a note written in Russian. I had someone translate the document: proof of payment for the get that had been performed in Russia. My mother called the translation "the greatest gift anyone has ever given me."

My maternal grandmother, frightened of the American medical system, refused to consult a doctor for what turned out to be colon cancer. On September 21, 1936, my mother found her lying in bed in a pool of blood. Rushing to get a neighbor, she fled the apartment, inadvertently locking the door behind her. Paramedics finally broke down the door, entered the apartment, and rushed Sarah to the hospital, where she died the next day. My mother was ten years old.

After waiting out the prescribed year of mourning, my grandfather narrowed the field of prospective brides and allowed my eleven-year-old mother to choose her stepmother. An only child, she was enticed by Lillian's large family and the many instant aunts, uncles, and cousins she'd acquire. But her selection only increased her loneliness. Her new stepmother destroyed all traces of Sarah, leaving my mother without evidence that her mother had ever lived. At the least amount of stress, Lillian would retreat to bed for several days at a time with migraine headaches. With Lillian ensconced in her bedroom and my grandfather at work all day, my mother was left to fend for herself. Like my grand-father, Lillian was distant and unaffectionate, and she had no idea how to raise a precocious child.

My mother left home at age seventeen, went to nurse's training school, and never looked back.

These life-altering events, combined with an upbringing lacking in empathy and tenderness, affected my mother's self-esteem—a fact I didn't appreciate until my adulthood. The lack of a role model for mothering left her without a road map for parenting her own daughters.

———

My parents met as high schoolers in Palisades Park, New Jersey, in May 1941. A group of girls who were picnicking there asked to borrow some salt from a group of young men also picnicking in the park. The two groups of students later went on to the park clubhouse, where they danced for several hours to the music of the jukebox. My mother often shared the story that on that day, she had told one of her girlfriends, "I'm going to marry that man," referring to my father. The pair began dating until, in April 1943, my father was drafted into the US Army. He had just turned eighteen years old. My parents married soon after he returned from Europe in 1946.

I was born three years later. It is a traditional Jewish custom to name a newborn after a deceased relative. In bestowing the name of an endeared family member, parents hope the child will emulate the virtues of the deceased namesake and identify with the history of her Jewish family. It is also believed that the soul of the loved one lives on in the child who now bears her name. As my mother had lost her mother, and my three other grandparents were living, there was never any doubt that, regardless of my gender, I would carry my grandmother Sarah's Hebrew name.

My mother followed the pattern of many American Jews by giving me a more anglicized first name, Sheila, which appears on my birth certificate, while I also carried Sarah as my Hebrew name. When I asked why she chose the name Sheila rather than simply using Sarah for my English and Hebrew names, she replied, "Sheila is a stronger name." I found that hard to believe since the biblical Sarah was a very strong woman. I wondered if my mother's decision centered on the rampant anti-Semitism of the day, or if she had a more personal reason related to her own mother's death. Her typical abrupt explanation left no room for further discussion. When I turned sixty, over my mother's objections, I legally changed my first name to that of my maternal grandmother. I carry her Hebrew name, Sarah, as my legal name, and I wear it with pride.

As men returned home from World War II in the early 1950s, the image of the stay-at-home mom became the universal ideal. The culture of the day implored women to give their jobs back to the returning soldiers, and rigid stereotypes became the norm. So after my birth, my mother, a registered nurse, gave up her career in public health and her undergraduate degree program to become a stay-at-home mom. I never knew and never asked if she made this choice willingly or resented it.

Two and a half years after my birth, my sister Lois was born, and two and a half years after that, my mother gave birth to Jane. The five of us lived in a tiny two-bedroom apartment on the Upper West Side of New York City, an area made famous by Lin-Manuel Miranda's *In the Heights*.

As a returning army veteran, my father got his undergraduate degree from Long Island University under the GI Bill. Jewish admission quotas thwarted his plans to enter dental school, despite the herculean efforts of his older brother, a second lieutenant in the Army Dental Corps. Discouraged, he resigned himself to working in his parents' furniture store, at least temporarily.

Located on Harlem's Amsterdam Avenue in New York City, the store sat amidst scenes of racial unrest, riots, lootings, and shootings in the 1960s. It was robbed on numerous occasions. My father detested that dusty, rat- and cockroach-infested place, which seemed to hold more importance to my grandfather than any of his three sons. Despite arguing vehemently with my grandfather for years over introducing appliances, linoleum, and other more profitable merchandise to the store, my father stayed—six days a week, for over twenty years—out of loyalty and commitment to his parents.

During the summers of my youth, my parents rented a duplex in Rockaway to escape the heat of "the city." My father remained behind to work and came out to the beach one night a week and on weekends. His love of the beach was infectious, and the ocean etched itself on my heart before I was old enough to walk. The Rockaway rentals ended after our family moved from the city.

When our miniscule shared bedroom became too tight for a seven-, five-, and two-year-old, we moved to Baldwin, Long Island, two doors down from family friends. In this neighborhood, known for its quality school system, my parents found a three-bedroom house with a fenced backyard, a towering maple tree, and flowering rose and hydrangea bushes that filled the air with their subtle perfumes in the spring and summer.

When Jane entered nursery school and I started third grade, my mother returned to her nursing career, working the 7:00 a.m. to 3:00 p.m. shift in a local hospital so she could be home when we returned from school. She brought home with her a temper frazzled by working all day on her feet and being demeaned by doctors—no doubt exacerbated by managing three young children who engaged in normal bouts of two-against-one sibling rivalry.

I suspect parenting exhausted her. By 1954, my mother, who had been independent since age seventeen, had three children and the financial and time constraints they imposed. Perhaps she was frustrated with my father for his lack of support for the daily tasks of running a household (not that such support was expected in the 1950s).

My father would leave the house at 7:30 a.m. and return twelve hours later, six days a week, unaware of the tension consuming the house in his absence. Unlike the many people who dislike lengthy commutes, he said he enjoyed the one-hour drive to and from the city as it gave him downtime to think and relax. I regret that I never asked him what he thought about, but I am certain he listened to Yankees games during baseball season.

He always entered the house as if, in crossing the threshold, he was leaving the day's woes behind him. He would find my mother in the kitchen preparing dinner and greet her with a quick kiss on the cheek.

———

If you were to talk with my sisters, their view of our family's history might differ from mine. But that history has played a significant role in my understanding of the world, my community, my family, and my place among them. The experiences, hardships, accomplishments, and celebrations that shaped the generations of my family—its traditions, culture, and religion—have shaped the woman I am today.

CHAPTER 3
My Journey into Judaism

Growing up in New York, I knew I was Jewish, but my involvement with Judaism was limited to two Passover *seders* a year and attending synagogue with my father on the High Holy Days, Rosh Hashanah and Yom Kippur.

Somewhere along the line, I learned about the three denominations of Judaism. Orthodox, Conservative, and Reform Jews differ in their attitudes and teachings about how closely to follow the Torah (the first five books of the Jewish Bible) on matters such as gender roles, kosher dietary rules, Sabbath restrictions, the amount of Hebrew used in services, the use of various types of music in services, and much more.

Orthodox Jews follow the most traditional interpretations of Jewish law, while Reform Jews—the most common denomination in the US—are the most liberal and least bound to traditional interpretations of Jewish law. Orthodox synagogues have morning and evening services seven days each week, while Reform synagogues typically have only Sabbath services on Friday nights or Saturday mornings. Conservative Jews have blended the traditional with the modern, maintaining Jewish law as binding while meeting the current cultural needs of Jewish people in varying circumstances. Like Orthodox Jews, many Conservative Jews still practice traditions such as observing dietary laws and honoring the Sabbath, but they have moved beyond traditional restrictions by giving women equal rights and responsibilities in all aspects of services, and by ordaining women as rabbis.

As the descendants of three Jewish immigrants who escaped religious persecution, one might think that our family would observe Jewish rituals and traditions. But other than Passover seders and observance of Rosh Hashanah and Yom Kippur, we didn't. I can only speculate that my immigrant grandparents were eager to assimilate into the culture of early-1900s America. Their escape from persecution would have left them fearful of anti-Semitism—enough to hide any outward symbols of their Judaism.

To assimilate into American culture, my paternal grandfather cut his payot (the sidelocks worn in keeping with the prohibition against shaving a prescribed area on each side of the face), stopped wearing his *tallit* (prayer shawl) under his clothes, and stopped wearing his *kippah* (the skullcap, also called yarmulke) except in synagogue. He sacrificed his Sabbath worship attendance in exchange for profitable Saturdays in retail, but he strictly observed Passover and the High Holy Days, closing his New York City furniture store only on Rosh Hashanah and Yom Kippur.

Although my parents belonged to a Conservative synagogue, at home we lived more like Reform Jews. My parents did not honor the Sabbath, we did not keep a kosher home, and my father attended synagogue only on the High Holy Days. My mother never attended. We never discussed religion, spirituality, or God. The most inclusive holiday observance in my family was Thanksgiving.

Given that I never had a religious education, I lacked any relationship with God. My grandma Rose always ended every visit, telephone call, and letter with "God Bless"; I considered it the same as someone saying "God bless you" when I sneezed. I never thought more of it. Not until I was well into my adulthood did my father share how his faith in God had crystallized during his earliest days on the front lines in World War II.

When I once asked my mother what she believed about God, she responded with "I believe in Pascal's Wager." She explained that Pascal, a seventeenth-century French philosopher, said people should live their lives as if God exists because, whether a Divine Being exists or not, people have nothing to lose by living as if there is a Holy Spirit. According to Pascal, if we believe in God and God actually exists, we have gained eternal happiness. But if God exists and we don't believe, we have lost the opportunity to reach heaven. On the other hand, if God doesn't exist, we have nothing to lose either way. Pascal suggested that by living as if one has faith, one might actually arrive at faith. I interpreted my mother's discussion of Pascal's Wager to mean she believed in living as if God exists, without explicitly saying whether or not she believed in the presence of an Almighty.

———

While attending George Washington University in the nation's capital during the late 1960s, I was more involved with the anti-war and civil rights movements than with Judaism. Participating in the protests and marches of the day eclipsed any thoughts of religious activities.

In my sophomore year, when my parents expressed dismay that I had forgotten Yom Kippur, the brief instant of shame I felt vanished as fast as it had arisen. Their judgment felt hypocritical, but I stifled my response; neither of my parents observed Jewish practices in our home throughout the rest of the year. Decades passed before I recognized my father's concern for his soul and its afterlife as different from the way he regarded other religious rituals.

In 1970, I married a man whose upbringing was as lacking in religious observance as my own. We dismissed any affiliation with Judaism, other than to write "Jewish" next to "Religious Preference" on census forms and medical questionnaires.

A decade after we married, we got the devastating report: my husband was unable to conceive a child. I began inseminations with donor sperm. In the late 1970s and early 1980s, information about the donor wasn't available to families as it is now.

When temperature charts, fertility drugs, and years of exhausting, emotionally and financially draining attempts continued to come to naught, and the emotional yo-yo had become unbearable, I started to pray for a baby. Petitioning God was a first for me.

I had never prayed before. It didn't occur to me to consult a rabbi or go to a synagogue. At that time, I had no books on Judaism or on prayer. I was too embarrassed to ask anyone for guidance. Instead, I agonized over how to stand, whether I needed to bow my head, how to hold my hands. All the television programs and movies I'd seen with children kneeling by their beds and putting their hands together to talk to God felt wrong for me—they depicted Christian children. I was a Jewish adult, and I didn't know how to pray. So I went to a park and spoke to God in the only way I knew how, stumbling over my words in the process.

"Please, God. I need your help. This is so hard. I take my temperature every morning before I even get out of bed. I race the seven miles to the doctor's office from work the minute I get the call that a semen donation has arrived. The waiting is agonizing, and then I get my period. I promise to raise my child with the religious upbringing that I never had. Please help me. I'm at my wit's end."

—

The seeds of life and of faith were planted simultaneously when I became pregnant, and the cloud of doubt, disappointment, and anxiety lifted. I felt God's spirit as alive within me as the growing baby. I believed God had blessed me, and something shifted inside me. A flame of new spiritual feelings kindled in my soul.

I became increasingly anxious as my pregnancy progressed and I contemplated the kind of mother I wanted to be. I knew I didn't want to be like my mother. I again turned to prayer, asking for the patience, wisdom, and strength to be a good mother. The years of fruitlessness ended, and at age thirty-two, holding my flawless newborn daughter in my arms, my gratitude for this blessing bubbled over as I thanked the God with whom I had only recently become acquainted.

My daughter's soft breathing sounded like God's whisper. The power of a love this deep induced a spiritual awakening, and I vowed to raise my daughter, Rachel, in a spirit of faith. I saw her birth as a miracle that came about with God's helping hand. Becoming pregnant after praying to God was transformative. My pregnancy solidified my belief in a higher power.

I became determined to bring Judaism into her life and to connect her with the generations of ancestors that preceded her. My husband and I set out to find a synagogue where we would both feel comfortable. Reform congregations lacked the rituals I wanted. Some Conservative synagogues were so traditional, so close to Orthodoxy, they felt more like "Conservadox."

When we visited Congregation Beth El of Montgomery County, we immediately felt welcomed; congregants radiated warmth, women had rights and responsibilities equal to men, and the synagogue had daily morning and evening services. The chanting of the Hebrew prayers echoed those I'd heard at my father's side in his synagogue years before. The blend of the traditional and the modern felt comfortable and familiar. And when I heard the lift in my father's voice after telling him I'd joined a Conservative synagogue, I felt I had come full circle to the days when sitting next to him in his synagogue had made me feel as special as a princess.

Despite my pleadings, my husband resisted the introduction of Jewish practices in our home. I acquiesced to preserve marital harmony.

Following more months of disheartening, unsuccessful attempts to conceive, David was born almost exactly two years after Rachel. The birth of this tiny, perfect little infant again felt like God's blessing. I overflowed with love for this miracle and felt my spiritual core grow deeper. At the *bris* (ritual circumcision), bliss radiated from my father's tear-stained face as he held his first grandson, and I felt God watching over the scene.

CHAPTER 4
My Father's Blessing

On December 23, 1993, when I was forty-four, the comforting illusion that my parents would live forever shattered—in an instant.

My father telephoned. Always one to bring levity to serious situations, he opened with "I've got good news and bad news. Which do you want first?"

Uh-oh. This is going to be bad news.

I tried to match his carefree demeanor, despite the wing beats of anxiety in my chest.

"Your call, Dad."

"Okay. I've been diagnosed with non-Hodgkin's lymphoma."

The *ticktock, ticktock* of the wall clock echoed, while anticipation pounded in my ears.

"The good news: it's a slow-growing cancer. The bad news: this form of lymphoma is not curable." He spoke as if delivering a weather report—cloudy skies are on the horizon.

Oh my God . . .

"The . . . prognosis . . . Dad?" I strained to temper my voice.

"Without treatment, I have possibly as much as seven years."

My father was trying to be his usual cheery self, but I was blindsided. Knowing he wouldn't want any gut-wrenching sobbing, I squeaked out, "Thanks for telling me, Dad. It's a lot to absorb. Can I give you a call back tomorrow?"

"Sure thing, sweetie."

I hung up not a second too soon, as the tsunami of anguish overtook me.

———

In early 1994, after obtaining second and third opinions about his prognosis, my father rejected treatment for the B-cell lymphoma that slowly permeated his body.

When he called to tell me, I felt like I was freefalling on a roller-coaster drop.

Oh my God, he's not going to fight this.

"But Dad, if it can prolong your life . . ." I was begging, like a child trying to justify all the reasons she should have the puppy she knew she'd never get.

"I refuse to take a cure that's worse than the disease. And I refuse to live as a cancer victim. I've done a lot of soul-searching. You may not agree with it, but it's my decision. I'd like to have your support."

What could I say? This was his life and his choice.

I didn't agree. I would have done anything to extend my father's life. I was being asked to join a game I didn't want to play. But crying and begging were futile.

"Of course, Dad. You have my support. And my love." I mustered my most confident and reassuring voice, glad he couldn't see my trembling.

Many days later, after pained phone calls with my sisters, the reality began to sink in, and I could hear my father's death whispering in my ear. I recalled the promise I'd made more than two decades earlier. Now it wasn't hypothetical. My father was going to die.

In that moment, I saw my agreement to hire a man to say Kaddish through a different lens. I did not want a proxy for my prayers. No stranger could show God the respect for my father that I could. I was not only a daughter; I would be a mourner. I was convinced that the salvation of my father's soul was an obligation of lineage, not gender, and I would not allow my gender to absolve me of this responsibility. *I* wanted to say Kaddish for him. *I* wanted to be the one to demonstrate that my father's soul was worthy of God's positive judgment.

In my mind, women's exemption from time-bound prayer did not mean exclusion. The word *exemption* leaves open the possibility that women *may* fulfill these *mitzvot* (commandments) if they choose to.

I had never broken a promise to my father, nor had I done something so contrary to his wishes. My father had always demonstrated and demanded the utmost respect for one's parents. As I pondered approaching him with such a radical idea, anxiety became my daily burden.

My father loved to engage his daughters in most any conversation—our schoolwork, extracurricular activities, friends, grandparents. Each evening, he'd ask my sisters and me, "How'd things go in school today?" or "How'd you do on that test?" And he listened attentively. When we were old enough, he debated politics with us, even confessing to having voted for Richard Nixon. "He's promised to bring our boys home from Vietnam," Dad said, "and I want our boys outta there."

But my father never opened up about his emotions, a reality I regret never having questioned. Engaging him in an open, two-way dialogue about his afterlife necessitated a surefire strategy.

If I couldn't convince him that I should say the Mourner's Kaddish for him, at the very least, I wanted his blessing. Even as an adult in my forties, I couldn't imagine deviating from my father's request.

———

I hungered to know more about this prayer that mattered so much to my father, and I began reading every book I could find. After I discovered Leon Wieseltier's book, *Kaddish*, considered the most well-researched treatise on the subject, my rabbi cautioned me that the book is so dense most rabbis don't even get through it. I was undeterred, thinking I had found a factual, historical context for women's recitation of the Kaddish.

From one page to another, I was validated one minute and invisible the next. "May a woman say kaddish? . . . It sounds to some like a feminist provocation. But ask the question differently. May a daughter say kaddish? Suddenly the controversy disappears. . . . If you deny the kaddish to a daughter, then you do not understand the kaddish. This kaddish is not an obligation of gender. It is an obligation of descent. This is not about men, this is about sons. This is not about women, this is about daughters."[iii]

Yes! Support for my argument! But my excitement burst like a popped balloon as Wieseltier then referenced the analysis of an influential eighteenth-century Talmudic scholar from Galicia: ". . . it is prohibited to allow her [the daughter] to recite the mourner's kaddish . . . she is forbidden . . . from making her voice heard in public. . . . A woman's voice is the very sound of lewdness, according to Jewish law. It is emphatically not to be heard."[iv]

"Lewdness" glared at me like a neon sign. Did my Galician grandfather believe this? I had never talked with him about his history or his views on religion, a neglect I now regret. Certainly, my father didn't consider *my* voice to be "lewd."

My teeth clenched so tightly my jaw ached. I couldn't focus. Had this been the basis for my father's original request? I fought the urge to rip the book to shreds and kept reading.

An "enlightened Galician rabbi"—another from my grandfather's home—wrote: ". . . only her lips should move, but her voice should not be heard. Otherwise the man who hears her may be aroused to an evil thought, which is worse than a sin. The woman must be very careful that she is not responsible for the failure of the men."[v]

What? How could a woman be held responsible for a man's sin? Aren't men responsible for their own failures? Was this a Jewish teaching? Could it be that my grandfather held these same views? And transmitted them to my father?

Ambushed by my own curiosity, I gripped the book so tightly I could hardly open my fingers. For the first time, I saw traditional Judaism as more than just patriarchal; I now considered traditional Judaism's exemption of women from time-designated prayer and other religious responsibilities to be a prohibition. Heat began radiating up my neck and across my cheeks. I couldn't reconcile my readings with the practices of my own Conservative and egalitarian synagogue, where men and women had equal rights and responsibilities.

My father believed in equality for women. Of that I was certain. He insisted on and financed college educations for each of his daughters, encouraging us to major in subjects that would lead to professional careers. He never considered college to be a husband hunting ground. He taught us financial management and repeatedly told us we could become anything we wanted to be, if we worked hard enough. Based on his unwavering support of my mother's career—as a nurse, as a professor of nursing after attaining her doctorate in her early sixties, and then as president of the New York State Nurses Association—he couldn't have thought a woman should not be heard. Not in a house with four women. But I never asked.

Then I read the 1916 letter that Henrietta Szold, the founder of Hadassah (the Women's Zionist Organization of America), wrote to Hayim Peretz, a family friend, declining his offer to recite the Kaddish for her after her mother's death:

> The Kaddish means to me that the survivor publicly manifests his wish and intention to assume the relation to the Jewish community which his parents had, and that the chain of tradition remains unbroken from generation to generation. . . . I believe that the elimination of women from such duties was never intended by our law and custom—women were freed from positive duties when they could not perform them, but not when they could. It was never intended . . . that

31

their performance of them should not be considered as valuable and valid as when one of the male sex performed them. And of the Kaddish I feel sure this is particularly true.[vi]

—

This would not be the first time I had challenged my father so strenuously. Thirty years earlier, when the Surgeon General's warning first appeared on cigarette packages—"Cigarette Smoking *May* Be Hazardous to Your Health"—my father was smoking three packs of Kent cigarettes a day. It was 1966, and I was seventeen years old. I nagged him relentlessly to stop. Although he called it a "dirty, disgusting habit," he claimed he couldn't quit.

One evening in my junior year of high school, as we sat together on the living room sofa watching *Perry Mason* on TV, I lifted a cigarette from the open pack lying on the end table.

"Can you show me how to smoke it, Dad?"

His jaw dropped open and his eyes widened.

"What . . . do you . . . think . . . you're . . . doing . . . young lady?" he asked, emphasizing every word.

"Well, if you can do it, so can I," I retorted smugly, rising to stand in front of him.

"I don't want you to smoke. It's a dirty, disgusting habit and you shouldn't start. Once you do, it's hard to stop. I know." He spoke with uncharacteristic passion.

"Well, I don't want you to smoke either. It can kill you and I'm not ready to lose my father." My heart kept pounding like a jackhammer, but I kept my voice from quivering. "So if you're going to smoke, I am, too. And you can't stop me," I pronounced with adolescent bravado.

My father stared at me in stunned silence. He must have seen my determination, because he made the promise that prolonged his life.

"I don't want you to smoke. Ever. Do . . . you . . . understand me?" Staccato words punctuated the air.

"I do, Dad, but I don't want you to smoke either." I put my hands on my hips, more to steady myself than to add emphasis. He stared wide-eyed.

"Well, if you'll promise me never to smoke, then I will stop."

"I promise, Dad. If you'll stop, I will never start." I put the cigarette back in the pack.

My father extinguished his cigarette and never lit another one. He went cold turkey, from three packs a day to zero. And I never again handled a cigarette.

———

Flashing back to that day fueled my resolve. I was confident that I could convince my father as long as I was passionate enough about reciting Kaddish for him, and I came at it logically.

I jotted down a list of justifications: I wasn't bound by the traditional constraints of earlier centuries; I belonged to an egalitarian synagogue; my children were old enough to stay by themselves while I worshipped; I had my own transportation; I had learned the Hebrew alphabet and a few basic prayers; my job afforded me flexibility. My list stretched on and on.

Still, I filled pages in my journal as I grappled with the questions: What if he doesn't give me his blessing? Then what will I do? What if he insists that I hire a male to say Kaddish? What if he holds tight to his belief that gender is more important than having his own child pray for his soul? And what if he's wrong? If there is a Gan Eden, as my father trusted, would God send his soul to that eternal home based only on the appeals of a male stranger?

But what if *I was* wrong? I could not accept that the Almighty viewed gender as my father did. Nor did I believe that a stranger's voice could carry the same passion as mine. I had listened to men in synagogue who rushed through the prayers with a monotone lightning speed. Surely God would hear my prayers, chanted with the richness of my love and intention.

I imagined Gan Eden to be like a theater—with the best seats down front, closest to God, and the nosebleed section reserved for those who lived less righteous lives. I wanted my father to have a front-row seat, to bask in God's mightiest embrace. When I shared this vision with my sister Jane, she joked that, given my father's distaste for theater, he'd probably prefer an obstructed view where he could sleep, away from God's sight, as he always had when accompanying my mother to Broadway productions.

I believed, as my father did, that the souls of Jews await God's judgment in *Gehinnom* (purgatory). Gehinnom is very different than the typical concept of Hell. Rather than being a place of fire and brimstone, it is the place where souls are cleansed and healed of their transgressions. The atonement process is not so much a punishment as it is a spiritual dry-cleaning to rid the wicked of any blemishes on his or her soul before entering the next phase—oneness with God.

The duration of God's judgment stage depends on the degree of goodness maintained in one's life. The maximum duration—twelve months—is reserved for the very wicked. Saying Kaddish for a full year would give God the impression that the deceased was an evil person who needed atonement for the entire twelve months. So traditional Jews recite Kaddish for only eleven months, ensuring God does not mistake our loved ones for the malevolent.

I did not want my father's soul to remain in Gehinnom for twelve months, stuck on a lower level of spiritual existence. I could not allow that to happen.

———

I finally mustered the courage to tell my father that I wanted to say Kaddish for him. I scheduled a visit to my parents' Florida home in

July 1996 to coincide with his seventy-second birthday. When my mother left to run errands, I jumped at the chance for private time with him. My father lay across the couch in his study, wearing his usual polo shirt and shorts, watching a golf tournament on his antiquated television set. Seeing the golfer's tan that rose above his ankles made me smile. As I stood in the doorway, listening to the whispered voices of the announcers, I thought, *Should I stay? Should I go? Maybe another time would be better* . . .

I silently counted to ten and stepped into the room, careful not to block the television.

"Dad, I want to talk to you about something serious."

Seeing my face, he sat up and immediately turned off the TV. I had his attention.

"What's up, sweetie?"

He angled his body toward me, his customary toothy smile replaced with a furrowed brow.

"I want you to release me from the promise I made to you to hire a Kaddish. I want to say Kaddish for you when you die."

I had said it. I took a deep breath and, as the air slipped slowly from my mouth, I felt my heart rate slowing.

"In the absence of sons, *I* am the best one to say Kaddish—not a stranger. It's not an obligation of gender; it's an obligation of family, and if you believe that reciting the prayer will bring calm to your soul, then *I* can do that better than any stranger can." The words tumbled out faster than I'd intended.

Dad knitted his thick, dark eyebrows. His direct gaze made me wonder if he was shocked at my forthrightness or just deep in thought about my proposition. I waited, struggling to maintain my slowly evaporating confidence. I glanced away toward the window and back at him as he shifted on the couch. He held his gaze.

"As your child, God will smile more on my efforts than on the prayers of someone who didn't even know you." I spoke with all the passion I could convey.

My father wore his poker face. I couldn't tell if my words touched his heart or not, so I tried one last approach.

"You know that Judaism emphasizes performing mitzvot—good deeds—rather than espousing beliefs. I want to demonstrate my love in actions, not just in words."

Finally, my father replied, "I'll have to think about it, sweetie. Is there anything else you wanted to say?"

"No, Dad, that's all." I felt like a slowly deflating balloon.

He gave the short, quick nod that signaled the end of the discussion. When he reached for the remote control, I knew to move on. I gave him a quick kiss on the top of his head and exited to the guest room, where I sat on the edge of the bed, burying my head in my hands.

At least he didn't give me an outright no.

My father, a man of simple pleasures and minimal needs, didn't drive expensive cars, buy fancy clothes or shoes, or own extravagant collectibles. Family meant more to him than any material possessions. The few things he wanted or needed, he provided himself. But the deceased cannot say Kaddish for themselves.

Lifting my head from my hands, I decided: With or without his blessing, I would recite Kaddish for my father. With this, my final gift, I would honor this man who had given so much for his family, his friends, his community, his synagogue, and his country. I would show my gratitude for my father's lifetime of generosity and put my love into action. With the decision made, I closed the door on my anxiety.

———

In 1999, ten months before his death, when our entire family congregated at Lois's house to celebrate Thanksgiving, Dad ushered us all into the cozy family room as he settled himself on the sofa. Lois, Jane, and I sat on the floor, huddled near the fireplace, facing him. Our mother, who had shrunk three inches to a diminutive 5'3", looked even tinier in contrast to the large wingback chair where she sat, close to the steps, leaving her out of our direct view.

Dad spoke candidly as he told us about the living will he'd just revised and where to find the copies. Then came the emotional jolt, without as much as a change in his tone: "I want a commitment from each of you to take no heroic measures," he said, emphasizing the last three words. "I don't want to be kept alive on machines or anything else that will compromise the quality of my life. I don't want there to be any arguing or hesitation when it comes time for that decision. Do you understand me?" He pursed his lips and stared directly at the three of us. "Promise me."

Three heads nodded in unison; we unanimously agreed without hesitation. But my sisters' downturned faces echoed their dejection. Promising was one thing. Imagining the day and time to carry it out was another.

"Good. I'm glad we all agree," my father stated.

I lingered in the family room as the others returned upstairs to the kitchen.

"Dad, did you ever think about my reciting Kaddish for you?"

"Yes," he said, nodding his head. "As a matter of fact, I've thought about it quite a bit."

Silence.

I craned my neck, awaiting words that didn't come.

"And . . ."

"And what?" He raised his eyebrows and tilted his head, as if oblivious to my meaning.

"Does that mean you're giving me your blessing, Dad?"

"You don't need my blessing, but if you feel you do, then you have it."

I wrapped my arms around his neck with a tight grip, as though willing him to stay alive forever. "Oh, Daddy . . . thank you. Thank you. So much. This will be my final gift to you."

"It's okay, sweetie. You have my blessing."

I don't know whether my father ever truly reconciled himself to the equality of women within Judaism or the importance of one's offspring over the stranger. I imagine he agonized between adhering to his father's traditional beliefs and accepting my feminist values—a grappling reminiscent of Tevye's conflict in *Fiddler on the Roof,* when his three daughters rebelled against his long-held traditions. But unlike Tevye, my father didn't share his internal contemplations with me.

My father and I got up to join the others, and as he wrapped his arm around my shoulder, his prognosis slipped from my mind.

CHAPTER 5
The Meal of Consolation

After a Jewish burial, mourners traditionally first wash their hands to disassociate from death and remember to serve God in a pure way. Then the family derives nourishment from the *seudat havra'ah* (meal of consolation). It is forbidden for mourners to eat food they themselves have prepared; it is considered a mitzvah (commandment, often used to refer to a good deed) for others to bring the food, demonstrating the community's concern for the welfare of the mourners. Eating immediately after the burial, surrounded by caring others, reminds the bereaved that life must go on.

Not so for us. As out-of-towners who would soon need to head to Kennedy Airport, we could only yearn for this source of comfort. Instead, I drove us to the diner-like restaurant closest to the cemetery in our rental van. The dimly lit interior contrasted starkly to the day's bright sunlight, and the bone-chilling temperature felt like a damp cave. Peering into the dining area, where most of the Formica tables were vacant, I fought the urge to turn and run. Emptiness filled the air.

I yearned to hold on to some semblance of Jewish tradition in this gloomy nexus between the cemetery and the airport. Rituals were an important part of my life, steadying me in uncertain times and linking me to a larger whole. They filled me with memories that soothed me.

Having prepared the seudat havra'ah for several friends whose parents had died, I knew and valued the power of drawing solace from this meal, and I wanted it for myself and my family. Having just buried my father, I needed to hold on to the customs of my faith the way a drowning woman clings to a life preserver. But that wasn't going to happen for me. This uninviting, austere restaurant was no place for a grieving family. We belonged at home, nestled in the familiarity of our environment, embraced by friends and loved ones who were not mourning. But we were still hours away from our three-hour flight back to South Florida, which would be followed by a long drive from the airport to my parents' house. We needed sustenance. Without food, we would be crankier and more fatigued than we already were.

I heard the hushed voices of my family and friends behind me as I searched for someone to seat us. Out of the corner of my eye, I saw my sister's nose wrinkle as she inhaled the musty odor.

Eventually a tall, middle-aged woman with an aloof air of authority approached us.

"Do ya have a resavation?"

Despite my disappointment in the surroundings, I chuckled at her New York accent, remembering when I sounded just like that.

"No, we don't," I said. "We just came from my father's funeral at Mount Ararat Cemetery."

"How many in yaw pawty?" The hostess sized up our group.

"Fourteen." I counted my family of eleven, including myself, and my three closest friends—Nancy, her husband, Alan, and Steven—who had flown together from Maryland to bolster me during the funeral.

She stepped back and her eyes widened. "Fawteen? Without a resavation?"

"Right. Can you seat us?" I asked, indicating the rows of empty tables beyond her. At any other time, I might have responded, "Are you kidding?" But I reminded myself that this should be a sacred time and stifled my sarcasm.

"Gimme a few minutes. We'll put some tables t'getha faw ya." The hostess summoned two servers, who promptly organized tables and chairs to accommodate our group.

At the meal of consolation, it is customary to serve foods that are round to symbolize the cyclical and continuous nature of life. Like the Passover seder meal, the meal of consolation typically begins with a hard-boiled egg. The egg, the only food that hardens the longer it is cooked, reminds us to be strong in troubled times. Dad always began our seder meals with this tradition, as his father had before him. And I wanted to do the same.

Once we were seated, I addressed the server while everyone else focused on their menus.

"We'll need fourteen hard-boiled eggs before the meal."

"You want *what*? Hard-boiled eggs?" The server, a thin twenty-something with blonde hair pulled back in a straggly ponytail, stared at me in disbelief.

"Yes, you know . . . eggs you boil for twelve to fifteen minutes so the yolks are solid."

"But we're finished serving breakfast."

While she was thinking only of the lunchtime menu and restaurant procedures, I was fending off grief and exhaustion to unearth my customary sensitivity.

"I know this isn't breakfast, but can you see if the chef has fourteen eggs in the kitchen that he can hard-boil?"

She turned and tramped to the kitchen.

While I deliberated between explaining our tradition or simply expediting the process, she returned.

"Do you want them with the shells or without?"

"If it will expedite the order, we'll shell them ourselves."

I felt like Jack Nicholson in the diner scene in *Five Easy Pieces*. I missed my father taking charge.

As the waitress paraded back and forth from our table to the kitchen, translating our needs to the kitchen staff, Mom repeatedly checked her watch and clicked her tongue, avoiding eye contact by rolling her eyes. Letting out deep, audible sighs, she made us aware of her irritation—as she typically did when she was not in control—without uttering a word.

I wanted to enjoy the company of my sisters, my children, my nieces, and my friends, but I seemed the only one vulnerable to Mom's dramatics. Even though I forced myself not to look in her direction, I was distracted by her behavior, picking up her unspoken criticism the way some people pick up a virus and are debilitated as it ravages their bodies.

Dad would have wanted his family cared for. That was always his priority. But my mother thought only of herself. Typical. I knew she wanted to get to the airport and was powerless because I held the car keys in my pocket. I could feel her increasing tension suffocating me like a pillow against my face, preventing even a modicum of sanctity in these bizarre surroundings.

As the waitress went around the table and slowly jotted down everyone's orders, my children and their cousins caught up on each other's lives, my sisters talked in hushed whispers (probably about our mother's disgruntled behavior), and my friends engaged my mother and me in lighthearted chitchat.

When the waitress finally brought the eggs, she dropped the bowl on the table with a thud. Everyone stared at it as if the eggs would explode. I took the first one, cracked and peeled the shell, sprinkled it with salt, and bit into it. The others joined in; Mom refused, as she always did when she was overridden. Throughout the meal that followed, she sat in steely silence, her grimace speaking volumes.

I'd anticipated that beginning our meal according to Jewish custom would offer comfort even as my sense of security was crumbling. But in the darkness of the malodorous restaurant, even though we had nourished our bodies, my soul remained desolate.

When the meal ended, my steadfast friend, Steven, fulfilled the traditional precept of providing the meal of consolation by paying for the entire meal, relieving us from thinking about money in the midst of our grief. I will never forget his kindness.

Steven's spirit of generosity reminded me of my father. If Dad were with us, he would have insisted on paying the bill; he never let anyone in the family open their wallets in his presence. Even after I became an adult with a managerial salary, my father refused to ever let me pay for a meal. He'd have called Steven a *mensch* (a person of honor).

As Steven settled the bill and my family began exiting the restaurant, I reflected on the many ways my life had been enriched by Dad's generosity. He had provided a fully paid undergraduate education, and I graduated without debt. He never wanted any of his daughters to work through school as he had. He made the sacrifices so we didn't have to. He supported my membership in a sorority and paid the dues. He financed the wedding of my dreams.

My daydream was cut short as my eyes adjusted to the sun's glare. Once outside, we said our goodbyes to my friends, then the family piled into the rental van and we settled in for the one-hour drive to the airport. Unlike the previous night's ride, when the joviality of my children and their cousins cut through the sorrow, this trip was filled with tension so thick it almost clouded the windows.

"We should have just driven to the airport without lunch and waited until we got home to eat. Now we're going to miss our flight," my mother carped. She never would have said that if Dad had been there, especially if he wanted to eat. Her temper flared when he wasn't around.

I could have pointed out that we had more than enough time to get to the airport, or that sitting at the airport for hours before our flight in a place bustling with people would have been more dispiriting, but I held my tongue—as I had so many times over the decades when she criticized or complained. Grief expunged any empathy I might have felt for my mother's anxiety. Knowing reassurances wouldn't help, I held the steering wheel with a white-knuckled grip and kept my eyes focused on the road ahead.

CHAPTER 6

Arriving

The funeral was over, the meal of consolation was disheartening, and the car ride to the airport was strained. Walking through JFK Airport, my mother clutched the ceremonial triangle-folded American flag to her chest as if afraid someone might snatch it. She proceeded through the terminal with the formal posture and gait of a soldier passing in review, oblivious to the children and grandchildren following behind her, looking like a unit commander leading a military color guard in parade. Throughout the three-hour flight to Florida, the reality that my father was never coming back inched into my psyche the way ounces, then pounds, had imperceptibly crept onto my waistline over the years.

It was late on Friday night (the beginning of the Jewish Sabbath) when we finally got to the house in my father's beloved Polo Club, the residential country club in Boca Raton that had given him a lifestyle he never thought he could afford. After his cancer prognosis had sunk in, Dad convinced my mother to sell the family home in New York, along with most of its contents, and move to a place where he never again had to scrape ice off his car windshield. He lived his happiest days in this golf community; he called it "paradise," in a way that made the word sound magical.

This home, once a source of great joy for my father, would now house his grieving wife and three daughters for the seven-day mourning period known as shiva.

Unlike Christian funerals, which are typically held a week after death, Jewish funerals traditionally take place within twenty-four to forty-eight hours after death. Embalming is not traditionally practiced in Judaism, making open coffins taboo. This prohibition against embalming allows the body to decompose naturally, following the biblical teaching, "For you come from dust and to dust you shall return." Nothing is allowed to slow the body's natural return to the elements.

In other faiths, a wake gives friends and loved ones the chance to visit with mourners (and often to view the body) before burial. In Judaism, the opportunity to receive visitors typically begins immediately after interment, during shiva.

The word *shiva* in Hebrew means "seven." During shiva, the mourners—the immediate family of the deceased, meaning the spouse, children, parents, and siblings—withdraw from the world for seven days to have a dedicated time and space to mourn the loss of their loved one. Throughout the weeklong shiva period, friends and relatives come together in the family's home to offer their condolences and support. Gathering together as a community is key during shiva, just as it is at the heart of many Jewish traditions. The strength and support of friends, family, and neighbors helps the bereaved through their grief.

Mourners are said to be "sitting shiva" because during the seven-day period, they traditionally sit on low stools or boxes while receiving visitors. This practice symbolizes the mourners being "brought low" by their grief.

This ritual derives from the story of Job, whose friends sat to the ground with him to comfort him in his grief.

Traditional Conservative and Orthodox Jews typically observe shiva for seven days. However, since shiva is always suspended during Shabbat (the Sabbath), many contemporary Jews now mark the end of shiva when Shabbat occurs, shortening the shiva period. In our case, our seven-day period would start at the end of Shabbat, after sundown on Saturday night. Sabbath joy traditionally supersedes mourning, but we had just buried my father and traveled more than 1,300 miles, and joy felt as remote as the New York cemetery we'd left behind.

Shiva is typically held in the home of the deceased, so no one discussed where we would sit shiva. The understanding that we would do
so in my parents' home and that my sisters and I would stay in Florida
with Mom for the full seven days was unspoken—absorbed as if by
osmosis.

We similarly understood that Lois would sit shiva despite her having
been baptized in the Protestant church many years earlier. Although
she had subsequently left the church, Lois had never returned to her
Jewish roots. Nevertheless, as with so many times in my life, she now
offered a grounding and soothing spirit. Dad always told us, "You three
sisters must stick together." In his death, his directive became reality.

———

Mom pulled into the driveway and pushed the button that raised the
garage door. My head hit the back of the seat as I gasped. There against
the right wall sat Dad's cherished golf cart, shiny and clean, still plugged
into the outlet and fully charged, ready for its next use that wouldn't be.
After years of dragging his clubs around in a leather bag, my father had
acted like a kid with a new toy when he bought his electric golf cart,
complete with roll-down sidewalls so he could golf even in the rain.

"I feel like I've won the lottery," he said, his face gleaming as he
drove that cart around the community.

Now he would never drive it again. I didn't know it then, but years
would pass before I could look at any golf cart without breaking into
a cold sweat.

Mom drove into the garage. There on the back wall hung Dad's collection of golf hats. The colors had mostly faded from multiple wash-
ings and the strong Florida sun, every brim stained with a ring of sweat.
When I saw the beige cap that my son, David, had given him—*Will
Golf for Food*—I gripped my sister's arm. Next to the caps hung the
Purple Heart license plate that Dad no longer used since the golf cart
eliminated his need for a second car. The wall on the left held his other

pride and joy—the workbench he had built, with his well-worn tools hanging from silver hooks in the brown pegboard.

We piled out of the car, no one uttering a word as we entered the house like zombies, our heels click-clacking on the white tile floor as we carried in suitcases laden with our sadness.

Beyond my parents' studies and the kitchen, we entered the large open space that incorporated the living and dining rooms. The white sofas and tiles were punctuated by tiny black pillows, a small round black area rug between the sofas, and the black shelves of the mirrored wall unit that ran the length of the left wall. The high-backed dining room chairs, covered in jet black cotton, sat around the large, rectangular glass table. The house looked like a black-and-white photo, devoid of all color. In this austere living room, my family would sit shiva.

I dragged myself to the kitchen, found the box of matches, and performed the first ritual act in a house of mourning—lighting the *ner daluk,* the large shiva candle that burns for seven days and seven nights as a symbol of the divine spark that inhabited the body. Mom placed it gently at the center of the dining room table.

I was ready to perform the other rituals that symbolize a Jewish home as a house of mourning, certain Dad would have wanted that. But I was soon to learn that my mother had other ideas.

In traditional Judaism, mirrors are covered during the shiva period to keep the soul of the deceased from being reflected in the glass. This centuries-old custom originated from the notion that mirrors attracted spirits and trapped them there. The modern interpretation claims the practice discourages vanity and fosters inner reflection, since mourners are not supposed to be concerned with their personal appearance during this time. Covering the mirrors also prevents us from seeing the lines of grief etched in our faces.

The mirrored floor-to-ceiling wall unit along the left side of the expansive room housed family photos and Mom's expensive collectibles.

"Mom, what should we use to cover the mirrors?" I asked. "I could get a couple of sheets."

"Cover the mirrors?" she grimaced at me as if I'd suggested jumping from a ten-story window. "We're not doing that."

"But it's tradition to hide mirrors in a shiva house," I pleaded. "If this is where we're going to be sitting shiva, can't we *please* cover them?"

I didn't add, "Dad covered the mirrors when each of his parents died." I knew to bite my tongue.

"It's impossible to cover all these mirrors, and I'm not about to move everything on these shelves. I can't think about it now. You'll just have to sit shiva in front of mirrors. That's all there is to it."

Quashed. A throwback to my childhood, when back-and-forth discussions with her didn't exist.

My mother gave out sleeping arrangements and bed linens with her typical demeanor of an army drill sergeant. Then she stiffened her back, walked into her bedroom, and shut the door, replicating the many times in my childhood when she had turned away rather than engage. I stood for slowly dragging minutes, staring at the closed door and longing for her comfort, thwarted as I so often had been by my mother's inability to cope with three young children and her need to always feel in control.

Maybe I should follow her and hug her, I thought.

But I remained glued to my spot as the others moved to their assigned places. My mother, the accomplished career nurse, could nurture the ill with the utmost compassion yet consistently denied empathy to her daughters.

I flashed back to the nine days when my father lay in a coma in intensive care after his double bypass surgery. Every time the steel gray doors of the ICU opened for visitors, my mother rushed in. Before seeing my father, she bombarded the head nurse with a barrage of questions.

"What's his oxygenation level? His current vitals? What's been done for him since we were here last? When did the doctor last see him?" Then she hugged every nurse who had cared for him, before going to his bedside.

I recalled those scenes, envious of those nurses for the daily hugs they received from my mother. From the moment I arrived in Florida until I left to go home twenty-one days later, she never once hugged me—the daughter who remained faithfully by her side.

At any other time, I might have acknowledged my mother's desolation. I might have reasoned that she did not embrace Jewish rituals as I did and would grieve differently. I might have remembered her trauma when, at only ten years old, she witnessed her young mother bleeding in bed from colon cancer and dying a day later. I might have recognized the ways my father's death was triggering memories of that death, knowing that any loss reminds us of the ones before. Or I might have been sensitive to the way my mother, enveloped in her own grief, couldn't recognize that my sisters and I had also suffered a life-altering loss.

But not that night. That night, I was reeling from the want of my father's love.

Despite overwhelming exhaustion, I couldn't sleep. Instead, I tiptoed into the dining room, yearning for consolation, and sat alone at the dining room table, staring into the tall glass jar containing the ner daluk candle and drawing solace from the flame dancing ever so slightly on the wick. The flame drew me from my grief to another place and time.

It is said that candlelight symbolizes the human being: the wick represents the body, and the flame the soul that brings light into darkness. The duality of the light against the darkness . . . my father had been that for me. He had been the light to my mother's darkness, but now he was gone.

The next morning, my sisters and I attended Shabbat services at my parents' synagogue in order to recite the Mourner's Kaddish. We three steadied each other like the wheels on a tricycle, and I imagined my father smiling.

Being in Dad's synagogue reminded me of sitting in *shul* (synagogue) with him as a young girl, when I understood nothing of the service, the prayers, or the Hebrew. Because my father worked six twelve-hour days each week, having alone time with him was like the thrill of a big birthday celebration. I sat quietly next to him, dutifully pretending to be engrossed in the service.

Then it hit me. I would never sit in shul with him again. I would never again hear the funny way he pronounced God's name, with his New York accent—"Adonoy" (to rhyme with "toy") rather than "Adonai" (to rhyme with "high"). I would never again feel the overwhelming pride I had when I prayed next to him as equals, after I learned a few Hebrew prayers as an adult. I would never again hear his voice, always off-key, in unison with mine.

As a child, I had stood with him, my voice silent from ignorance of the blessings. Now I rose in his house of worship, his voice the silent one.

When the time came for the Mourner's Kaddish, the three of us read the transliteration. In *siddurim* (prayer books), the Hebrew words of the Mourner's Kaddish are transliterated to the English alphabet so that those unfamiliar with the prayer can articulate it. Side by side, my sisters and I were as connected as the three sides of a triangle. We'd had our periods of sibling rivalry over the years, but in this we were one.

———

Back at my parents' house later that afternoon, we set up the small folding table with coffee and refreshments for the guests we anticipated. On Saturday night, when sundown marked the end of Shabbat, we would have our first prayer service at the house. It is a sacred obligation to hold daily services—both morning and evening—in the shiva home, and for that, we needed the ten-person minyan to say Kaddish.

"I don't know if you three girls should be counted in the minyan." My mother spoke so casually, I wasn't sure I'd heard her correctly.

"What do you mean?" I turned and looked directly at her, stunned.

"It might be difficult for some of the old-timers who are coming to be part of the minyan to handle."

I felt my feminism stir and my childhood wounds reopen as I remembered all the other times she'd left me feeling invisible. Once again, her concern about others' perceptions eclipsed any thought of her daughter's feelings.

But my focus was on my father's soul. Besides, my father had given me his blessing. It didn't occur to me then to pose the question, "And if ten men aren't available, then will we count?" Much later, I chuckled, realizing we'd forgotten that on the first night, our own family constituted a minyan—we were more than ten.

Rather than allow resentment to fester like an infected wound, I stood as straight as I could, and with a soft but authoritative voice, I asserted, "In Dad's house, his daughters and his wife will count for the minyan."

Mom, unaccustomed to such boldness on my part, glared wide-eyed, her lower jaw dropping open as if in shock, then turned her back and walked away without a word.

CHAPTER 7
Duality

Watching my mother walk away reminded me of another time, many years earlier, when she also turned her back on me.

Growing up with my mother was like living with Dr. Jekyll and Mr. Hyde. During the day, she was tyrannical. But when my father was home, peace reigned, and my mother softened.

During my elementary- and middle-school days, I would watch the hours tick away until my father came home from work. I would crouch down at the living room window, hidden from my mother's view by the thick brown-and-gold drapes, staring at the street, watching for his car to pull into the driveway when he returned from work.

The glow of his headlights shone into my heart. I watched him climb the three steps onto the front porch, reach into his pocket for the leather pouch that held his keys, and choose the house key from the bunch. Just as he was about to put the key in the lock, I would fling open the door, letting the heavy claustrophobic air drift out.

As he entered the living room, my sisters and I would pounce on him, and he pretended we were strong enough to knock him over. With the grace of an acrobat, he would tumble to the floor, allowing us to jump on him. Believing in my youthful naïveté that I could topple him made me feel strong and powerful at a time when I was, in reality, powerless.

When we were very small, he would lie on his back on the floor, put his feet flat on the floor, and bend his knees, creating an indoor human slide that was more fun than the slides on the playground. Gales of laughter would fill the living room.

Sometimes, he would roll over and get on all fours; we took turns getting on his back, wrapping our legs around his waist, and shouting "Giddyup, horsey," while he pranced around the living room, nickering and mouthing "Neigh, neigh," until our mother yelled for us to come to dinner.

Years later, I learned that my father's merrymaking was a relief from the doldrums of a job he hated, working for a father who stifled his intelligence and creativity. Perhaps that explains why my mother never intervened in our revelries when he was home, given her intolerance for our noise.

I didn't know enough about my parents' relationship to understand why this was, but I noticed that my mother's sullen grimaces disappeared and her voice softened as soon as my father entered the house. Was she embarrassed for him to see her anger? Was his presence as calming for her as it was for us?

I tried everything to avoid my mother's wrath, from clearing the dinner table, washing dinner dishes, cleaning the house, doing the ironing, and getting good grades. But no matter how good I tried to be, I could never do things right enough. I could never make her happy, no matter how hard I tried.

I lived in fear of my mother's angry outbursts and insults. When her yelling started, for no reason I could ever fathom, dread would creep up from the pit of my stomach, and my body would start to tremble like the leaves on our maple tree when the wind picks up.

Her beatings were worse. One Saturday afternoon in March 1959, something set my mother off. I can't remember now what precipitated the event; maybe I forgot to hang up my coat or put away my books or school papers, or perhaps I didn't dust the fake plant leaves to her satisfaction. Maybe I was arguing with one of my sisters, or my tone of voice was misinterpreted—a common occurrence that always resulted in a thrashing.

I was ten years old that day when, standing in the dining room of our house—the room we had to walk through to get to the kitchen—she began hitting me. She slammed me against the doorframe, and I heard the sound, like breaking a carrot in two, before my brain could compute what had happened. As I lay on the floor gasping for breath, my mother turned her back and walked away, and I heard her bedroom door creaking as it closed.

I hobbled as far as the living room couch, sobbing. I watched my leg swell as the patches on my ankle went from red to blue to purple, and the bone began to protrude from my skin; I couldn't tell whether the searing pain in my chest came more from the beating or my mother's abandonment. I was alone, convulsions wracking my body, and terrified. My sisters stayed cowering in their bedroom, weeping quietly while they listened to my shrieking.

When my father came home from work hours later, he took one look at me.

"*What* happened?"

My mother raced out of their bedroom and told him I'd fallen. She told him that the floor had just been waxed (something my mother paid a man named Mr. Ryan to do every other Saturday) and that I slid and fell.

I wanted to tell my father, "She's lying. She beat me like she beats all three of us," but I felt like a rottweiler was digging its canine teeth into my heart. My throat constricted as I glared at my mother in horror, immobilized.

If my father wondered why my mother, a trained nurse, had done nothing to care for me, he didn't ask in that moment. Wasting no time, he lifted me from the sofa, carried me to the car, and rushed me to the local emergency clinic. I imagine his army experience taught him not to hesitate, not to stand around asking questions, when seeing a wounded comrade. In his presence, I was freed from danger. He had rescued me. At the clinic, an X-ray validated what we knew to be true: the fibula was broken.

People have asked if my father knew the truth. What I know is that I never told him. Considering the culture of the times, the idea that spanking a child could constitute child abuse was still unheard of. And in the 1945 edition of *Baby and Child Care*, Dr. Benjamin Spock considered spanking "less poisonous than lengthy disapproval, because it clears the air, for parents and child." But there is a big difference between a spanking and a beating.

Fearing my mother's reprisal, I never asked my father if he knew of her abuse. Certainly, he knew of her narcissism, as he had to live with it, too. But in all the years I lived at home, I never saw my mother turn her back on my father.

My father was the light of my life. And now he was gone.

CHAPTER 8

Shiva

On the first night of shiva, many of my parents' longtime friends, new community friends, and local cousins came to the house to pay their respects. One of the functions of a shiva call (also called a condolence call) is to share recollections of the loved one. Doing so is one of the greatest gifts a person can give to a mourner.

I listened happily to the stories of the golfers, who talked about the way Dad always smiled and never said a negative word about anyone. The corners of their eyes crinkled as they told of calling him "Slim" and "Stilts" because of his long, thin legs. And I learned that Dad, who never used profanity around his daughters, loved dirty jokes.

"You know, it's unusual for a golfer, especially a competitive one like your father, to rejoice in others' accomplishments," said Norman, one of Dad's golf buddies who had played in, and won, multiple tournaments with him. "Your dad was always happier for others' good shots and good scores than he was for his own." The affection for Dad shown by his golf buddies consoled me, like my father's hugs after I'd tumbled from my bicycle as a child.

A friend of Dad's from way back, who'd played pinochle with him during my formative years, talked about the three holes-in-one Dad had shot between May 1999 and August 2000.

"Your father actually looked embarrassed when he hit his third hole-in-one; he wouldn't acknowledge that the ball had sailed into the cup," he reported.

At that point, I excused myself and scurried to Dad's study to retrieve his three trophies. I saw the black leather sofa where he used to lie on his right hip, watching his cherished golf on the outmoded television set. A shiver coursed through me when I saw his desk and the old computer he had learned to master in his midsixties. I envisioned him leaning back in his black desk chair, holding the phone as we talked and staring at the colorful bird-of-paradise flowers outside his window, delighting in knowing he never again had to shovel snow from his driveway. I remembered the lilt in his voice as he told me, "I'm absolutely in awe of this newfangled device [the computer]. It saves me hours of time and energy . . . more time on the golf course."

I'd been proud of my father. In the earliest days of personal computers, he'd mastered them. While many people his age resisted the new technology, he was fearless and undaunted. In the credit finance company he established in the early 1960s, before Visa and Mastercard became household words, he replaced his decades-long process of typing letters, one at a time on a manual typewriter, with computer-generated letters. He created spreadsheets to monitor collections and even learned to print envelopes using his then state-of-the-art printer. I stared at the black screen until I recalled why I had entered his study.

On top of the entertainment unit stood the three hole-in-one trophies, five and a half inches high, each containing the ball that landed in the cup in one shot. Each ball sat on a faux gold tee, encased in the number 1 and mounted on a wood base, with an engraved gold plate bearing his name and the date. I heard myself moan: the third one was dated August 31, 2000, only eleven days before he walked into the hospital and only twenty days before he died.

I smiled, picturing his buddies cheering for his third hole-in-one and my father standing humbly on the green. My father, not an overly exuberant man, wouldn't have wanted his shot to affect the pace of play, but he would have been quick to say, "The first round of drinks is on me!"

I presumed my father would be embarrassed at displaying his awards, but I was beaming as I carried them reverently to the living room, as though they were sacred objects.

"The candle always burns brightest before it goes out," said another of Dad's friends as I displayed the trophies.

Another characterization came from Lieutenant Al Cone, Dad's commanding officer from Company C of the 406th Regiment of the 102nd Infantry Division, who telephoned as soon as he heard the news. He told us, "Your father was a brave soldier. He never hesitated from any command I gave him, and he carried out several very dangerous combat operations. You can be very proud of your father's service to the army and the country."

In the stories, my father came alive. In the stories, I could let go of him more gently.

———

Sunday, September 24 marked our first full day of sitting shiva. Realizing the date, I startled as if awakened from a deep sleep by a loud alarm. Today was my son David's seventeenth birthday. I had completely forgotten it and done nothing to prepare. According to Jewish tradition, as a mourner, I couldn't celebrate. Caught between the proverbial rock and hard place, between honoring my dead father and my living son, "bad mother" guilt bubbled to the surface.

David, dressed in his usual T-shirt and shorts, was searching through the refrigerator for something to eat.

"David, I need to talk with you." My voice cracked.

He half turned and eyed me with a quizzical expression.

"David, I'm so sorry. I completely forgot your birthday. I don't have a card or a gift for you." My son, at six feet tall, now towered over me.

"It's okay, Mom, I'm good. I'm just hungry." He turned back to the refrigerator as if to end the conversation.

I needed to continue, even though my commentaries usually made my son tune out.

"When my grandfather died, two days before my twenty-first birthday, my father sat shiva and everyone forgot my birthday. I never wanted this to happen to you."

"I'm all right. Really," he said in a reassuring voice.

His crescent moon smile matched his gentle but matter-of-fact tone, and his sincerity diminished my self-reproach. I relaxed.

"Some life events take priority," he said as he put his arm around my shoulder, the child comforting the parent. Drawing closer to his strong frame, I felt the same gentle spirit that had been my father's.

My father had had a special relationship with his only grandson. He and David shared a love of sports—all sports. They made friendly wagers on the Super Bowl and the World Series, and razzed each other on the weaknesses of the other's favorite teams. They played basketball, racquetball, and golf together over the years, and once, when I told my son that my father had never uttered a word of profanity, he replied, "You've never played golf with him."

Since David rarely, if ever, showed emotion, I couldn't know how he was coping with his grandfather's death. Rachel, on the other hand— my more expressive child—removed herself to a closet so she could break down without disturbing anyone.

———

By the second night of shiva, my uncle had shuttled our children to their various flights so they could return to school for Monday morning classes. Rachel had flown back to college in California and David had arranged to stay with his father until I got home. After all the visitors had left, Lois, Jane, and I retreated to our parents' bedroom and sprawled out in our pajamas across the king-size bed.

The bedroom faced the back of the house, where a sliding glass door opened to the screened lanai and the soothing burbling sound of the water fountain as it emptied into a small one-person-size pool. The lush green grass and tall palm trees beyond the lanai reminded me that I could count on nature's consistency even when my life was changing; I could behold beauty even during shiva.

"I see you finally gave up wearing those old-lady flannel nightgowns," Lois teased.

I don't remember what else we talked about, but the three of us got silly. We joked, laughed, and knocked into each other, roughhousing and releasing our pent-up emotions. Such playfulness was rare for us. Even though we had long ago put our sibling rivalries behind us, we three lived far apart from each other. We each had a full-time job and children living at home, making visits difficult.

"Stop that noise! I can't stand it. What do you think you're doing?" Our mother's voice rang through the house, curtailing our fun. Her squinted eyes and threatening voice took us back to our childhoods, when her intolerance for noise resulted in severe beatings. We just never knew when her anger would erupt; my mother could take me from age fifty-one to five as fast as a tornado could level a town.

We silenced immediately and peeked at one another from bowed heads, like shamed children, but behind the solemnity, giggles waited to explode again. Our eyes spoke what words didn't: "She's scolding us, but I'm not sorry, and I can tell you're not sorry either."

Later, away from Mom's glare, I thanked my sisters for our restorative time together. I could almost feel Dad's delight in our combined hilarity and closeness. He always relished our playfulness as kids.

I was profoundly grateful for my two sisters, the bond between us more cemented than ever. Sharing grief's burden lightened it. I thought about people without siblings to rely on at times like this, and my heart ached for them.

The third day of shiva dragged on, time hanging like a dead weight. The seven-day period is supposed to bring peace to mourners by providing them the opportunity to remember the deceased and free them from distractions such as work, bills, television and movies, and current events. But on this day, peace eluded me.

Mom's women friends, many of them acquaintances from her various volunteer organizations who never knew my father, collectively decided to visit on this one afternoon. Carloads of women descended on the house together, and before one group left, another arrived. The well-dressed women in their seventies and eighties, with manicured nails, carefully styled hairdos, and Saks Fifth Avenue clothing, sat gracefully in the living room, as if convening for a board meeting. They stayed for hours, talking about one woman's husband, another woman's illnesses, someone's grandchild who had gotten in trouble—their voices droning on endlessly, setting my nerves on edge.

Unlike a wake, where the mood can be festive, the atmosphere in a typical shiva home is subdued. The fitting topic of conversation is the deceased. These women seemed oblivious to both.

I didn't want to appear antisocial or unappreciative, so I sat, along with my sisters, making eye contact with various ladies, nodding at the appropriate times and offering "Um-hum" and "Interesting" at the proper intervals. But the incessant chatter was sucking the air out of the room, and with it the threadlike remnants of my physical and emotional energy. As shadows moved across the floor, I ached for solitude.

Mom, on the other hand, was animated and smiling, distracted from her sorrow, the center of attention. Her face softened as she joined in the small talk. The women, seeing my mother's delight in their company, kept chatting, reassuring me that my mother would have support after the three of us returned home. I imagined my father telling me, "It's okay. Let her have her friends around her. You'll soon be going home, and she'll be alone."

Finally, I pardoned myself and tiptoed from the room like a small child trying to escape the watchful eye of an adult after taking forbidden candy. My sisters, wide-eyed at my gumption, followed me into our parents' bedroom like children behind the Pied Piper. We shut the window blinds, climbed into the king-size bed, pulled back the covers, and silently consoled one another until we fell into a deep afternoon sleep.

———

"What are we going to do with all this food?" my mother yelled from the kitchen. "There's no more room in the refrigerator. I can't fit it all in here." Panic laced each word.

More food deliveries arrived daily from well-meaning friends and family—platters with cold cuts and bread and condiments, trays of cookies and pastries, assortments of bagels with cream cheeses and fish, and disposable foil pans of cooked meats and potatoes. We had enough food to last for weeks. But with each subsequent delivery, my mother became more obsessed. Her refrigerator, which typically resembled Old Mother Hubbard's cupboard, became an anathema.

"How are we going to store this food? We're never going to be able to eat it all," she groused.

Without a moment's hesitation, or time to take the pulse of my feelings, I defaulted to my usual knee-jerk reaction: take care of Mom's anxiety so it doesn't get worse. "I'll take care of it, Mom," I said, trying to reassure her. I immediately found people to deliver the overflow food to a local food bank. Right then I decided, although it is customary to send food to a shiva home, in the future I would first check to see what, if anything, the family needed. If food was abundant, I would bring coffee or soft drinks and send a donation to the family's charity of choice.

———

In a traditional shiva home, the hostess and mourner roles are separate. The mourner's primary focus is moving through grief, so friends or members of the mourner's synagogue typically host, serve, and clean up. But my mother had different expectations, discounting my grief.

I was to ensure that those who came for the morning minyan had coffee, tea, or juice, and a pastry or bagel. I woke each morning while the others slept and put up the coffee and water for tea, checked the supply of cream and sugar, and arranged the food in a tempting display.

Mom charged me with making daily telephone calls to ensure we had the requisite ten people for morning and evening *minyanim* (plural of *minyan*). Her constant worry that we might not have two daily quorums manifested itself in relentless instructions to "call this person" or "call that person." It would only be later, after I returned home to Maryland, that I realized I could have contacted my parents' synagogue for help. These insights are elusive when grief clouds one's brain.

After everyone left, I cleaned up and prepared the house for the next guests. I looked on the outside like a party hostess, rather than a daughter who had just buried her father. The pressure of these chores felt like an elephant sitting on an already crushed heart.

It never occurred to me to say no to the responsibilities being placed on me, or suggest that my sisters carry some of the load, or ask for assistance from any of Mom's many friends who would have been only too thrilled to help. Strange as it may seem, despite feeling I was trudging through quicksand, I never questioned my province as the responsible eldest. Shedding the lifelong role of the dependable firstborn is not easy. Shiva was not the time to abdicate that function.

"Respect your mother," I could hear my father telling me, his counsel ineradicable.

And putting my grief aside, I did just that.

———

Friday morning was *erev* Rosh Hashanah—the day before Rosh Hashanah. Since days on the Jewish calendar begin at sunset, the holiday would begin that evening. Cantor Levy, the prayer leader from Mom and Dad's synagogue, came to the house to conduct the *shacharit* (morning) service and mark the end of shiva. I assumed him to be late sixties-ish, with a round potbelly and scraggly white whiskers that formed a thin, V-shaped beard on his chin. He and my mother had a mutual respect born of many shared conversations.

After the service, following tradition, the cantor escorted my mother, my sisters, and me for a walk around the block. We had donned our leather shoes, which, traditionally associated with vanity, are not worn during shiva. Walking outdoors symbolized our return to the "real world" from which we'd withdrawn, while also escorting Dad's soul as it leaves the house. One of the aspects of Judaism that gives me great comfort is its symbolic rituals for every important life event.

Being in the open air after being in my mother's black-and-white home for a week felt like Dorothy's awakening from the black and white of Kansas to the glorious colors of Munchkinland in *The Wizard of Oz*. As I took in the cloudless blue sky, the emerald of the grass, and the bright salmon hues of the bird-of-paradise flowers, I felt the same excitement as I did when NBC introduced its colorful peacock logo after years of black-and-white TV. The trickling water splashing in the fountains that dotted the community soothed me; I marveled at the towering palm trees, their feather-like fronds fanning out in a way I had never noticed before. I vaguely recalled a blessing for the beginning of spring, where we thank God for creating "good trees that give pleasure to mankind through them," and I uttered a silent prayer of gratitude for Adonai's gifts of nature that surrounded me.

I drew the clean, fresh air into my lungs. As my chest rose and fell with each inhale and exhale, my mind flashed to my father and how his chest expanded and contracted in the same way at the very end of his life. Even after doctors pronounced him gone, the respirator continued pumping air into his lungs, creating a steady, rhythmic rise and fall of his chest. The colors of the Florida landscape gave way to the nightmarish image—my father's skin had turned a gruesome shade of yellow, his face rounded and puffed up like the Pillsbury Doughboy, and his luminous brown eyes, opened for the first time in those nine days, were covered with thick, cloudy, oatmeal-colored mucus. I'd been unprepared for the gurgling, gasping sounds of the death rattle, the jaundiced color of his face, and the way my father's always-warm hands had turned cold.

Neither television nor movies had prepared me for his final moments. As much as I tried to erase those horrific images from my brain, they reappeared unpredictably. If I could rewind the clock, I would still choose to be at my father's bedside as he died. But I wondered aloud to my sisters, "Why don't we, as a society, prepare people for the awful look of death? I can't get it out of my mind."

"When we get back to the house, we can look at Dad's smiling face in some photos I brought. Hopefully they'll wipe out the bad memory," Jane offered, embracing me.

My sisters and I strolled back to the house in silence while our mother walked in front, conversing with the cantor. After he left, my sisters and I slipped into our father's study to enjoy Jane's photos. Her favorite—showing her and our dad sitting side by side, celebrating their joint birthdays in 1984, when she turned thirty and he turned sixty— revealed the two of them wearing toothy grins, a birthday cake in front of them. Other images showed Dad holding his infant granddaughters, a happy man who loved being a grandpa.

"Do you think Dad anticipated the worst? Do you think he suspected he was sick enough to die?" I turned toward my sisters.

Lois shrugged with puddling eyes.

"We'll never know." Jane's voice was almost inaudible.

What fears had my father wrestled with? I wondered.

I recalled a conversation from earlier that summer, when he casually confessed to no longer being worried about outliving his money. I hadn't thought much about it at the time, but now I was sorry I hadn't asked more questions.

Thinking about what I could have, should have, and would have talked about, I began shivering. Lois and Jane wrapped their arms around me so tightly, the tension in my body loosened like a taut cable gone slack. Hindsight can birth enormous regrets.

Later that morning, in an empty house, my sisters and I sat quietly in the living room, relieved and grateful that the frenzy of activity, meal preparations, housekeeping, and ensuring minyanim was over.

"I miss not having my own support group around me," Jane said wistfully.

We all agreed.

"True," I asserted. "Shiva would have been more spiritual for me if I'd been at home, surrounded by people who care about me—people to coordinate all the arrangements, handle all the food preparations, clean up, and ensure a minyan twice daily—people who aren't also mourners. At home, I could have focused on grieving."

"I wouldn't have sat shiva if I'd been home," Lois revealed. "But I'm really glad I stayed here. I love you two."

"We're Mom and Dad's best gifts to each other," I admitted, feeling the blessing of my sisters.

That afternoon, I drove Lois and Jane to West Palm Beach Airport while Mom stayed home. Amidst weepy farewells and promises of telephone calls for support, I reluctantly waved goodbye as each boarded her homebound flight, feeling the crack in my heart widen as I turned toward the airport exit.

I was staying behind to support my mother through myriad legal and financial matters that are prohibited during shiva, and to accompany her to synagogue that evening, Rosh Hashanah, the beginning of Jewish New Year 5761.

Sitting in the car in the corner of the airport parking lot, preparing to drive back to my mother's house, I was alone for the first time in more than three weeks. I finally had the peace I'd craved. But in the hushed silence, facing the idea of being alone with my mother, I felt only desolation. She and I shared this common tragedy, yet we were like two trains running on parallel tracks: both going in the same direction but never meeting; both needing comfort, neither having the capacity to give. This truth was almost as painful to me as my father's death.

CHAPTER 9
Entering a Man's World

"*Women* do not wear tallit," growled the small octogenarian man as he hurried to where I stood. My mother and I had just entered the small chapel in my parents' synagogue, Temple Anshei Shalom, in Delray Beach. While the synagogue advertised itself as "The Friendly Conservative Synagogue," the members behaved more like Orthodox Jews.

The little man glared at me while I froze in place, every muscle stiffening, uncertain how to respond. His squinted eyes bore into me as he stared without blinking.

"You will remove it," he hissed, a demand rather than a request.

This was my first visit to the morning minyan at Anshei Shalom. I had just wrapped my tallit—the traditional Jewish prayer shawl—around my shoulders.

Wearing the sacred garment, I felt enveloped in a warm embrace, the way a small child feels when she holds her soft, velvety blanket up to her nose, inhaling the smell of the fabric and drawing peace from the familiar. Donning the tallit prepares me to pray. It reminds me of God's commandments and demonstrates my belief in, and love for, God. Praying without my tallit felt as sacrilegious as praying without clothes on.

—

My fascination with the sacred garment began when I was a young child, when I watched my father wrap himself in his tallit. Even then,

69

I felt I was watching a hallowed ritual. Sitting next to my father in synagogue, unfamiliar with the service, the prayers, and the Hebrew, the only available discreet distraction, other than squirming in my seat, was braiding the *tzitzit* (fringes) on his tallit. As the service wore on, I would braid the fringes, take out the braids, and then braid them again. Dad occasionally glanced down at me with his half smile, as though braiding, unbraiding, and rebraiding this religious garment was the most natural child's activity. His patience never waned.

The commandments to wear the tzitzit are found in the Hebrew Bible (in Deuteronomy 22:12 and Numbers 15:37–41). The fringes hang from each of the four corners of the prayer shawl, each with eight strands and five knots on each corner. The central purpose of the tzitzit is remembering—to look at the tassels is to remember God's commandments. There are stories in the New Testament of sick people kissing the hem of Jesus's tallit. Historically, the tallit was exclusively the providence of males, who received their tallits at their bar mitzvahs. But in 1990, I began wearing one, too. Shrouded in that spiritual garment, I felt equal to the men.

———

I looked to my mother, standing at my elbow, for support. She said nothing, her blank expression noncommittal, and left me standing as if alone. *Why isn't she speaking up for me?* I wrapped my arms across my chest, hoping to feel less exposed.

I peered into the small chapel and saw only white males whose average age exceeded eighty, a marked contrast to my synagogue with its wide range of different age groups. They were glaring at me with scowls, furrowed brows, grimaces. Not one smile. Certainly, the men saw the black keriah ribbons over our hearts designating us as mourners. Not one word of welcome or condolence. The air thickened as they held their collective breath, awaiting my reaction.

Options flew through my brain. Protest or not? Wear the tallit and take my seat or take it off? Confront or acquiesce?

Do you really want to cause a scene in your parents' synagogue, Sarah, when you'll be here for several more days? Do you want one of these octogenarians to have a heart attack right here in the synagogue? Remember: your purpose for being here is to honor your father and show God his soul should be elevated to the highest spiritual plane in Gan Eden.

Making a scene would be the antithesis of my goal to bring merit to my father's soul. Besides, my mother would remain in this synagogue long after I went home, and I didn't want the elders to make her uncomfortable. So I relinquished this meaningful and holy source of comfort. Slowly and deliberately, I removed my tallit, taking my time to fold it in half and in half again, carefully tucking the fringes into the creases and smoothing it with my fingers so it didn't wrinkle, then gently replaced it in its matching bag, all the while staring at the men who continued to glare at me.

My mother and I took seats in the back row of the chapel and opened our prayer books. But my mind flooded with unanswered questions.

How could my father have joined a synagogue where women weren't accepted as equals, when he always advocated for the professional growth of his wife and daughters? What made him affiliate with men who were so unaccepting of women? It just didn't make sense.

I kept my head down, staring into the prayer book. When the time came to recite the Mourner's Kaddish, my mother and I rose. I stood erect like a soldier, kept my eyes focused on the transliteration, and enunciated each word in my most assertive voice, proud of my ability to sanctify God and honor my father. When the Kaddish ended, I sat down, eyes focused on my lap. When the service ended, I whisked my mother from the synagogue, eager to escape before I said something I would later regret.

"What made you and Dad choose this synagogue over others in the area?" I asked my mother after we got back to the house. She stared into space as if reminiscing.

"When we came to Florida, we had very good friends who belonged here. They invited us to come with them for Sabbath services and then for the High Holidays. Your dad and I had visited other nearby synagogues. He felt comfortable here; it mattered more to him than it did to me. So with our friends urging us to join them, we did."

My mother's explanation slowly diffused my resentment at the treatment I received that morning, but it didn't lessen my chagrin that she did not come to my defense nor share my outrage at being told to remove my tallit.

"Your father and I never expected you to come here. We knew you loved your own synagogue," she elaborated. "You were at home there. I guess we just didn't anticipate this situation."

"It's okay, Mom. As long as you're reciting Kaddish while I'm here, I'll come to this synagogue with you." And with that, I put aside any ideas of looking elsewhere to pray.

"I'll recite the Kaddish for the thirty days. Your father was proud that you wanted to pray for him for the whole eleven months."

According to tradition, widows and widowers chant the Mourner's Kaddish for only thirty days (as do siblings and parents), a time frame I have never understood. For a woman who had loved and been married to the same man for fifty-four years, thirty days seemed insufficient.

Later that evening, I spoke to my father as if he were in the room.

"Dad, in asking me to hire a Kaddish, were you trying to protect me from the patriarchy of Judaism? And this disparate treatment?"

Silence.

I had been so determined to bring honor to my father's soul, I had unwittingly exposed myself to the more traditional side of Judaism, never considering that I might not always be welcomed. I had forgotten the chauvinism that lies at the core of patriarchal Judaism and that Orthodox Jewish men recite a blessing each morning, praising God "who has not made me a woman." Contemporary scholars argue that the blessing does not disparage women or imply their inferiority, but rather expresses gratitude for men's obligation to perform the religious commandments. But given the behavior and collective ages of the men in Anshei Shalom's sanctuary that morning, they clearly did not hold contemporary views.

Months passed before benevolence replaced the sting of rejection and I could recognize the challenge I had brought to the elderly worshippers by walking into their midst wearing the sacred cloth that had been the exclusive right of men.

This face-to-face encounter with patriarchal Judaism was just the first of many to come.

CHAPTER 10

Respite from Grief

The day after Rosh Hashanah, I was still in Florida, wilting like a plant without enough water. I'd been away from home for twenty-one days; I'd spent nine of them sitting in the dreary waiting room outside the ICU of the hospital, listening to the creeping cadence of the clock as life slowly ebbed from my father's body. I'd arranged his funeral, flown to New York for the burial, and spent seven days playing hostess during shiva in my parents' home. I'd been embarrassed in my parents' synagogue and sat respectfully through Rosh Hashanah services in an unwelcoming synagogue where I was treated as if I were invisible.

More than anything else, I needed time to grieve and begin to heal—time away from my mother and the endless rounds of post-death administrative tasks. The burdensome logistics of death—phone calls with my parents' lawyer, credit card and life insurance companies, banks, social security, and the Veterans Administration—made me feel my father's loss more poignantly. I wanted to escape from this house where I'd sat shiva. I wanted to be taken care of and I craved connection with people who weren't mourners.

Now my wish was about to come true.

My friend Morey came to take me out. Our relationship went back ten years, to the days we dated—before agreeing we'd make better friends than lovers. Back then, he lived in the Washington, DC, area, before retiring and moving to Florida.

When I opened the door and saw my tall, thin, slightly balding friend, he gave me an affectionate hug. With a big smile, he announced, "I am your slave for the day. Your wish is my command." These were the most curative words I'd heard in three weeks.

Shedding the role of caretaker, even for the briefest of moments, felt euphoric. I buried my face in the fabric of his T-shirt, releasing my tension and hiding any display of emotion from my mother.

"Morey, I've been so confined. I just crave fresh air."

"Well, it's warm and sunny outside and I know how much you love the beach. Delray Beach isn't far; I'll take you there."

Nearing the beach, the smell of the salt air rekindled my love affair with the ocean. Many of my happiest memories were of days at the beach with Dad. I let myself be led by that sea-salt aroma into fifty-year-old joyful memories. Reminiscing was like a balm on my wounded heart.

—

Living near the Atlantic Ocean as a child was a blessing. On hot summer Long Island Sundays, my father and I would wake early and go to the Buttercrest Bakery to buy fresh seeded rolls for our beach lunches. We would stand side by side in the kitchen, preparing sandwiches, always the same menu. I marveled as he cut the Hebrew National salami into thin slices and heaped them onto the rolls, adding Gulden's spicy mustard only for those, like me, who preferred it. He'd wrap each sandwich into a little baggie with the precision of an engineer, then I'd pack the fruit—fresh plums, peaches, and nectarines.

His shining achievement was the lemonade he made in the two-gallon Coleman jug with its black screw-on top. He knew precisely how much ice and water to add to the frozen pink lemonade to ensure it tasted delicious, no matter the time of day. In that, he was like a magician. No watered-down lemonade for our palates in the late afternoon. Not on his watch.

Dad drove the family to the private beach at Point Lookout, reserved only for residents of our town. After parking the car, we unloaded the beach paraphernalia—folding chairs, beach blankets, towels, pails, shovels, lunch, and our multicolored striped umbrella—then crossed the concrete onto the sand. I wiggled my toes in the white softness, delighting in the immense freedom from the constraint of shoes.

After we marked our spot, always close to the water's edge, Dad set up the chairs and planted the umbrella pole, pushing and pulling it back and forth—first north to south, then east to west—until it made a hole deep enough to support the umbrella against the strongest wind. My sisters and I stripped down to our bathing suits and ran as fast as we could toward the ocean, giggling with excitement.

Dad took his time, methodically hanging his little transistor radio on the arm of his beach chair so it would be ready when the Yankees game began, and carefully placing the business section of the *New York Times* on the seat. Only after everything was set to his satisfaction did he sprint into the ocean, wearing his trademark beige bathing trunks.

Mom would sit under our umbrella, completing the Sunday *Times* crossword puzzle—in ink. She never joined our frivolity in the water.

My favorite activity was jumping into the waves from the diving board of my father's shoulders. He stood 6'2" with a thin frame. But he was strong—a strength gained from moving and delivering furniture in my grandparents' store and from playing weekly racquetball and baseball games.

Dad crouched down in the water, his back to me, and raised his hands for me to grab. Steadied by his confidence and his gentle hands with their firm grip, I placed the arch of my right foot onto his right shoulder, then slowly lifted my left foot from the ocean floor and placed it on his left shoulder. I paused there, enthralled by the kaleidoscope of colors formed by beach umbrellas stretched as far as my eye could see, the sea breeze brushing against my face and the salty air filling my nostrils. Ten feet off the ocean floor, I saw the larger world—the one beyond our beach blanket, where the ocean and sky met and blended into one enormous space. In those split seconds, I was the queen of that expansive world.

"Ready," my father shouted above the roar of the ocean. It was both a question and a statement. All the while, I wobbled, struggling to maintain my balance.

"Ready!" I shouted. Then, mirroring the spring of a diving board, he straightened his knees and stood upright, balancing on his thin legs, and pushed on my hands as he let go, tossing me through the air and into the cold, vast ocean and teaching me a fearlessness that, to this day, makes risk-taking as natural as falling off his shoulders.

———

"I'm so glad I can bring you to a place that holds so many happy memories for you," Morey said, sensing my elation as we neared the ocean.

"And I'm so grateful to you. I feel like a prisoner out on parole."

As Morey pulled the car into the parking space, I took off my shoes and put them on the floor of his car.

"I want to wiggle my toes in the sand," I chuckled.

Morey's smile lit his face.

We walked the beach for almost an hour, the sun caressing my skin while the gentle wind ruffled my hair. Watching the ocean kiss the shore, withdraw, and return to meet the shore again, I stared into the ocean, imagining my father with outstretched arms, riding in the waves that rose higher than my shoulders and showed their white frothy caps before breaking. My urge to go into the water grew stronger with each step.

In my black slacks and white blouse, I clearly wasn't dressed for swimming. When I'd learned of my father's pending surgery, I'd packed hastily, never thinking to toss a bathing suit into my suitcase.

Finally, the impulse got so powerful that I let go of respectability and ran, squealing with delight, into the ocean, clothes and all. Morey stared, incredulous.

Dad was always a dive-right-in-and-get-wet guy. I, on the other hand, typically put one foot into the water at a time, slowly getting knee-deep, then waist-deep, and gradually chest-deep, before diving under water. But today, Dad would have been proud as I tossed caution to the wind and jumped into the waves, matching his exuberance.

I ignored my initial shivering and the goosebumps peaking on my arms. The waves were strong and tall, just as I loved them. My blouse expanded like a sail as I let the swells jostle me. I floated, I swam, I bodysurfed. I jumped into the waves, catching them as they broke, feeling a sorely missed joy. All the while, Morey watched from the shore, grinning, while others looked at me quizzically.

As the sun drew closer to the horizon and seagulls began pecking at scraps left by departed sunbathers, I finally abandoned my escapade. I don't know how long I played in the surf, nor did I ask where Morey got the towel he wrapped around me as we walked back to his car, my teeth chattering. I took a last glance at the ocean, a glow radiating from inside me. The rush of the waves filled the emptiness created by Dad's death. In this respite of laughing and dancing in the ocean, grief released its hold, and I felt my father at my side . . . and he was smiling.

CHAPTER 11

Returning

"I am so disorganized," my mother fretted the next morning. I watched my typically highly organized mother walk aimlessly from one room to another, numb and bewildered.

"How will I live without him? How will I go on?" Her voice quavered and her worry created creases in her forehead. Never had she expressed fear of any kind.

"Mom, you'll be okay. You're a strong woman with a strong will to live, and you have hundreds of friends to support you."

"Easy for you to say. You've never been widowed. You have no idea what I'm going through."

Whoa! A verbal slap.

Her despair reminded me that my mother was no longer part of a couple. Her identity was being redefined, and I was watching her falter. My attempts to comfort her proved futile.

I had occupied myself with myriad practical post-death matters—ordering additional death certificates, calling the Veterans Administration and the insurance company to begin claims processes, writing thank-you notes, and sending letters informing various organizations of my father's death. I bought a trash can on wheels so my mother could transport her garbage to the street on her own—a job previously reserved for my father. Focusing on the countless details kept me from fully absorbing the magnitude of our loss.

Gradually, I began thinking about my life back home. Rachel had returned to college in California, but David had just started his junior year in high school. I felt guilty about missing his soccer games and not being home when school let out. I knew he was safe at his father's house, but I missed our dinners together, and especially driving carpool. When I shuttled David and his friends, I learned the full scoop about what went on at school (like the fact that some kids were playing cards in biology class). Eavesdropping is easy when driving a van full of teenagers, and I learned more from hearing their chatter than I learned directly from David.

I needed to go home. My consulting firm and my therapy work, along with single parenting and managing a household, required my attention.

When Dad was hospitalized, I had cancelled a workshop with a long-standing client—something I had never done in my twenty years in business—along with all client sessions at the courthouse. Now I was imagining all that awaited me after an unanticipated three weeks away: attending to stacks of bills, mail, phone and email messages; rescheduling postponed appointments; preparing for my upcoming workshops; handling the backlog of paperwork and reports required at the courthouse; meeting my clients' needs; dealing with the upcoming Jewish fall holidays; and tackling a refrigerator full of food that had probably morphed into gross-looking science experiments. I had left home hurriedly on September 11, anticipating I'd be in Florida for only a few days. By October 3, I wanted to go home, even though I cringed to think of the effort I'd need to face all that had been put on hold.

When would I find the time to grieve?

The time had come for me to resume my life. I needed quiet, private time and a space to deal with my grief in my own way, unbothered by my mother's expectations.

A staggering number of decisions preoccupied me, wreaking havoc on any chance of serenity: *How will I oversee David's needs—his homework, extracurricular activities, and dinner—when I need to go to synagogue every evening? Where will I say Kaddish when my job takes me to other states? How will I find a place to pray in those different cities? How will I explain to clients of other faiths my need to orchestrate my work life around morning and evening services?*

I was stalled at an interminable series of red lights, eager for each one to turn green and give me the go-ahead.

"Leaving will be hard," Lois warned me on the phone. "I cried almost the entire way home. I hope you have an easier time." Even with her warning, I didn't anticipate the onslaught of emotions.

On the way to the airport, Mom and I didn't speak. The car felt airless. Stifling. Even though she had acknowledged my need to return home, she wanted me to stay with her. I knew she was unprepared for the deafening silence that would now fill her house. At the airport, she simply dropped me off at the curb, gave me a quick kiss on the cheek, and drove away, rather than walking to my gate and staying until I boarded my plane—a decades-old ritual of my dad's in the days before 9/11.

Waiting for my flight, I saw a man, a woman, and two young girls sitting in the waiting area. When the gate agent announced, "We'll soon begin boarding," the girls kissed the man goodbye, and as the woman and the girls walked away toward the exit, the older girl turned back and called out, "Bye, Dad. I love you."

Bye, Dad. I love you.

So simple. So casual. How many hundreds of times had I spoken those same words to my father? No sentimentality to reveal the depth of my feelings. Anything more demonstrative made him uncomfortable.

"We know how we each feel," he used to say, when I tried to express my love.

Suddenly those words felt inadequate, and it was too late to add any more. Would I ever again be able to witness a loving father and daughter without envy?

I yanked my journal from my bag and wrote to my father:

> I miss you, Dad. I love you. I know I'll never see you
> again, but my heart refuses to concede. Remember all
> those times you met me at LaGuardia Airport when I

came to visit? I can still envision you waiting for me at the bottom of the escalator, towering over the other greeters, in your drab, mismatched plaid clothes, wearing that brown cloth hat you loved. Can you believe Lois actually wants it? I can still hear your distinct, lilting three-note whistle and see the corners of your eyes crinkle the way they did when you flashed your broad smile the minute you saw me.

I stopped writing when the agent called the flight, composing myself enough to board the plane. Like Lois, I sobbed inconsolably for the entire two-hour flight from West Palm Beach to Washington, DC. The undeniability of my father's death was creeping in slowly, like fog on a cool, humid morning.

Arriving at Ronald Reagan National Airport, time and season had slipped away from me. I had frantically left Washington summer and flown to Florida, then flown to New York for the funeral, back to Southern Florida for shiva. When I finally landed back in Washington, DC, early autumn crispness filled the air. I felt disoriented, like I'd awoken in an unfamiliar hotel room and was trying to remember where I was. Moving from one space to another, I had lost a step along the way—and my dad in the process.

I walked into my dark house, wading through the sea of mail that had collected on the floor after the mailman dropped it through the mail slot. Since David was with his father that night, I had quiet time to myself. Unable to think about the countless decisions, tasks, and commitments facing me, I chose Scarlett O'Hara's approach: "I'll think about all this tomorrow. Tomorrow is another day." Without unpacking my suitcase, I set my alarm to rise in time for morning services. I climbed into bed, snuggled under my blanket, hugged the spare pillow to my chest, and cried into it.

CHAPTER 12
The Morning Minyan

Standing in the doorway of the small chapel, I checked my watch: 7:27 a.m. on Wednesday, October 4, 2000. I had returned to my own synagogue—Congregation Beth El of Montgomery County—in the suburbs of Washington, DC, I had spent many hours in that chapel when my daughter and son were enrolled in religious school. But crossing the threshold on this morning felt very different. Now I was a mourner coming for the morning prayer service. Alone. Familiar and yet unfamiliar, old and yet new.

The minyan is made up of individuals who blend into a fellowship that shares the sorrow of its members. In Judaism, when a person suffers loss, we come together as a community to support the mourner. Each person's individual grief resonates throughout the group, enveloping the mourner with the warmth of its collective sympathy. No Jew has to stand alone in his or her grief.

While the word *minyan* refers to the ten-person quorum (traditionally males who have had their bar mitzvah) required for prayer, the term has often been used to refer to the morning and evening prayer services. People can be heard saying, "I'm going to minyan."

I stood at the back, surveying the quiet hodgepodge of activity and counting more than a dozen people. Some congregants were already seated. Two men were removing their tallit bags from a cabinet in the rear of the chapel. Others were at various stages of putting on their *tefillin,* the two small black leather boxes worn on the forehead and forearm containing parchment scrolls with passages from the Torah. "Laying" tefillin fulfills the commandment (Deuteronomy 6:8) to "bind [God's commandments] as a sign upon your hand and a reminder above your eyes." This practice is intended to connect one's heart and mind to God and inspire mindfulness.

I remembered watching wide-eyed as a child when my father donned his tefillin. Dad had explained to me that the pattern of the strap on the hand and fingers represented *Shaddai*—one of God's names—and that when he wore his tefillin, he felt God's closeness.

The chapel had only six rows of benches on both sides of a center aisle, and an accordion door in the back separating it from the synagogue's tiny library. The Torah scrolls, containing the first five books of the Jewish Bible, were housed in a nondescript wooden ark at the front and hidden by a plain, thin white cotton curtain. Above the ark hung the eternal light (*ner tamid*) that hangs in every synagogue, representing God's eternal presence. Historically, the ner tamid was an oil lamp, but ours was an unpretentious, metal light fixture lit with electric lightbulbs. A worn, unadorned lectern covered by a cobalt velvet cloth stood on the *bimah* (elevated platform). Windows along the left wall, revealing the center courtyard, made the room seem larger and airier than it actually was.

After watching the scene for another moment, I put on my kippah (head covering, also called a yarmulke), whispered the prayer for donning the tallit, then draped it over my shoulders and entered the sanctuary. When people saw the small black ribbon with its ragged tear on my chest, they knew why I had come. The minyaneers (my expression for those who regularly come to the weekday morning service) acknowledged me with nods and eyes that said, "I understand; I've been there." I knew they had walked in my shoes.

Scanning the room, recognizing no one, I noticed three women seated in the front. As I approached, they immediately made space on the bench.

"Come join us," invited a lady whose name I learned was Fran, a woman orphaned by the death of her second parent within one year. Her angelic voice and warm smile made me feel at ease. The women embodied the Jewish value of *hachnasat orchim,* of openheartedly welcoming the stranger, a primary value of our synagogue and a clear, much-welcomed departure from my experience at Anshei Shalom.

"Thanks."

Fran handed me a prayer book as I sat next to her.

"Who's *davening* [praying] today?" came a voice from the back, requesting a volunteer to begin the lay-led service. I heard muffled voices; a man rose and came to the bimah, and announced, "Page one." My first service in my own synagogue as an avelah (female mourner) had begun.

Sitting among the morning minyaneers, many of whom were of my father's generation, felt like being near him. Surrounded by men whose faces had the same deep lines of time, whose hairlines had receded in the same way, who joked in a similar manner, and who pronounced the name of the Sabbath as "Shabbos" (the more traditional pronunciation), versus "Shabbat" (the more modern pronunciation), felt almost like being with Dad—blanketed in a big hug.

The leader chanted so quickly that because of my limited Hebrew, I couldn't keep up. I watched Fran out of the corner of my eye during the service; when she turned the page in her prayer book, I mirrored her, feigning that I was following the text. When the people stood, I followed suit like a kid playing Simon Says. But when the leader announced the Mourner's Kaddish, I knew exactly what to do.

The time-honored act of rising and reciting the Mourner's Kaddish told everyone in the room of the love, commitment, and faith we shared. Even though the leader slowed the cadence, I stumbled over the Aramaic words of the prayer, my mouth and tongue failing to keep pace.

When the service ended, I replaced my prayer book into the back of the seat in front of me, like the magazine pocket on an airplane, then carefully folded my tallit and gently returned it to its bag. As the men began removing their tefillin, the women encircled me.

"Who are you here for?" asked one of the older women, with her arm on mine.

"My father," I replied. "He died on September 20. I've just gotten back from Florida."

"May your father's memory be for a blessing." The woman, whose name I later learned was also Sarah, warmly conveyed the English translation of a traditional Hebrew affirmation often inscribed on Jewish tombstones.

"I hope you'll stay and join us for breakfast," invited Fran with a heartfelt voice.

"Absolutely." I followed the women, grateful for their company and swathed in their compassion.

In the social hall, eight-foot-long tables were covered with white paper tablecloths. One held a vast array of food—bagels, cream cheese, herring, tuna salad, egg salad, vegetables, and cookies. There was coffee, and even my favorite brand of decaffeinated tea. I felt pride that my synagogue offered food after prayer; I found this show of abundance comforting. I hadn't known that Beth El provided a synagogue-sponsored breakfast every day. I learned later how highly unusual this was.

Breakfast was always preceded by *schnapps*—the word misused by the minyaneers to refer to the Scotch whiskey that Ralph, a veteran minyaneer, poured into plastic jigger-size cups. And a blessing.

As I carried my plate of food to a seat beside Fran, I carried it with a sense of peace—a first since my dad's funeral.

The majority of worshippers lingered after the service to eat and schmooze. Topics covered every imaginable subject—jobs, children, politics, weather, travel, medicine, current events, and even religion. Some of the minyaneers held diametrically opposed views, but their undeniable goodness remained evident through their smiles, back pats, and high fives.

Over the weeks and months, breakfast became much more than tea and previously frozen bagels. The predictability and rhythm of these daily breakfasts soothed my spirit, helping me to heal. The dependability of the minyaneers (and the kitchen staff that arranged the breakfasts) offered stability at a time I struggled to keep myself steady.

Breakfast became a respite between the reflective solemnity of prayer and the rush of my daily activities, helping me shift from the peace and solace of the sanctuary to the complex demands of my fast-paced life. Sharing this gentle transition through time and space with empathic others consoled me in a way my mother couldn't. And I was grateful.

CHAPTER 13
Embraced by Community

As I was leaving my first morning service at Beth El, my rabbi approached me.

"I know you stayed in Florida for shiva. Have you considered inviting your friends to come and pay their respects by having an evening minyan in your home?"

"No. . . . Can I do that?" I had assumed that once shiva ended, I had missed the chance to be consoled by my own community.

"Of course. You've often welcomed people to your home for Jewish holidays. You can certainly hold open houses for them to pay their respects. Give me a few dates you're available. We'll select two and I'll come and lead the evening service, and you can recite Kaddish with a minyan in your home."

A minyan in my own home . . . I could have what I had missed in Florida—the nurturing support of my friends.

"And I have a suggestion," he continued. "Why don't you put some pictures of your father in the room where we'll recite the evening prayers? That will bring his spirit into the room."

"Oh, I love that idea," I exclaimed, my heart expanding. "Thank you."

I left the synagogue with a broad smile and a sense that my feet were hardly touching the carpet.

I knew right away where we'd gather. My favorite place in the house was the room where I snuggled into my dusty rose–colored sofa to write in my journals. My stereo, with my favorite new age music, sat on a credenza opposite the sofa. The sliding glass door opened onto a wooden deck and the grassy, fenced-in backyard. My "journaling room" was the only place in the house off-limits to my children.

Now my challenge: choosing pictures that would best reflect my father's love of life. Because his funeral took place in New York only two days after he died, I hadn't had time to prepare the kind of collage that I've often seen at Christian wakes. And now I didn't have the time I wished for to peruse fifty years of photos, most of which were in albums and boxes—like the one of my father leaning over my baby carriage in April 1949, or the ones of him and me at the beach in the summers of my youth, or the ones of Dad walking me down the aisle at my wedding. Magical moments preserved in a box.

It seemed fitting to choose the last picture ever taken of him. My parents had decided to celebrate the turning of the millennium on a Caribbean cruise. On December 31, 1999, Dad was photographed descending the staircase of the *Princess* ship dressed in his tuxedo. With his left hand on the bannister and his upright posture, he carried himself like royalty, as if he actually liked dressing up. In fact, he hated it and did it only to please my mother. "Happy wife, happy life," he used to say.

Staring at his infectious smile and the wrinkles scrunched around his eyes, I smiled back, as though he could see me. I touched the image as if caressing an infant's face, focusing on it as if by gazing hard enough, I could will him back to life.

Another treasured photo was taken by my niece on the weekend of Dad's seventy-fifth birthday, when our entire clan gathered at a historic bed-and-breakfast to celebrate him. He was dressed casually, as he always preferred, wearing his favorite gray T-shirt and his huge, broad grin. The close-up of his face revealed a chin dimple reminiscent of Kirk Douglas and sagging jowls. His overly large eyeglasses reflected his total disregard for style and fashion.

But both photos portrayed a seventy-five-year-old man; I wanted to show him as the vibrant young man he had been.

On my dresser stood the leather picture frame containing a black-

and-white 8″ × 10″ photo of my father in January 1942, on his graduation from George Washington High School in New York City, just weeks before he enlisted in the US Army. He was eighteen.

His skin was tight then. His upper lip was shaped like Cupid's bow, and the brown of his eyes, indiscernible in the photo, reflected an innocence to the horrors he would witness as his army platoon liberated death camps in war-torn Europe. The commencement cap hid the thick, curly black hair he would lose after returning from the war, leaving only the horseshoe-shaped ring at the back of his head.

I also retrieved the gift he had given to me when I left home at eighteen—the Purple Heart medal he'd earned in November 1944, after being hit by a German mortar shell.

I remembered him knocking gently on my open bedroom door in August 1967. The solemnity in his deep-set brown eyes told me we were on the brink of something serious. His right hand was clenched uncharacteristically in a fist.

I was getting ready to leave home for my freshman year at college. Piles of clothes and stacks of books were spread around my room.

"I want to give you something," my father said in a soft whisper.

I sat on my clothes-strewn bed and waited.

"You're leaving home for the first time," he had said, "the same age I was when I shipped overseas. You might get scared and lonely. I certainly did. I want you to have this medal to remind you that no matter how alone you may feel, I'll always be here for you." He slowly opened his hand and there rested the medal.

Tears filled his eyes. Lost for words, I rose from my bed and wrapped my arms around my father's neck in a tight hug. The following week, I left home.

I had the medal mounted onto purple velvet and placed it in a shadow box with a gold wood frame, highlighting the color of the heart that surrounds George Washington's profile. Whenever scared, I would hold it, remember my father's heroism, and garner my courage. No matter how alone I was, I never felt lonely. Until now.

I put the photos and the Purple Heart medal on the coffee table just as my friend Louise arrived. She had graciously offered to come early to set up coffee, tea, and soft drinks, relieving me of the role I'd had to assume in our shiva home in Florida. As she and I worked to ready the house, friends began trickling in, carrying pastries, cookies, and meals that would sustain David and me for days. The abundance of food meant I could take grocery shopping off my lengthy to-do list for a while.

Being with my friends for the first time since my father died, their warm embraces reminded me of the hugs I used to get from Dad when he came home from work—a bittersweet memory that left me grateful and heartbroken at the same time. Most of my friends had been to my home many times and knew to make themselves comfortable. I didn't have to serve as hostess.

David stood along the back wall of the living room, looking increasingly uncomfortable with each new arrival. I remembered how awkward I felt during shiva when I didn't know any of my mother's colleagues. And although David knew some of my friends, I sensed his discomfort and let him return to his bedroom as soon as I knew we had our minyan.

At 7:30 p.m., my rabbi came in carrying a vintage black suitcase filled with enough prayer books and kippot for everyone. He gave the group the chance to continue schmoozing, and at precisely 8:00 p.m., he said, "Let's go ahead and start the service." Everyone moved into my journaling room; prayer books and head coverings were distributed, and we all stood facing east, toward Jerusalem—the contemporary practice for Jews around the world when praying.

As the rabbi began to pray, I felt swaddled in the love of God, of my father, and of those who had come to support me. I glanced at the images of my father in his seventies, the ones where crow's-feet were etched around his eyes, reflecting a joyful man who wore life well. And that made me smile.

CHAPTER 14

Coming into Being

Almost immediately after Rachel's birth, I began taking classes in Jewish history, studying Jewish life-cycle events and holidays, learning the Hebrew alphabet, and immersing myself in learning about the role of women in Judaism.

On May 30, 1987, after years of study, I became an adult bat mitzvah (daughter of the commandments). My growth and development as a Jew were coming together like the pieces of a jigsaw puzzle, and as I stood in front of the congregation, I basked in the glow of my father's pride and joy. As I read a short selection from the Prophets, the picture of a feminist Conservative Jew was clear for all, including my parents and my children, to see.

It is a tradition, when called to the sacred scroll, to take the tallit, use the tzitzit (fringes) to touch the word where the reader is to begin, and then touch them to one's lips before reciting the blessing, to show reverence to the words of God. At that time, women in my congregation had not yet begun to wear a tallit. I was in a quandary. What would I use to touch the Torah scroll? When I consulted my father for guidance, he loaned me my grandfather's tallit. And while I dared not wear it, I touched its fringes to the Torah before chanting the prayers.

Holding my grandfather's tzitzit in my hand, I felt the tradition of Jews passed down through the centuries. Nevertheless, I imagined he would be horrified to see a woman holding his tallit while being honored at the Torah. On that day, the cloth became a talisman for my conflict between my feminist leanings and traditional Judaism. I wanted to fashion a Jewish life for myself and my children that incorporated both *Halakhah* (Jewish law) and my feminism—to interpret these traditions and apply the commandments to my current life, an important component of Conservative Judaism.

Then, in 1989, I was inspired to see Marilyn Wind, the president of our congregation, sitting on the bimah (elevated platform) and wearing a tallit. The next year, during a visit to Israel, I bought a handloomed, textured wool tallit from the woman who had woven it. I was among the first, but not the last, of women to begin wearing a prayer shawl at my synagogue. Three years later, I taught a workshop at Beth El about the history of women wearing the tallit and collaborated with an artist who taught women to make their own prayer shawls. This workshop has been ongoing now for decades.

By 1981, I had become the youngest vice president in the history of the fourth largest bank in Washington, DC. But when I realized that the president and I held very different visions of the importance of human resources, I left and launched my own human resource management consulting service.

The more successful I became, the more threatened my husband grew. It was clear that I had married a man as narcissistic as my mother. Lacking the confidence to be on my own and wanting to protect the two children I had brought into the world, I remained, unhappy, until his abuse became unbearable. Despite our mutual love for our children and my attempts to preserve any remnant of marital harmony, in 1988, my husband and I decided to separate after eighteen years of marriage.

My father, who valued family above most else, expressed his dismay at the news.

"Have you done everything in your power to save this marriage?"

It didn't take long to convince him that my sanity depended on divorce. After he witnessed my husband's relentless acrimony, his support never waned.

Out of my marriage, I felt free to embrace a more spiritual path.

I resolved to sanctify my new home and bring religion, rituals, and spirituality into my children's lives on more than just a few holidays. A core principle of Judaism—to translate our beliefs and values into actions, exemplifying the adage "actions speak louder than words"— became my own, and I looked for ways to make mundane activities sacred.

I started by *kashering* (making kosher) my kitchen—scrubbing every inch of it; cleaning every cabinet and appliance; buying separate pots, dishes, and silverware for meat and dairy meals; and purchasing only kosher foods. The cleaning, emptying, and refilling symbolized the beginning of my new life as a single mother and Conservative Jewish feminist woman.

I had a ten-foot-high tree painted on the wall in our foyer. We called it our mitzvah (commandment) tree, and each time Rachel and David did a good deed, fulfilling the Jewish value of *tikkun olam* (performing acts of kindness to repair the world), they added a green paper leaf to one of the branches. Over the years, the tree changed from the bare branches of winter to the full, lush greens of summer foliage. Visitors marveled.

Every Sabbath, the imaginary "Shabbat Queen" visited with a treat for the children. On Saturday nights, we honored the end of the Sabbath and its distinction from the other days of the week by standing at the kitchen counter, lighting the braided *Havdalah* (separation) candle, and reciting blessings to usher in the new week. I enrolled both children in religious school, rejecting my grandfather's belief about not educating daughters, and actively participated in their religious educations by working with them on schoolwork, joining them in learning to write the Hebrew alphabet, and attending services with them.

A few years into my consulting career, a workshop participant sought me out to ask my advice on personal matters. I felt unequipped to counsel her about her private life. I decided then that, if workshop attendees were going to seek my guidance, I needed to be sure I could help them appropriately.

I returned to graduate school in 1992, and I received a master's degree in social work from the University of Maryland in 1996. My father and mother, who sat in the graduation assembly, beamed with pride.

I interned at the Fairfax County Juvenile and Domestic Relations Court, which relied on the family systems model developed by Murray Bowen. At the courthouse, I worked with families who were court-ordered into therapy for domestic assault, custody and visitation disputes, and with adolescents in trouble with the law. I loved the work, my supervisor, and my coworkers, and I went on to become a county employee, fulfilling the three-thousand-hour requirement for certification as a licensed clinical social worker while continuing my consulting business. By the time the county stopped funding the therapy program, I had become an excellent therapist. I had come into my own not only spiritually, but professionally as well.

And my father had died.

CHAPTER 15

Candle of the Lord

Three days after coming home from my stay in Florida, while standing in the kitchen preparing dinner, I realized I didn't own a *Yahrzeit* candle—the memorial candle Jews light in memory of the dead. According to tradition, on the eve of Yom Kippur, Jews light the Yahrzeit candle for a deceased loved one. Yom Kippur was forty-eight hours away, and I was unprepared.

Yom Kippur, the "Day of Atonement," is the holiest day on the Jewish calendar. It marks the end of a ten-day period of introspection and repentance that starts on Rosh Hashanah. Together, Rosh Hashanah and Yom Kippur are known as Judaism's "High Holy Days." Yom Kippur is devoted to making amends and asking God's forgiveness for sins committed during the past year.

Most traditional Jews spend the entire day in synagogue, fasting and abstaining from normal activities. The fast is believed to cleanse the body and spirit; other restrictions, such as avoiding bathing, shaving, applying cosmetics, and wearing leather shoes, are intended to keep worshippers from focusing on material possessions and comforts and focus instead on spiritual matters.

The holiday includes a special memorial prayer service called *Yizkor*, meaning "to remember." During this brief service, which is also conducted on the last days of Passover, Shavuot, and Sukkot, we ask God to remember the souls of our departed relatives and vow to give charity in their names. Committing to acts of beneficence fulfills a vital

Jewish belief—that through acts of kindness and goodness, the living can bring honor to and redeem the dead.

Candles are integral to Judaism. The flickering candlelight reminds us of the fragility of life and encourages us to embrace life and the lives of our loved ones. A candle, believed to be a symbol of the human soul, reminds us of God's divine presence. Jews believe that by lighting a Yahrzeit candle, we help elevate the soul of our deceased loved one. To light the candle is to keep the promise: I will remember you all the days of my life.

On the eve of each Yizkor holiday, it is a revered custom to kindle a Yahrzeit candle for the departed.

The small candle sits in a glass jar three inches high and burns for twenty-four hours. As a very young girl, I saw my mother light the candle for her mother and set it on the Westinghouse stove in the kitchen to burn. As years passed, my mother lit Yahrzeit candles for both parents, then my father began lighting one for his father and, eight years later, also for his mother.

In need of the special candle, I frantically called a friend.

"Where am I going to find a Yahrzeit candle when I'm working all day and going to synagogue every night? Synagogue gift shops and stores with Judaica just aren't open when I need them."

"You can buy them at the grocery store," she confided. "And they're open twenty-four hours."

After much searching in the kosher aisle of the supermarket, I finally found the candles on the bottom shelf, relegated to a lowly place, thus denigrating their sacredness. Bottom shelves are where things like seven-pound cans of pork and beans and twenty-pound bags of rice are kept, along with huge bags of sugar cereals with obscure names like Berry Krunch Heads and Cocoa Magic. An item of such religious significance should have a more respectable place. I made a mental note to share my opinion with the store manager at another time, when I could talk less emotionally about the lack of consideration in putting Yahrzeit candles close to the dirt and grime of the floor.

I took the candle from the shelf, holding it reverently as I walked to the checkout line. The cashier put it into a small brown paper bag, which I handled with the same care as a carton of eggs. Once at home, I wondered, *Where should I light it? What prayer do I say? How do I make the moment sacred? And where do I keep the candle burning while I'm away from home, so the house is safe?*

Then I chided myself. *Really, Sarah . . . Jews all over the world, for hundreds of years, have left their candles burning unattended and* their *houses haven't burned down. What are you worried about?* I chuckled to myself; Dad would have found my worry laughable.

I combed through my collection of books on Jewish ritual practice, looking for the blessing my parents repeated when they lit Yahrzeit candles. I learned that, because lighting the candle is a time-honored tradition rather than a commandment, there is no prescribed blessing. Maybe I was supposed to focus on my father or speak my own prayer to the Almighty, a notion that escaped me at the time.

Before sunset on the eve of Yom Kippur, I took the candle into my journaling room, where we had held the two evening minyanim. Light still streamed into the room from the sliding glass door. Alone with thoughts of my youthful, vigorous father and his death at only age seventy-six, my heart began pounding like a drummer in a marching band.

"Why, God? Why did you have to take him? Why did you take such a good man—a brave army soldier, a loving father, devoted son and husband, a man of such integrity and dedication? How could you take him and leave me without protection from Mom, whose unrealistic expectations would now likely multiply?

"I shouldn't be lighting this candle for you, Dad. You should still be alive."

I had to pull myself together; I'd be going to synagogue soon. I began taking slow, steady deep breaths, stunned that my anger could erupt so suddenly . . . like lightning on a summer day.

Then, just as suddenly, the thought: *How can I be angry at you, God, when you spared my father the anguish of a battle with cancer?*

I cleared my head enough to retrieve the box of kitchen matches. With a quivering hand, I swooshed the match across the striking surface. It didn't ignite. A second failed attempt. Finally, on the third try, I heard the sizzle. The flame danced on the end of the match as I picked up the little jar, struggling to hold the match still, until the flame met the wick. I extinguished the match, sniffing the sulfur, mumbling words I don't remember, and gently placed the candle on the coffee table, tiny and alone on its surface. I moved two pictures of my father—the one in his golf T-shirt on his seventy-fifth birthday and the one in his tuxedo on the millennium New Year's Eve cruise—next to the candle, to remind it for whom it burned.

Watching the flickering blue-and-yellow flame reminded me of the night we returned from the cemetery, when I stared at a similar flame in the large ner daluk candle that burned in my mother's home during shiva. Once again, watery eyes fixed on the glow, mesmerized.

Performing this ritual at home, alone, was a stark contrast to reciting the Mourner's Kaddish surrounded by a supportive community. The emptiness of my house echoed the enormous emptiness of my heart.

I gradually regained my composure, reminding myself that this hollow feeling would not get me through the following twenty-five hours of fasting and atonement. I needed fortitude to remain in synagogue the entire next day without food or water.

In years past, my father and I would call each other from our respective homes as we began to break our twenty-five-hour fast. For the first time in my life, I wouldn't be able to share lighthearted bantering with my father when Yom Kippur ended.

"What did your rabbi speak about in his sermon?" "How many people fell asleep during it?" "Did you have an easy fast?" "Did you get a headache?" Those exchanges, a contrast to the solemnity and introspection of the long day, always left both of us chuckling. They were even more recuperative than the food and water.

I miss you, Daddy.

I dragged myself to the bathroom sink, splashed cold water on my face, and left to join the warm embrace of friends who had invited me for the pre-fast dinner. Later that night, sitting in synagogue as the sun set, I thought of the Yahrzeit candle illuminating the dark of my home. I prayed that memories of my father, like the candle aglow in my journaling room, would continue to light up my life.

CHAPTER 16

Remembrance

Sometimes, we're compelled to be in a place we don't want to be.

I didn't want to be in the group that recited Yizkor, the prayer service in which we ask God to remember our departed loved ones. I wanted to be in the other group, the one for people with two living parents. Now I would always remain inside the sanctuary, as if a member of an exclusive club, reciting the special memorial prayers. My commitment to the traditions of my faith and to my father's memory necessitated my presence.

My father believed, as many traditional Jews do, that you leave the sanctuary during the Yizkor service if both parents are alive. As a child, when the rabbi announced, "Yizkor will begin shortly," my father and I joined the ensuing shuffle of congregants rising from their seats, crowding the aisles, and exiting like patrons at the end of a theater performance. When the memorial service concluded, we returned to our seats inside. After my grandfather died, that changed. Dad ushered me out of the synagogue while he stayed inside to pray.

As a teen, I had asked my father, "Why do people with both living parents leave the synagogue during Yizkor?"

"It would be tempting fate to remain," he answered. "If children with two living parents stayed in the synagogue, it could tempt the evil eye and bring bad luck to those parents."

Although Dad's explanation was a common understanding, for my logical father to subscribe to an old superstition was so out of character, I couldn't help but chuckle.

I figured there had to be other explanations. Maybe children would be frightened to see so many adults weeping. Or maybe those who left were showing respect by letting mourners grieve with only those who shared their sorrow. Nowadays, some Jews who haven't lost a loved one remain during Yizkor to recite the Mourner's Kaddish for the six million Jews who perished in the Holocaust and have no one to recite the prayer for them.

Standing for the short Yizkor service, the words of the rabbi faded into the background as I recalled the light my father brought to my life. The rabbi instructed us to take time for silent prayer; I reflected on the many ways my father had shaped the woman I am today.

If my father's playfulness was transmittable, then I caught it. I thrived on the way he played in the ocean with us during summer days at the beach, the way he lovingly created nicknames for our friends, and how he cheerfully teased us about our musical icons of the day, the haircuts of the Beatles, and the length of time my sisters and I could spend on the one telephone line in the house. His light-heartedness was ever present, no matter what other challenges were on his mind.

My father modeled commitment to family. He remained at a job he detested out of loyalty to his parents. He cared for his mother to her dying day, taking charge of her needs despite having two older brothers, bringing her out of the hospital so she could die in our home. He insisted that we eat dinner as a family when he returned home from work, listening as we recounted our days and asking questions about our studies and our friends.

I remembered that in high school, I tried out for a leadership role in our Girls' Week activities, and even though I was more qualified, I was passed over for one of the more popular girls. To assuage my crushed heart, my father agreed to do something that he hated with a passion. He stood up in front of the entire assembly—on his league championship bowling night!—and delivered the "Ode to Daughter" speech, a tradition reserved to only one father each year. Seated behind the lectern on the stage, listening to the poem he crafted after Lincoln's Gettysburg Address, I thought my chest would burst with pride as I watched him, his knees shaking, behind the lectern. Seeing my father do something for me that so frightened him—writing and delivering a speech—I walked from the assembly that evening standing taller than I ever had before, heightened by my father's act of love.

I sought my father's wisdom when problems or worries plagued me. His undivided attention and gentle way of questioning made me feel special. I recalled a time during high school when his advice proved judicious.

I was being mercilessly teased and tormented by the boy who sat in front of me in homeroom. One night at our dinner table, my father sensed my agitation as I relayed that day's bullying.

"What's the boy's name?" my father asked.

"Alan Bader. We sit in alphabetical order—Alan Bader, Sarah Birnbach, Betty Black."

"Well, that's an easy problem to fix," he said as a big smile lit his face. "If you follow my instruction, he will *never ever* bother you again."

"Okay, Dad," I conceded, doubtful. "I'll take your advice."

"The next time he annoys you," my father began, "you say the following: 'Leave me alone, Master Bader.' Use a voice loud enough for everyone in the class to hear and say it like you mean it. And I promise you, he will leave you alone from then on."

Being completely naïve to the meaning behind the message, I couldn't fathom how my father could be so sure. But pretty soon, the opportunity presented itself.

Two days later, when Alan Bader turned in his chair and made fun of me, I announced in a clear, loud, and affirmative voice, "Leave me alone, Master Bader!" He turned beet red and shrank down in his seat. The class broke out in uproarious laughter, and true to my father's words, Alan Bader never bothered me again. That day, I decided my father possessed the wisdom of the sages.

All these years later, no longer ignorant of the meaning behind my father's advice, I blushed and hoped God appreciated my father's sense of humor.

The rabbi continued chanting the Yizkor service, his voice fading in and out as my mind returned to reminiscing.

My father had infinite patience, especially while he taught me to drive. Actually, my driving didn't test his patience as much as my multiple failed attempts at parallel parking. Each time I tried to pull up against the curb, the car ended more than two feet from it. After gently and repeatedly saying, "Turn the wheel now . . . now . . . *now* . . ." he always reassured me that I would master the mechanics. To this day, I can parallel park perfectly without the benefit of modern rear-park-assist features.

But my father wasn't the perfect model. He drove with his left foot on the brake and his right foot on the gas pedal. When I tried driving that way, my father scolded me.

"But you drive that way, Dad."

"Don't do as I do, just do as I say" became a frequent mantra.

From my father, I gained my entrepreneurial spirit. In his mid-forties, he started a credit company—before Mastercard and Visa became household words—in a corner of the furniture store basement, with only a rickety metal desk and broken-down chair. In 1981, at age thirty-two, I left my promising career in commercial banking to launch my own company—a human resource management consulting firm that thrived for thirty-four years, until I retired. Like my dad, I started my business in the basement—but in our home, with only a gray metal desk, a wobbly chair, an IBM Selectric typewriter, and a warped secondhand Steelcase filing cabinet.

"I know you can launch this business and succeed," my father assured me. "All it will take is your intelligence and some very hard work. If I could do it, you can do it. I have every confidence in you." As the only female in our family to go into business as a solo entrepreneur, I shared with my father a common language and experience that bonded us.

I jolted back to the present when I heard the rabbi say, "Please rise for the Mourner's Kaddish."

"Yitgadal v'yitkadash sh'mei raba . . ."

Glorified and sanctified be God's great name . . .

After the Mourner's Kaddish, my thoughts again returned to my father. I remembered all the time he spent teaching me about investing. He subscribed to Value Line investment reports, which I read at the library. Then we'd discuss various stocks and mutual funds.

"Did you read the commentary? How did you evaluate the prognosis for this company?" His questions always opened a dialogue that taught me how to discern quality investments.

"You must have a diversified portfolio. And you must do dollar-cost averaging."

"Yes, Dad," I responded, bewildered by the unfamiliar vocabulary.

I remembered the frustration I caused him by my inability to calculate cost bases of mutual funds in the days before computers. Back then my father kept green multiple-column ledger sheets where he wrote the number of shares, the per-share value, and the fair market value of each mutual fund he owned . . . in pencil. At year end, he calculated and entered the cost basis of each fund in red ink. He taught me, against great resistance and perpetual confusion, to do the same. He would be awestruck by current software programs that now do these calculations.

Today, when many of my female friends tell me they know nothing about investing, I thank my father for his unrelenting patience. While many fathers of his generation anticipated that their daughters would marry someone who would handle their finances, my father committed to teaching my sisters and me money management, enabling us to be independent. The result: a portfolio that secures my future.

I prayed that God would remember the sweet musk smell of my father's Old Spice aftershave, the warmth of his hugs, and the way he made me feel safe. And his exuberant laughter when my sisters and I wrestled him to the living room floor—this man who was strong enough to carry refrigerators up four flights of stairs in city brownstones as part of his delivery responsibilities but who acted like he could be easily overcome by three little girls—all the time chortling and modeling the playfulness that I have inherited. I prayed that God would remember how he filled his pockets with change before coming home and, after dinner, would lie on his side on the sofa, making sure the change fell between the cushions for us to find. And his strength as he'd lift us up on his shoulders in the ocean, tossing us into the waves and teaching us to be unafraid.

As Yizkor ended, I was jarred from my musings by people moving around me, some returning to the sanctuary for the remainder of the service and others departing. The Yizkor service had given me time to reflect on my father, nourishing me with memories. And this was a blessing.

CHAPTER 17
Sukkot

I had begun thinking ahead to Sukkot, which falls only five days after Yom Kippur. This year, it would begin at sundown on October 13.

Sukkot, which takes place in autumn, marks the end of the harvest time and the agricultural year in Israel. The seven-day holiday also commemorates the forty years that the Israelites wandered in the desert after their exodus from slavery in Egypt. We are commanded in the book of Leviticus (23:42) to dwell during Sukkot in temporary structures, called *sukkahs*, to remind us of the fragile dwellings farmers lived in during the harvest and in which the Israelites lived in the desert. This year, I felt like the Israelites, wandering through an unfamiliar landscape, trying to find my way.

Growing up, my family didn't acknowledge Sukkot, nor did my husband and I during our marriage. Many Jews consider it a minor Jewish holiday and ignore it today. Coming after the major religious holidays of Rosh Hashanah and Yom Kippur, widely observed by Jews, it is like the forgotten, left-behind stepchild. But in 1988, as part of my commitment to make Judaism more accessible to my young children following my divorce, I decided to build a sukkah, indisputably the major symbol of this festival.

I purchased a sukkah kit, complete with seventeen spruce beams, all the necessary hardware—hex bolts, wing nuts, washers, and mending plates—and a sixteen-page instruction booklet, which I painstakingly followed, step by step.

Building the freestanding wooden structure took hours. Laying the eight-foot beams on the floor of my deck, I constructed the two short side panels first. While they lay facing each other foot to foot, I attached what would become the long side of the sukkah so it stood up straight. Raising the walls while working alone required every ounce of energy and resourcefulness I had, and my children were too small to help during those first few years. I had to lean the beams against the deck railing while I connected them together, all the while teetering on a ladder, clenching my teeth. But when I stepped back and saw the completed 8' × 8' sukkah, I giggled and clapped my hands like a small child. I imagine that same joy is felt by those who bring home and stand up their Christmas tree each year.

Assembling the roof also took diligence. Jewish law prescribes that the roof covering provide more shade than light, to shield its inhabitants from the sun, while still allowing the moon and stars to be visible at night. Material for the roof must be earth-grown and cut from the ground, meaning that wood, branches of trees, cornstalks, reeds, or bamboo sticks can be used. Living in a major metropolitan area, the likelihood of finding bamboo sticks growing in soil was near zero. The good news: given that Sukkot often comes near Halloween, cornstalks were easier to find at many local retailers. But dragging them home and raising them onto the roof reminded me why my high school gymnastics had been important to master.

Constructing it by myself became an enormous source of pride, as I could barely distinguish a wrench from a pair of pliers. Having never done anything like that before, I discovered I loved working with my hands and being more self-sufficient than I had been during my marriage. Since then, Sukkot has become one of my favorite Jewish holidays.

Every year, Rachel and David would invite their friends to decorate the sukkah. The annual fun fest resulted in construction-paper decorations, paper chains, pipe-cleaner figurines, cutouts from magazines and Jewish New Year cards, and strings of gumdrops and popcorn that adorned the sukkah. I carefully stored those treasures year after year. But all that remains is the lone string of gumdrops, now as hard as little rocks.

While the Torah instructs us to "dwell in booths for seven days," I have only slept in the shanty once, preferring the comfort and warmth of my bed. But weather permitting, the children and I have, after carefully transporting food from the kitchen, eaten most meals on folding chairs and tables in the sukkah during the festival. And while there are no specific foods recommended during Sukkot, I try to honor that the holiday commemorates the harvest by filling up on fruits, vegetables, and grains.

An essential element of the holiday is extending hospitality. I loved having friends and family eat in the sukkah—a second home each fall— some years in winter coats, and other years in shirtsleeves. In 1996, when David became a bar mitzvah during Sukkot, the weather was so warm that family and friends celebrated his occasion in shirtsleeves.

But this year, I was mired in uncertainty. *Where do I find the energy to erect this structure once again? How do I carve out the hours? And how do I celebrate the weeklong holiday when hosting festive gatherings during* avelut *[the mourning period] is considered improper?* Inviting myself into others' sukkahs seemed a bit forward; I could hear the *tsk tsk* inside my head.

"I don't have the stamina to build my sukkah this year," I confided to my friend Louise one day, after I'd returned from Florida. "Grief has taken more than my father. It's taken my energy, like a tiny hole in a bucket that loses water one drop at a time, leaving nothing behind."

"I get it." Louise's voice exuded empathy, born of the loss of both of her parents.

"Celebrating the holiday without the sukkah will be another loss. I love building it and eating in it every year, but trying to fit that in while going to synagogue every day feels overwhelming." My voice trailed off as Louise listened attentively.

"You know, you don't have to build it alone. You have so many friends who'd be glad to help you. I'm sure your father would approve."

She was right. Dad always supported my celebrating Jewish rituals. And I did have many people I could ask.

Louise's compassionate listening helped me untangle my jumbled thoughts. Life had to go on.

I immediately called my friends from my *havurah*. In Hebrew, the word *haver* means "friend"; a havurah is a fellowship—a small, informal group of friends typically with a common interest, who study and celebrate Judaism together. Celebrating Jewish holidays alone after my divorce became lonely. So, in 1994, I started a havurah of Jewish men and women who were either separated or divorced and who, like me, had no local family with whom to celebrate the Jewish holidays. During years when I didn't travel to Florida, I hosted the group in my home for Passover seders, and subsequently for Yom Kippur break-the-fast meals and Chanukah celebrations.

When I called them, their eagerness and willingness overwhelmed me. Responses like "I'd love to help," "Count me in," and "What time do you want me?" made me feel almost weightless. Reaching out to others was a long-overdue and much-needed lesson.

On one of the evenings between Yom Kippur and Sukkot, several members of my havurah joined me on the deck behind my home to erect my sukkah. The friendly exchanges as we constructed the dwelling were like uplifting music: "Pass me one of those wing nuts, please" and "Who just took the wrench?" and "Hold that wall steady." The only other time I felt that happy since Dad died was the day my sisters and I laughed and wrestled on Mom's bed during shiva—and that was short-lived. I relished watching the walls go up one at a time. Even though I participated in the building, I mostly observed—a first.

When the structure was stable, we attached wooden lattices on three sides, allowing space for the doorway. A few years earlier, after I'd walled the sukkah with blue plastic tarps, a strong wind blew the little hut more than three-hundred feet away from the house. Dragging my sukkah back to my deck from the corner of the backyard taught me never to enclose it completely.

We left the fourth side open to view the backyard and the flower boxes, filled with pink and white geraniums, which hung from my deck railings. This also let the rose and mint scents of the backyard flowers drift into the sukkah. We balanced wooden slats across the top and covered them with branches, leaves, and cornstalks. With the construction finished, I reserved the job of decorating for myself. That task, a labor of love, always filled me with joy.

After everyone left, I attached years' worth of Rachel's and David's artwork, and that of their various friends, to the wooden beams and lattice and tacked the construction-paper *mezuzah* to the doorframe. Then the sukkah was complete.

On the first Saturday night during the eight days of Sukkot, ten friends from the havurah joined me for a potluck dinner in the sukkah. Each came laden with food. Two men carried lamps onto the deck, shining light into the dwelling; others brought in chairs; everyone pitched in. I did nothing to prepare, unashamedly uncharacteristic for me. Things fell into place without my needing to take charge of every detail.

As I stood back, watching the burst of activity, I realized that I could carve out a bit of joy if only I got out of my own way. I could enjoy the beauty and sanctity of the sukkah, even within thirty days of my father's death, just by reaching out to others. I had spent a lifetime doing for others, always trying to be the "good girl." To relinquish that role and realize I didn't have to do everything myself and that others would be there for me, was a dramatic change. In allowing myself to be cared for, I had received the long-overdue meal of consolation—food prepared by caring others—that I had missed in that dingy Long Island restaurant following my father's funeral. The evening air was just cool enough to need a light sweater. The sky was clear, the moon was full, and the light of the stars, like little sparkles, shone through the openings in the roof.

When a wave of sadness briefly washed over me, Reva, a small grayhaired woman who had been at every havurah event I had hosted, put her arm around me. My friend Steven came around the table and gave me a hug. Before I could focus, my neighbor Judy took out her guitar.

"Why don't we sing?" She changed the mood with just four words.

Singing in the moonlight reminded me of contented days at Girl Scout campouts.

"Yes, let's. That sounds great," I said, wanting to shift the focus from myself.

We sang Jewish songs—"Oseh Shalom," "Shalom Aleichem," and "Y'rushalayem Shel Zahav," which translates to "Jerusalem of Gold."

We also sang some American folk songs—"He's Got the Whole World in His Hands," "By the Light of the Silvery Moon," "Michael, Row Your Boat Ashore"—then listened to Judy strum her guitar until it became too chilly to stay outdoors.

Everyone helped clean up, and after everything was put away, we exchanged fond goodbyes. After the last person left, I put on a warm fleece jacket, made a cup of tea, and sat alone in the sukkah, looking at the decorations and remembering the many happy times I'd had in that wobbly structure, grateful for the companionship and blessing of my friends. By letting go of control and allowing others to support me, I had been embraced by their spirit, a joy I would have otherwise missed. In the stillness of the evening, it was easy to focus on my many blessings and the beauty of my sukkah.

CHAPTER 18

Women *Do* Say Kaddish

Before our father died, Lois and I had been planning for months to make an October visit to the homes of our favorite writers—Louisa May Alcott, Ralph Waldo Emerson, and Henry David Thoreau—in Concord, Massachusetts. But six weeks after Dad's death, the excursion seemed like a burden. Grief had stolen my enthusiasm.

With some hesitation, I called my sister.

"Lois, would you be okay if we postpone our trip to Concord?" I asked. "My excitement vanished somewhere between Dad's funeral and today."

"No problem. We'll just do something else." Her response was instantaneous.

We brainstormed possibilities until, almost simultaneously, the idea came to us: "Let's go to the beach!" I heard an animation in my voice that had been missing for almost two months. Lois and I both loved the murmur of the ocean waves lapping the shore, the smell of salt hanging in the air, and the warmth of the sun beating down on our lotioned skin.

"Daddy would have loved that idea," she reminded me, as if I needed reminding.

"He sure would have. I'll get a place in Ocean City here in Maryland. That will rejuvenate both of us."

"That's a great idea. I'll come to you," she said without pause. "We can head to the beach from there."

I changed my airline tickets and reserved a hotel room in Ocean City. Lois booked a ticket from her home in Rochester to Reagan National Airport. One thing left—locating a place to say Kaddish. The only synagogue with a Saturday night and Sunday morning minyan within fifty miles of the beach was affiliated with Chabad, the ultra-Orthodox denomination of Judaism. I called to check their service times, and a gentleman answered.

"Can you please tell me your service times? I'm going to be in Ocean City, and I'm reciting Kaddish for my father and want to . . ."

"*Women* don't say Kaddish."

"I'm sorry? I don't think I heard you."

"*Women* don't say Kaddish," he repeated. Did I imagine anger in his voice?

"I'm saying Kaddish for my father. He had no . . ." Before I could explain, he cut me off.

"*Women* don't say Kaddish," he echoed.

"Yes. We. Do." I replied, my calm eroding. "My father had no sons, and I am praying for his soul."

"I'm sorry. You'll have to find someone else to say Kaddish for him."

"How can you say that?" Steadying my voice was futile. "How can you turn away a Jew who wants to pray for her father's soul?"

Silence.

I wanted to be acknowledged as the loving child of an honorable man, rather than be punished for being his daughter rather than his son.

I had anticipated having to sit apart from the men—to sit behind a *mechitzah* (the partition separating men and women in Orthodox synagogues). I had anticipated needing ten men to recite the Kaddish. I had not anticipated an outright refusal to allow me to pray for my father's soul.

A primary goal of Chabad is to bring more Jews into the fold, but that didn't seem to include me. I wanted to say, "I thought you wanted more observant Jews. Well, I am one. I'm honoring the Fifth Commandment." But I didn't. Instead, I switched to talking about my dad.

"My father was a good man. How can you deny his soul the benefit of the prayers of his own child?" My voice sounded shrill in the silence on the other end.

Silence.

The futility of debating with him hit me like a wrecking ball. Arguing about my right to pray would not bring honor to my father's soul. Besides, Dad didn't like arguing.

I placed the handset back into its cradle, then cringed as I recognized I'd done something I had never done—I had hung up on someone.

I stomped in circles around the house, my feminism galvanized. The hall mirror reflected the story; in front of me stood a red-faced woman with a clenched jaw and fisted hands. Male mourners didn't have this problem; they could go into any synagogue, including the ultra-Orthodox, and pray and be welcomed with open arms.

My purpose slowly came back into focus, the way an image appears on a Polaroid photo. I stopped pacing, grabbed the phone, and cancelled the hotel room in Ocean City. Rather than going to the beach, we would stay home and share rich, fun-filled days enjoying all that the Washington, DC, area offers.

Leon Wieseltier wrote that some seventeenth- and eighteenth-century Talmudist scholars prohibited a woman from reciting the Kaddish. But this was the twentieth century. I had erroneously assumed that because my father had blessed my efforts after hearing my passion and determination, others would too. Mine was a childlike wishfulness. My bubble of naïveté had burst open.

I sat on the sofa in my journaling room, trying to calm down and recover from my disappointment. I nuzzled my spine into the crease in the cushions, hugged by the pillows.

"Did you see this coming, Dad?" I didn't want to be annoyed with him, but he hadn't prepared me for this rejection.

"You told me how to deal with your death and your funeral arrangements, Dad. You explained what to anticipate at the funeral home and warned me they would try to sell me the most expensive coffin, preying on my grief. You told me you wanted the American flag on your casket.

You prepared me for all that. Why didn't you tell me what to anticipate as a woman trying to say Kaddish?" As soon as the words left my lips, heat moved up my neck and across my face. Shame rising. How could I be annoyed at my father?

After all, *I* was the one who wanted to say Kaddish for him. *I* was the one with the false expectations. Just six weeks into my eleven-month commitment, I hit a wall of opposition I hadn't anticipated. Naïvely, I had assumed that even the ultra-Orthodox would welcome my effort. I hadn't been prepared to be completely denied.

Despite being caught off guard, the feeling was familiar. I had grown up having my needs discounted.

As a preadolescent and teen, my bedroom was painted brown, with my mother's gloomy, pallid artwork hanging on the walls. When I wanted to put up teenage posters and paint the room a more feminine color, my mother responded, "It's my house and I'll choose the way the room looks." I had no voice.

Begging this man to let me pray felt as futile as begging my mother to hang a Beatles poster in my bedroom. The emotional sting of being devalued, this time by my own religion, felt just as sharp.

Lois flew to Maryland and we spent the weekend doing things we most enjoyed. We combed the shelves at Barnes & Noble like two kids in a candy store. As voracious readers, we always shared our reactions to the books we read and recommended our favorites to each other. We filled our arms with the books we wanted and then, following our decades-long custom, put back the ones we considered excessive. Waiting in line for the cashier, we chatted excitedly about our purchases.

Later in the day, we walked along the C&O Canal, sometimes arm in arm, reminiscing about Dad and basking in each other's company. We ate out for meals, and in the evenings, we slipped into our pajamas and snuggled up on the sofa to watch movies and share popcorn out of a single bowl.

And I recited the Mourner's Kaddish every morning and evening in my hometown synagogue where my prayers are welcomed, where I am not invisible, and where women *do* say Kaddish.

CHAPTER 19

Traditions Transformed

The day after Lois left, my mother called as I was cleaning the house.

"I'm not going to make seders anymore," she declared, as if it were nonnegotiable. Wham! Out of the blue. No discussion. So typical of my mother, discounting that I might have feelings about our family's tradition.

The seder, the central ritual of the eight-day Passover holiday, is one of the most widely observed rites in Judaism, and it had been a hallowed tradition in our family for generations. Passover commemorates the freedom of the Israelites from persecution by the Egyptians, a story captured by Hollywood in *The Ten Commandments* and told in the Jewish Bible in the book of Exodus. According to the book of Exodus, we are commanded to retell our history, which is read at the seder from a book called the *Haggadah,* which means "telling."

Before I could say anything, my mother continued.

"I'm going to divide the *kiddush* cups between you and your sister, Jane. She'll get the velvet *matzoh* cover, and you'll get the new one you bought for your father in Israel in May. He never got to use it." Her voice had the emotion of someone reading her grocery list.

I should have been used to Mom's this-is-the-way-it-is edicts after all these years, but strangely, I never ceased to be stunned by them.

I felt like saying, "Really, Mom? Dad's gone only six weeks, and already you're divvying up the Passover ritual items?" But disbelief muted me.

"I've already spoken to Jane, and she's going to make seders next year. I'm going to go to her house for Passover."

Arrangements are already made? I felt like a passenger on a hijacked plane. My mother had unilaterally cancelled a family tradition that I loved without input, further snapping my already broken heart. On top of losing my father, gone now was my beloved religious ceremony.

Any other time, I could have understood that my mother wouldn't want to continue to make seders without my father. But that day, her timing and matter-of-fact tone blindsided me, leaving me wondering how much more sorrow one heart could bear.

—

Could it really have been only six months since we had gathered in Mom and Dad's living room at the Passover table, with Mom's light-blue china and the silver kiddush cups polished so brightly that our reflections shone in them? Could that really have been the last time I would hear my father read from the Haggadah, or see him pour the four cups of wine from his mother's antique, cut-crystal wine decanters? Or hear him dramatize the words of his favorite passage from the Haggadah—"God took us from Egypt with a *mighty hand and an outstretched arm.*" Could that really have been our last seder together?

Passover had been my father's favorite holiday since his boyhood, when my grandmother would extend tables the entire length of their Bronx apartment and fill them with family members, the women dressed in their finest dresses adorned with strands of pearls, and the men in coats and ties, heads covered with fedoras. In later years, as my father and his brothers had their own families, as many as thirty people gathered in my grandparents' tiny apartment to celebrate our freedom from oppression and injustice.

Until my grandfather's death in 1970, our entire extended family congregated every year for two Passover seders at my paternal grandparents' apartment. The table would be adorned with my grandmother's finest china and her wine decanters. My grandfather, dressed in the traditional white *kittel* (robe) and positioned at the head of the long set of tables, conducted the entire seder in Hebrew. Since my cousins, my siblings, and I didn't know the language, we spent most of the time daydreaming, playing with the silverware, annoying each other under the table, and counting the minutes until the festive meal began.

Along the table were piles of matzoh—cracker-like flatbreads known as the "bread of affliction." Because the Israelites departed from Egypt in such haste, without time for their dough to rise, we are commanded during Passover to eat only unleavened bread to recall the plight of our ancestors. Observant Jews remove leavened products (wheat, barley, spelt, rye, and oats) from their homes during the holiday. As for the taste, Michael Wex aptly wrote in his book *Rhapsody in Schmaltz*: ". . . God gave us cardboard so that we could describe the taste of matzoh."

The meal always began with hard-boiled eggs, just as during the meal of consolation after the funeral. My cousin, who disliked the egg white, and I, who disliked the yolk, surreptitiously swapped egg sections with each other, evading the adults' eyes and their expectation to eat the entire egg. To this day, that remains one of our fondest memories.

The comforting smell of my grandmother's homemade matzoh ball soup would waft from the kitchen during the seder. She always made the lightest, fluffiest matzoh balls—compared to others I had in later years, which would sink in my stomach like a rock. After the soup course, she would serve a scrumptious turkey dinner complete with matzoh stuffing and all the trimmings. For years I believed my grandmother when she told me she had purchased a four-legged turkey from the local butcher because so many members of the family, including my father and I, liked the turkey leg the best.

After my grandfather's death, our family's Passover seders transformed. Gradually, the extended family stopped gathering to celebrate the holiday, and my father began leading his own seders for our nuclear family. As grandchildren expanded our family tree and then became old enough to read, my father eliminated much of the Hebrew and incorporated more English into the storytelling, conducting a more "user-friendly" seder than his father had, and ensuring his grandchildren understood the meaning of Passover. In making it his own, he preserved many of my grandfather's rituals while introducing new ones.

The seder table is covered with symbolic foods: a green leafy vegetable (in our case, parsley) to represent the fruit of the earth, horseradish to represent the bitterness of the lives of the Israelites as they toiled in slavery, a lamb shank bone to represent the Passover sacrifice, *charoset*—a mixture of apples, walnuts, and wine—to represent the mortar the Israelites used to make bricks during slavery, and a roasted hard-boiled egg to remind us of the cycle of life.

When my father cut the pieces of fresh horseradish for the ritual of eating bitter herbs, he invariably cut one piece larger than the others. With a glint in his eye, my father would hand David the largest piece and watch as my son's eyes widened, then teared up. I imagined David intuiting that his grandfather was getting even for all the times he beat his elder in sports. The teasing nature of their relationship endured even on Passover.

I loved watching the good-natured back-and-forth negotiations for the *afikomen*. That small piece of matzoh, hidden for the children to find and then bargain for its return to the leader, is required to resume the post-meal service. The game of hiding the broken piece of matzoh and the accompanying haggling originated as a way to keep children engaged during a long evening. Over the years, my children and nieces became savvy negotiators, having learned from the best.

"I'll give you each fifty cents for the afikomen." Dad always started low.

"Fifty cents? You've got to be kidding, Grandpa. We want ten dollars each. There's inflation, you know." They always started high.

"You're the ones who must be kidding. I can't afford ten bucks for all six of you. Okay . . . I'll give you a dollar each. That's gonna cost me six bucks." There was never any question that, no matter who found the afikomen, every child got the same reward. No favoritism.

I cherished the drama. My father could never hide his joviality, and I giggled as my children and nieces whispered with one another in a tightly formed circle, glancing at my father from the corners of their eyes, trying not to let him hear their deliberations. Back and forth they haggled, until a crisp five-dollar bill was handed to each child and the piece of matzoh was turned over to my father to resume the seder.

—

I came back from reminiscing when I realized my mother was still rambling about attending Jane's seder. Her decision to stop making seders and disburse the ritual items hammered the final nail into the coffin of my father's custom.

"Thank you, Mom." I tried to sound grateful. "I'll gladly accept any items you've earmarked for me, and I'll use them with pride."

"Good. One more thing off my mind."

And with that, I wished my mother an easy evening and ended the conversation.

—

In the years when the children wouldn't miss school and we could travel to Florida, being with my parents was the highest priority. But beginning in 1994, in years when we didn't travel to Florida, I began making seders of my own.

When my father began conducting seders, he had made the Passover story more accessible and the seder more inclusive, melding his father's Orthodox traditions with our modern realities. My grandfather's death had freed Dad to make the ritual his own. I adopted my father's model.

Passover is a celebration of freedom. With Dad's death, I felt a newfound freedom to create a unique celebration—free of my mother's expectations and my grandfather's traditions. Instead of driving 190 miles to Philadelphia to my sister's seder, I decided to make my own and to write my own Haggadah, one more accessible to my children. I collected and read more than a dozen Haggadot, then took the best of each to retain the essence of the Passover story, and included more explanations for each tradition and ritual. I removed archaic terms such as "thee" and "thou," replaced male-oriented language with gender-neutral language, and used smaller words. I printed it from the computer and had copies bound at the local Kinko's.

Like my grandmother, who extended hospitality to many, I invited friends and havurah members who had no one to share the holiday with. Those who accepted expressed gratitude and relief at not having to be alone on the holiday.

I wondered if and how my two grandfathers, both immigrants, celebrated Passover in their early years in America. I reached out to the Jewish Federation and invited newly settled Russian immigrants to my home to partake in this time-honored ritual. When the four Russians arrived holding Russian-language Haggadot, I pictured my Russian-born maternal grandfather, who had died suddenly when I was thirteen, smiling.

I moved all the living room furniture into another room, creating one long open area, as my grandmother had, and joined six-foot-long tables until they filled the space. I borrowed chairs. But unlike my working grandmother who did everything herself, I had guests contribute either food or sweat equity—a helping hand with setup or cleanup.

To honor the importance of women in the history of the Jewish people, I added a Miriam's cup to the table, symbolizing Miriam's well, believed to have provided water for the Israelites in the desert. I imagine my grandfather would be aghast, but this action made me feel as liberated as the Israelites must have felt in leaving Egypt. I had held on to traditions yet no longer felt constrained by them.

On the night of the first seder, I felt rapturous looking out at the long row of twenty-eight people who were bound to each other to perpetuate a tradition handed down to us by our parents and grandparents, eager to repeat the story that had been told for generations. All the while,

I knew Jews the world over were simultaneously retelling the story of our liberation from slavery, anchoring us in a shared past that made those of us around the table feel almost like family.

As I continue to conduct Passover seders, I have given my children, and now my grandchildren, a foothold in the history of our people. And I've shared the lesson I learned: when loss closes the door on long-held customs, it creates opportunities to establish new and meaningful rituals within our own traditions.

Top: My father and me (five months old),
September 1949

Center: My father
transmitted his love of
the beach when I was
only fifteen months old,
July 1950

Bottom: My father and me,
Mother's Day, May 1953

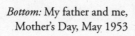

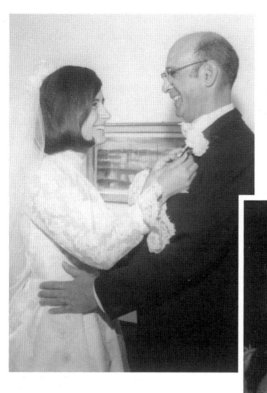

Top: My father and me on my wedding day, May 30, 1970

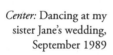

Center: Dancing at my sister Jane's wedding, September 1989

Bottom: My father and me in front of the sacred scroll at Congregation Beth El during Rachel's bat mitzvah, August 1994

Top: My father took Rachel and David for a spin in his golf cart and let Rachel drive (note: he's holding on tight), July 1995

Bottom: My father in front of his home in his beloved Polo Club, Florida, June 2000

Top left: My father's graduation photo from George Washington High School, New York City, January 1942

Top right: My father, the infantry soldier, 1st Platoon, Company C, 1st Battalion, 406th Regiment, 102nd Infantry Division, date unknown

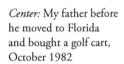

Center: My father before he moved to Florida and bought a golf cart, October 1982

Bottom left: My father at his seventy-fifth birthday celebration (he loved that golf T-shirt), July 1999

Bottom right: My father aboard the *Princess* cruise ship, New Year's Eve, 1999–2000

CHAPTER 20

Prayer and Then the Laundry

Eight weeks after my father's death, I struggled to balance the multiple demands of my spiritual and secular lives—as a single mother, a part-time therapist in a juvenile court, and an entrepreneur whose job required extensive domestic travel. Life went on, even if on autopilot.

Arranging work-related travel was now a logistics nightmare. Finding and ensuring morning and evening minyanim in every city where clients sent me became a time-consuming investment of research and planning before the advent of GPS and Google. For help, I bought Oscar Israelowitz's *United States Jewish Travel Guide,* which identified synagogues alphabetically by states and then cities across the country. When a client offered a job opportunity, I opened the book, found the correct city, and called the Conservative synagogue most likely to have morning and evening services in that city. The calls usually went something like this:

"Can you tell me if your synagogue has a morning or evening minyan?"

"I'm sorry . . . we don't have a morning minyan here" and "We only have a minyan on Shabbat" were frequent responses. But I remained relentless.

Airline schedules dictated whether I could arrive home in time for the evening worship service at my synagogue, Congregation Beth El, or whether I had to stay out of town an extra night in order to pray. Finding and coordinating flights before travel search engines like Expedia, Orbitz, and Priceline required the patience and discipline of a yogi.

Evenings were especially exhausting. After praying every evening, I still had much to do before I could sleep. Stopping at the grocery store on the way home, I lugged my body through the aisles. The loneliness of late-night shopping was intensified by the bright store lights pressing on my eyes, contrasting the darkness outside the windows. The wheels of my grocery cart glided along the waxed floors as I searched for easy, quick-to-fix meals.

Many nights I huffed and puffed as I carried the laundry up the steps, dragging my legs and wondering why builders put laundry rooms so far from the source of dirty laundry. As I paid bills and carried out other household chores, I fought the urge to ignore it all. Fog took permanent residency in my brain. A friend accurately characterized the sensations as "an altered state."

One day, I received a letter from one of my dearest and oldest friends:

> Dear Sarah,
>
> I love you and I wish I could find a way to ease your burden as you grieve the loss of your father. I have to say I find the idea that it takes ten people to get a message to God very foreign. I find prayer of great value in my life, particularly when I have a heavy heart. It's personal. Me . . . just me alone . . . speaking into the heart of the Great Spirit. I wish you could find a way to retain the support of your faith without having to endure the burden of twice-a-day worship at a synagogue with at least nine other people. Does this strengthen you or drain you? If your religious observances do not strengthen you, do they serve a purpose?
>
> Much Love,
> Barb

I stared at the words, immobilized. In my grief, I didn't recognize the letter as her attempt to comprehend my chosen path. I didn't see it as the gentle concern of a heart sister, but as a challenge to my spiritual practice. I felt inadequate to articulate my heart's path, and as I didn't feel I could respond in a way that would deepen our relationship and build mutual understanding, I tucked her letter away in the back of my journal.

One evening, to nurture myself and gain some needed perspective, I turned to writing in my journal, a habit I'd cultivated since my teens. My journal had always been my friend—allowing me to release emotions, clarify ideas that were always swirling uncontrolled in my brain, consider the pros and cons of major decisions, and decompress when stressed. My commitment to the power of writing in a journal inspired me to become one of the country's earliest certified journal therapists in 2010, a designation painstakingly earned at the Center for Journal Therapy.

I made a pot of tea and nestled myself into my favorite sofa. I calculated the number of hours (including commuting time) required to recite Kaddish in synagogue for the full eleven months: 816 hours!

I wrote, *Would I give up 816 hours of my life to elevate Dad's soul to Gan Eden?*

The answer to my own question flowed immediately onto the paper: *Absolutely!*

After all, my father had done so much for me and my sisters over the years.

I remembered the time my children and I returned home from a weeklong visit to my parents' house to find four feet of water flooding our lower level. Someone had put a hose through a basement window and turned on the faucet. Fortunately, our guinea pig cage floated on top of the water, the rodent seeming to consider it an adventure. Everything else—my son's valuable baseball card collection, our guest bedroom, all of our furniture, and my entire office—was destroyed. My father, on hearing my voice on the telephone, wasted no time getting on the next plane and flying to Maryland to help me clear water-soaked items from the basement. When he arrived, he said, "I don't know what I can do to be helpful, but I'm here for you."

I stared out the window, absorbed in thought, and then put my pen back to the paper.

I wrote:

> Dad spent more than eighteen months fighting on the front lines of Germany during World War II, living in squalid trenches, being shot at and wounded to make our world a safer place. He worked six days a week for more than twenty years in Grandpa's nasty furniture store, in a job he hated, to feed, clothe, and shelter us. He saved and paid for the college educations of all three of us, so we wouldn't have to work our way through school as he'd had to. He never shrank from responsibility. Isn't this the least I can do for a man who sacrificed so much for his country and his family?

I knew my life would be easier if I didn't recite Kaddish twice daily. But my father never took the easy road, and I felt I shouldn't either. I was struggling to emulate his commitment.

Of course, when my father recited Kaddish twice daily, he wasn't a single parent traveling the country for his career. He also wasn't doing the grocery shopping or the laundry, paying the bills, or making dinner. He was never encumbered with those functions. I doubt they ever crossed his mind to offer. Growing up, he had a mother who worked and performed all those household rituals; then he had a wife who did the same.

I didn't want to concede that grief had stolen my stamina. I'd always juggled multiple priorities simultaneously without letting a single ball drop, as if I were Superwoman. The words *no* and *I can't* had never been part of my vocabulary—until now. Now I needed to make emotional and physical space to mourn and pray, to slow down, and accept the limitations of my endurance.

But I had underestimated the challenge of being in synagogue every morning and evening. I couldn't remember ever orchestrating my life so strictly.

It is hard, in twenty-first-century America, to make grieving a priority. Society expects us to suppress sorrow. Many people are uncomfortable seeing grief's manifestations. But in committing to attend the morning and evening minyanim, I gave myself a time to grieve and a place to cry with others who understood. In the minyan, we make space for our own pain and bear witness to the pain of others. This was a drastic contrast from my youth, when if I cried, my mother would say, "Stop that crying, or I'll give you something to really cry about." Even at my father's funeral, she had dictated, "There will be no crying."

Reciting Kaddish at my synagogue gave me designated times for quiet and prayer, introspection and reflection, and a chance to connect with my father and God. No honking horns, no blaring televisions, no ringing phones, no roaring lawn mowers, no jets taking off and landing. My spiritual community offered a safe place to release my grief every morning and evening, making it easier to tuck it away during the day.

As I began to shed some of grief's self-centeredness, I was able to respond to my friend's letter with equal compassion.

> Dear Barb,
>
> I am moved by your love and concern for me and for my challenge in attending services twice each day in synagogue. To answer your question, twice daily participation in the minyan both drains and energizes me. Some days I find it physically wearying, but I am comforted and uplifted, emotionally and spiritually, by the support of other minyaneers.
>
> I have faith, as you do, that God hears our individual prayers. With other voices joining mine, I feel we

are a mightier cry for God's attention. Even if untrue that God hears collective voices more than the solitary voice, I'm unwilling to take the chance on my father's soul. If his soul will be elevated to Gan Eden as a result of my prayers with nine others, then every ounce of energy is worth the effort. This is the final gift I can give to my father.

Much love,
Sarah

I began to see, in a new way, what was most important. I remembered how, after Dad's cancer diagnosis, he had reassessed his lived life. He left the fast pace of the New York City environs and moved to a golf community in Florida, a place more fulfilling than he dreamed possible. My commitment to him was giving me the chance to do the same—to slow the pace of my life and bring tranquility to my soul, even while managing the laundry.

That was Dad's gift. And I treasure it. Still.

CHAPTER 21

The Minyaneers

By late winter of that year, the world seemed a precarious place to take my feelings of loss. Several people outside the minyan expected me to "move on," "stop living in the past," or, as one colleague told me, "Just let go already." By contrast, the minyaneers provided refuge, emotional support, and a container for my grief. Their gestures, subtle but genuine—a gentle touch on the arm, the quiet passing of a tissue when tears fell discreetly, or a look of mutual sympathy—made me feel cared for. In their presence, I was safe to express my emotions without criticism or ridicule: a safety my father had provided and which I had thought I had lost forever.

The minyaneers understood how our emotions can catch us off guard, overpowering us without warning. Even the most stalwart of the veterans could be seen shedding silent tears on the Yahrzeit (anniversary of death) of their loved ones. One regular minyaneer, Ralph, rose one day in January to recite the Mourner's Kaddish. A broad-shouldered man who stood over six feet tall, he had the same thinning gray hair on the back of his head as my father had, and the same infectious smile. Tears clouded his eyes.

"This is the sixty-sixth Yahrzeit for my father," he told me.

"Ralph, have you really been saying Kaddish for sixty-six years?" I leaned closer, astonished by his years of grief, commitment, and loyalty.

"My father died when I was very young, and I've said Kaddish for him every year on his Yahrzeit. Today is the sixty-sixth anniversary of his death."

His solemn bass voice and downcast eyes kindled my compassion. I wanted to offer my condolences, but no words came. I just stared.

"Many years ago, Rabbi Scolnic, the first rabbi of our congregation, started the minyan here at Beth El," Ralph explained. "Some days we had only three people, but the rabbi said, 'If we keep it up, eventually the people will come.'

"I came to synagogue one time to recite Kaddish for my father, but we didn't have ten people. I decided then, if I wanted to have a minyan on my father's Yahrzeit, I had to become a regular minyaneer. And that's what I did. I come every morning. And the rabbi's words came true. Now we have more than ten every day."

"Your being here is a gift, Ralph," I said gratefully.

———

I experienced many blessings during my avelut (mourning period), but one of the most special was the deep friendships I made with three other minyaneers.

Soon after I started saying Kaddish, three people began coming every morning to recite the Mourner's Kaddish for their parents. Rick, an engineer who looked younger than his forty-something years, began saying Kaddish for his mother days after I started. A short time later, Roslyn ("Roz" for short), a tall, blonde, blue-eyed doctor at the National Institutes of Health, started coming each morning to recite Kaddish for her father. Then Jonathan, an economist and active member of our synagogue, whose casual attire contrasted with Rick's meticulous grooming and professional dress, lost his father. We four were a motley crew, as different in our physical appearances as in our occupations and life stages.

Despite our outward differences, we coalesced in our shared intention to bring honor to our deceased parents. We sat together in the chapel each morning and stood side by side as we chanted the Mourner's Kaddish, our voices blending in prayer. Seated together at breakfast in the small social hall, we talked about our upbringings, our beliefs, our children, our full-time jobs, our life challenges, and our commitment to this tradition; this sharing solidified our friendship the way glue binds broken pieces. Our bond became so close and so apparent, other minyaneers teasingly called us "the Four Musketeers." We were inseparable and wore the nickname with pride. This friendship, which deepened over the months, has continued to this day.

———

On an otherwise ordinary morning during services at Beth El, grief stormed me for no apparent reason, and I started shaking. Rick put his hand on my shoulder and softly whispered, "Are you okay?" After I nodded, his hand remained, a gentle touch radiating caring, a small gesture with a powerful impact. One mourner to another. Tenderheartedness transcending words.

Each day, we recounted a different psalm. On Mondays, we recited Psalm 48:

> The kings conspired and advanced,
> but when they saw her they were astounded.
> Panic stunned them, they fled in fright,
>
> Seized with trembling like a woman in labor,
> shattered like a fleet wrecked by an east wind.[vii]

One particular Monday, Roz had us in stitches. "How did the authors of the Psalms, all men no doubt, know what it felt like to be 'a woman in labor'?" Restraining our laughter became impossible.

And when she asked, "How do you compare labor with an east wind? What were those guys thinking?" I laughed until my sides ached.

Laughing amidst mourners had felt irreverent until Roz pointed out how funny the Psalms really were—something I had never considered.

I leaned over and whispered, "Thank you, Roz."

During the morning minyan on the seventh day of Passover, the leader selected Rick to read the abridged version of the Song of Songs:

> Oh, for a kiss from your lips,
> For your love is better than wine . . .
> How beautiful your sandaled feet, daughter of nobles.
> Your rounded thighs are jewels, the work of a master-hand.

"These verses are a little spicy, don't you agree?" asked Roz in a voice just louder than a whisper. Rick went on, struggling to maintain composure.

> Your navel is a rounded goblet . . .
> Your belly is a heap of wheat encircled by lilies.
> Your breasts are like two fawns, twins of a gazelle.[viii]

"That's some juicy language for a blessing," Roz said.

She was right; I'd never considered how risqué those verses were. She continued until the sanctuary filled with the sounds of uncontrollable laughter. Rick chuckled so hard that he could barely read the page. I hadn't laughed that much in months.

I began to see that frivolity could coexist with solemnity and that life didn't have to be an either/or. The rigidity I had no doubt inherited from my mother often prevented me from seeing life's "both/and" opportunities. When you share such sorrow as grief elicits, humor is as binding as the grief. Laughing with those who had cried beside me was the best elixir for sorrow.

———

One Wednesday morning, this community of worshippers affirmed to me the importance of compassionate others for our own healing.

The previous day had begun like any other, until a conversation with a friend drifted into a discussion of his love of baseball. In a flash, I visualized my father playing baseball on Sunday mornings during my childhood. But I couldn't remember the position he played. I called my mother; she didn't remember. Neither did my sisters. Memories gone. Lost.

If Dad's experiences and passions are forgotten, then what? If I can't remember, how can I ever transmit recollections of him to my children— and someday to my grandchildren? Then it will be like he never lived. Do our lives not matter? Do we mean nothing in the long run?

My distress poured out in nonstop sobbing. Rick and Jonathan consoled me. Sonja, a longtime member of our congregation, held me. Her broad frame and large, soft bosom reminded me of the soothing hugs of my buxom grandmother. Inhaling Sonja's flowery cologne and feeling the softness of her cashmere sweater against my face, my muscles loosened, and I went limp like a rag doll.

"I can see him standing over home plate with the bat in his hand; I can see him swinging at pitches, and the clay-colored dirt flying as he slid into home base. But I can't remember what position he played when his team was on the field. Maybe I didn't pay enough attention then. It feels so much more important now, to remember. If those memories fade, what will be left of him? How will he live on?"

"You're creating a beautiful legacy for your father by being here every day. That's a greater testimony to him than remembering his baseball position." Sonja's tenderness consoled me.

"Those Sunday mornings, having him all to myself for the drive to and from Van Cortlandt Park in the Bronx, were precious. He listened as I shared about my schoolwork, my friends, and my adolescent worries. He used to tell me things like 'Be sure to seek out the good and beauty in the world'; 'Life is short, so you must live it to the fullest'; and 'Life is sometimes filled with sadness and difficulties, but that's what makes the good times even better.'"

"Aren't these beautiful recollections of his words more important than his position?" Sonja whispered, stroking my back.

"You're right," I mumbled. Hearing his words pour from my lips, I knew that he was still alive inside me.

The intimacy in Sonja's lingering hug, and her gentle wisdom, softened my heartache. When she and I finally loosened our embrace, I knew my father would live forever in my heart—even if his baseball position didn't. Looking into her eyes, I felt God had touched my soul.

—

Other relationships developed as well. Judi Canter, whose mother died before my father, began saying Kaddish before me. We became fast friends over the months we prayed together, and Judi helped advance my Jewish education.

One day, I closed my prayer book before the final Mourner's Kaddish, proud that I could now recite the blessing without the transliteration. The accomplishment seemed sudden; in reality, the prayer had crept into my consciousness gradually, unnoticeably. It had become part of me.

"Keep your book open to the correct page," counseled Judi.

"But I've memorized the Kaddish. I don't have to read it anymore," I boasted.

"We keep the book open to the Mourner's Kaddish so newcomers and mourners who don't know the prayer aren't embarrassed at having to read it. It equalizes all mourners," she replied.

I immediately reopened my prayer book. No one-upmanship among mourners. Sensitivity to others is a prominent Jewish value.

In that moment, I realized that repeating small (and possibly difficult) behaviors consistently over an extended period of time can produce what seems like sudden, dramatic change.

A few days later, Judi rose for the final Mourner's Kaddish of her avelut (mourning period). Her obligation was complete.

Because her synagogue didn't have daily minyanim, she had come to Beth El each morning, but she wouldn't be returning. We held hands, delaying our goodbyes. And even though we committed to seeing each other, I expected that the demands of our respective lives would override our best intentions. Our hand clasp expressed the consolation of two mourners whose shared path was now diverging.

"It's kind of strange and hard to explain," she said after the service. "I'm relieved it's over, but I'm nervous about moving on without this community. I'll miss you and the togetherness of the minyaneers. It makes me sad, but I'm sure looking forward to the hours I'll regain each week."

"Letting go of the support network must feel a little scary," I said.

"The problem is, there's no real way to mark the ending," Judi noted. "It feels kind of incomplete."

I just nodded. In a religion so filled with ritual, Judaism lacks a custom to honor the end of an eleven-month journey along grief's highway. Judi and I shared a tight, lingering hug in the synagogue parking lot, and as we parted, I vowed to make my ending more tangible.

———

When another minyaneer had the last day of his avelut (mourning period) a few days later, I became the senior—the avelah who had been saying Kaddish the longest. Months had passed since my father died. Mourners who were reciting Kaddish when I first returned from Florida had left. New mourners had come.

Becoming the tenured mourner in the minyan mirrors the natural order of life. Elders pass; newborns arrive. If we live long enough, we gradually become the seniors in our social circles and families—the matriarchs and patriarchs—typically positions of esteem. *I should find that notion consoling*, I thought. But being the grande dame among mourners didn't feel like such an honored position, given the price paid for it.

CHAPTER 22

Nine Is the Loneliest Number

Just as the strength of any chain is as strong as its individual links, so too does the solidity of the minyan depend on its ten individual members. And when one link is missing, the bond of communal prayer is broken.

Waiting for the evening service to begin one Sunday night in winter, all heads turned toward the door each time we heard a noise, hoping for new arrivals. The nine of us, sitting in the small chapel at Congregation Beth El, watched the minutes tick away, waiting for a tenth to be able to start the service. By 8:10 p.m., it had become clear: for the first time in the three months since I'd begun reciting the Mourner's Kaddish, we didn't have a minyan.

What do I do now? I can't not say Kaddish.

In the back of the small chapel hung a call list—people living near the synagogue who agreed to be phoned at the last minute when we needed a minyan. Scanning the list for addresses closest to the synagogue, I garnered my spunk and dialed the first number.

"Hello. This is Sarah Birnbach. I'm at Beth El. We don't have enough people for the evening minyan. Can you help us out?"

"How many do you need?" asked the first congregant I called.

"Just one." My voice was almost a question. "We have nine."

"I'm on my way." Not a moment's hesitation.

Fifteen minutes later, the man arrived, and we began to pray.

Reciting the Mourner's Kaddish for my father changed me. Previously, I hadn't been someone who reached out for what she needed.

I had allowed the rejections and punishments from my childhood to become a self-fulfilling prophecy. In the magnifying glass of hindsight, I saw that my newfound fearlessness came from my determination to elevate my father's soul. Would I have made the call if the stakes hadn't been as high? I wasn't sure. My father's death emboldened me with a mettle I carry to this day.

That Sunday evening, I vowed that when my Kaddish period ended, I'd put my name on the call list and consider my responsibility to minyan duty as seriously as my commitment to jury duty. And that's what I did.

Over the following months, whenever we had less than ten people, I would scour the synagogue's classrooms and offices in search of others to complete the minyan. If the rest of the building was empty, I called those on the call list, delaying the service until we had ten. I never got resistance. I remained undeterred.

"Before I started saying Kaddish, what did you do when you didn't get a minyan?" I asked Sam, a kind of unspoken Sunday evening minyan captain.

"Whenever we only had nine people and someone needed to say Kaddish, we opened the ark and counted the Torah as the 'tenth man,'" he responded.

I was aghast. That alternative was as unacceptable to me as it had been to my father. After reciting the Mourner's Kaddish twice daily for eleven months for each of his parents, he then served as his synagogue's unofficial Monday morning minyan captain for ten years, ensuring a minyan each Monday morning. He stayed on the telephone every Sunday night, sometimes for hours, calling until he had firm commitments from at least ten congregants. He could not imagine conducting the service with less than the requisite number of people. In this one aspect of Judaism, my father did not deviate from tradition. This acorn had not fallen far from the tree.

I naïvely believed that my father's dedication to the minyan was standard in Jewish communities everywhere. I saw his devotion and assumed, erroneously, that most observant Jews did the same for their parents. But I would soon learn that many who mourn do not share this practice.

My expectations for other congregations were distorted by my ability to phone our congregants until we had ten, and by belonging to a synagogue where I unfailingly counted in the minyan. When other synagogues didn't include me in the ten-person count, I was thwarted in my ability to pray for my father's soul.

My first experience of a service with just nine men and me happened when I went on a business trip to Raleigh, North Carolina, later in the year.

Before the trip, I turned to my trusted *United States Jewish Travel Guide.* Chabad, an ultra-Orthodox sect of Judaism that excluded women for making up the minyan, was the sole place in Raleigh offering a morning service. With great trepidation, I called the rabbi.

"We don't always get ten men for our morning service, so I'm glad you've called me ahead of time. I'll make some calls to ensure a minyan for you when you're here." His commitment reminded me of my father.

On the morning of my workshop, I arrived at the Chabad center well before the 6:45 a.m. start time. Right on the dot, the rabbi arrived and unlocked the door. His dark brimmed hat cast a shadow on a kind face with sparkling eyes. His smile radiated from a bushy reddish beard that revealed early signs of graying. He directed me to a small room, where I sat, my eyes remaining fixed on the door. One . . . two . . . three . . . until the men, including the rabbi, numbered nine. At 6:55 a.m., my hopefulness ebbed. No minyan. I drooped down in my seat as the number nine became final.

"Since we don't have a minyan, I'm terribly sorry. You won't be able to recite Kaddish." The rabbi looked directly at me.

Nine men had shown up, and I didn't count. I was present but extraneous, disheartened, and stuck. I had nowhere else to go and no call list to contact nearby congregants.

"Instead, I'll read a portion from the *Mishnah* [Jewish law]." The rabbi's words brought me back from my thoughts.

Since study is one of the highest mitzvot in Judaism, in the absence of a minyan and in lieu of saying Kaddish, it is customary to study a passage from the Mishnah. The rabbi was providing his best alternative.

In my youth, I erroneously believed that if I did everything "right," things would work out well. Decades passed before I realized that being the so-called good girl did not guarantee my desired outcomes. Nevertheless, my childhood hopefulness remained as much a part of me as my skeleton was. I had assumed that since I'd called ahead, the rabbi, like my father, would ensure ten men were present.

Thinking about Dad in that moment gave me a blueprint for kindness: nine men had come out to honor my father's memory, and the rabbi had performed an act of holiness to bring merit to my father. The spirit of their mitzvah softened my disappointment. I shifted my focus to the service, and when the rabbi finished, I remembered my manners.

I recalled that, according to the Torah, Orthodox men are forbidden to touch any woman outside their family. So, instead of shaking their hands, I put my hands together in the namaste pose and bowed my head slightly, showing my respect to those who had shown up for me. Before leaving, I thanked each of them with heartfelt sincerity and gave a special thanks to the rabbi. My father would have expected no less of me.

As I drove from the Chabad center to my client's facility, I wondered, *Would God penalize my father for something out of my control?*

Despite my best intentions, I had failed. To relieve my chagrin, I reached out to God.

"Please, God. Please judge my efforts to be as praiseworthy as reciting Kaddish, and don't let this situation influence your determination for my father's soul."

———

The number nine would haunt me throughout the eleven months. On a Sunday morning a few months later, in a Conservative synagogue in Frederick, Maryland, another woman and I sat with nine men.

"We don't have enough men to recite the Mourner's Kaddish," the rabbi announced.

I wanted to speak up that I wanted to be counted, but I stayed quiet out of respect. After all, I was in a synagogue.

We two women shared a wordless look. I shrugged my shoulders, all the while biting my lip. Visible to each other and in full view of the men, we were discounted, treated as if we didn't exist. We were alone in a congregation of fellow Jews, contrary to the very purpose of praying in community.

When the time came for the Mourner's Kaddish, the rabbi skipped over it. I moaned quietly, my hand tightening its grip on my prayer book. The other woman's lower jaw started to quiver. I stayed until the service ended and then left the synagogue without a glance or a word to anyone, flight the only recourse for my sick heart.

Nine was only one person short to pray for my father's spirit: only one missing soul to help me bring honor to my father in God's sight. Nine left me powerless. Nine deepened my grief.

CHAPTER 23
Accepting Reality

When I first saw the Beeler's Mill property in Charles Town, West Virginia, in the spring of 2000, I fell in love at first sight. As I drove through the white wooden gate, my eyes flew open at the twenty-two-foot waterwheel turning slowly in the millrace only a few feet from the road. The historic steel waterwheel, one of the first in the country, was built shortly after the Civil War, after the original wooden wheel burned in a fire. The wheel was the sole reminder of the mill that had operated there until just after World War II.

Driving up the long gravel driveway, hearing the pebbles crunching under the wheels of my car, I was captivated by the way the sunlight shone through the leaves of the majestic seventy-five-foot sycamores that reached toward the sky like a beanstalk.

The stream, Evitts Run, ran along the acreage and powered the waterwheel, humming a soothing lullaby. Hearing the burbling of the two twelve-foot waterfalls as they cascaded over their rocky ledges, I set my heart on the property before I even reached the house—called the Mill House—which was built in 1751.

The home had three enormous stone fireplaces; the one in the dining room had been the cooking hearth with the original wrought iron crane, which held the cooking pot, still attached to its side wall. The other two were located in spacious great rooms.

As I climbed the narrow wooden stairs, creaking with the weight of their history, to the bedrooms on the top floor, I knew I had to

153

buy the Mill House. Now I just had to convince the owners to sell it to me.

When the owners accepted my offer over two others, I started dancing feverishly around the room. Signing the contract marked the end of my five-year search for a home in a more rural area large enough to conduct journaling retreats. I had no problem with their request to leave the settlement date open. In early September, the owners told me they wanted to close on the day before Thanksgiving.

Two weeks later, my father was dead.

———

November 22, 2000, the day I closed on my idyllic property, should have been a joyous occasion; but sitting at the settlement table in the attorney's office, the elation of my first visit to Beeler's Mill and the acceptance of my offer were overshadowed by the realization that my father would never see my historic home. He'd never hear the gushing water tumbling over the rocks or the creaking of the rickety wooden bridge that crossed the stream. He'd never feel the crisp West Virginia air on his skin or revel in the millions of brilliant stars that lit the night sky, a spectacle impossible in New York City. He'd never share this part of my life . . .

My sadness coexisted with joy.

But now, grief manifested itself in a new and different way. Realizing that I'd not only lost my father's physical presence but also his inclusion in the rest of my life hit me hard. I ached for all the future events, accomplishments, difficult decisions, and *simchas* (happy occasions) I would have to experience without him. With the keys in my hand, the Mill House became a three-acre reminder of the immense void he left behind.

———

A few weeks after I became the newest owner of the Mill House, while on my way home from work, I debated whether or not to stop at the grocery store before going home for a quick dinner and then on to evening worship.

What the heck, I thought. *I need bread, milk, and lunch fixings for David. How much time can it take to get a couple of items?*

Despite the lack of vacant parking spaces, which should have been a clue to me, I went in.

The supermarket was unusually crowded; people congregated in every aisle, perusing the shelves while their carts stood waiting for them to resume steering, blocking easy passage.

Are they giving something away for free here tonight?

All I wanted to do was get in and out. Quickly. The nightly pressure I felt to be on time for the evening service was ratcheting up by the minute. As I steered my grocery cart through the aisles at a pretty good pace, the wheels wobbled in every direction except the one I wanted, and time ticked away.

Carts clogged both directions of the bottled-water aisle, my typical route between the dairy department and the bread aisle. To bypass the congestion and keep moving, I detoured down the cookie aisle, one I never went into. That was my big mistake.

I was pushing my grocery cart like a NASCAR driver when the bright yellow packaging struck me like a jolt of electricity. There on the shelf sat my father's favorite cookies—Mallomars. I came to a screeching halt.

Mallomars are like s'mores without the need for a campfire or fireplace—graham cracker cookies topped with marshmallow and covered in dark chocolate. Nabisco only sells them between September and March, a throwback to the early twentieth century when they were delivered in unrefrigerated trucks. The company did not produce the cookies in the summer to avoid chocolate melting in their delivery trucks and customers finding a gooey mess in the box.

My father loved Mallomars. He used to say they accompanied a cup of coffee perfectly, the way a glass of Merlot pairs with a steak dinner. And just as some people have a preferred system for eating

Oreos—either eating the cookie whole or taking the layers apart and eating them one at a time—my father followed a strict set of steps for eating Mallomars: first, he bit off the top chocolate layer, letting the chocolate melt in his mouth and revealing the fluffy white marshmallow below; then he carefully ate just the marshmallow, exposing the caramel-colored graham cracker base; finally, he finished the cookie with its last coating of chocolate around the rim. It was a serious matter of familial duty to eat Mallomars one layer at a time, a tradition I have followed all my life.

Wait 'til I tell Dad his favorite cookies are back on the shelves!

I reached for my cell phone.

Then it hit me. He was gone.

The sounds of the people, the screeching wheels of the grocery carts on the linoleum floor, and the synthetic, piped-in Muzak all faded into the distance. I clutched the handle of the grocery cart and bent over the cart, pressing the handle into my stomach to steady myself.

How could something like a box of cookies trigger grief? Right in the middle of a busy supermarket, too.

I struggled to maintain my composure, all the time staring at the golden wrapping on the Mallomars boxes, silent elephant tears streaming down my face. In that moment, I learned that the tiniest trigger can evoke a memory that destroys our illusion of control and hurls grief upon us like a surprise avalanche.

I stood up slowly, staring at the bright wrapping that had thrown off my equilibrium.

"Okay, Dad," I spoke aloud, wondering if I was crazy as I gently put a box of Mallomars into my cart.

Later that night, after the evening service, I sat at my kitchen table and stared at the box, remembering how my father looked as he enjoyed a Mallomar. I slowly slit open the paper wrapper on the box of cookies and lifted the cardboard lid. I took one Mallomar from the box and turned it around in my hand before carefully nibbling the chocolate off the top, as my father had done. I studied the marshmallow below, smiling at the imprint of my teeth marks, and ate the spongy white middle. Then, just before biting into the bottom layer of cookie, I paused, as my father always did. I gazed through the window at the night sky beyond, held the remainder of the cookie up in my right hand, and declared, "This one's for you, Dad. I wish you were here. I love you."

CHAPTER 24

Thanksgiving

It was my sister Jane's turn to host our family for Thanksgiving—the only time each year that my entire nuclear family came together. Driving up Interstate 95 to Philadelphia in day-before-Thanksgiving traffic, David dozing next to me, I had time to reflect. Dad loved this holiday, and especially loved seeing his three daughters tend to the family's needs without the bickering that had characterized our childhoods. We three put on scrumptious meals, fit for a king—and he was our king. I imagine he secretly enjoyed being waited on hand and foot, though he never admitted it. His greatest happiness lay in seeing all six of his grandchildren together.

When I arrived at Jane's, her puffy eyes and red nose told me I wasn't alone in my sorrow. She greeted me at the door with an uncharacteristically tight embrace, bridging the divide that had often existed between us in the past. Our five-year age difference frequently felt like a generational schism when we were growing up.

We had often given the term *sibling rivalry* its ultimate definition; I was the responsible firstborn child, Jane the rebellious youngest. We constantly vied for our one bathroom, our one telephone, and our father's affection. We quarreled over who got to sit in the front seat of the car. We'd argue, then we'd argue over who'd started the argument.

But in the pure warmth of our embrace, we left all that behind. Shared grief assuaged old wounds.

One by one, family members arrived: first, our mother; then Lois and her two daughters, Lindsey and Chelsea; then Rachel; and finally, Jane's oldest daughter, Bronwyn. The hour was late and talking sparse as Jane assigned beds and gave everyone towels, and we gradually found our way to sleep.

On Thanksgiving morning, Jane and I rose early, and she drove us to her synagogue to recite the Mourner's Kaddish. I imagined Dad beaming with joy at two of his daughters praying in synagogue together, side by side, bonded in a common purpose. By joining our voices in showing God our love for our father, I felt an invisible force drawing us closer to one another. Another gift from Dad's death.

The Torah is taken from its place in the ark and read aloud to the congregation on Mondays, Thursdays, and Saturdays (the Sabbath). Congregants are called to the Torah to receive an *aliyah* (honor) prior to the reading of each portion of the text. When the rabbi called my name, I jumped like I'd just been named Best Actress at the Academy Awards. The twinkle in Jane's eyes and her broad smile spoke volumes. She had prearranged for me to receive the honor. Walking up to the bimah (Torah podium), I felt taller than my five and a half feet, and I paced my steps to reflect the solemnity of being called to the holy scroll in a congregation where I was unknown.

"I hope you know how much that meant to me," I said when I returned to my seat. My sister's gesture sealed my view of her as a gracious and thoughtful woman who knew what it symbolized to receive an honor on a day devoted to giving thanks.

"I do." Along with her satisfied smile, she gave me a heartfelt hug.

After we returned to Jane's house, Lois joined us as we started preparing the festive meal. Cooking Thanksgiving dinner as a threesome had become a tradition several years earlier, after the workload became more than our mother could handle. As all three of us were adults with homes of our own, and cooking for our family for an entire weekend was labor intensive, we all agreed that the time had come to pass the workload to the next generation. My sisters and I took turns hosting, rotating in birth order.

I worked side by side with my sisters, hoping that I'd avoid thinking about Dad by staying busy. But distraction didn't work. No amount of bustle in the kitchen could erase the vacancy in the family room, where the men watched football and shouted at the television set: "Just throw the ball!" "Let 'em play, ref."

When we sat down for the meal, Jane's husband, Stuart, occupied Dad's customary seat at the head of the table. Another reminder of Dad's absence.

My children and nieces, a generation removed from the grief, chatted cheerfully, catching up on each other's lives. Stuart's jokes and frivolity added some much-appreciated levity.

Jane's meal would delight the palate of the most discerning gourmand—turkey, homemade stuffing and gravy, cranberry muffins, sweet potato casserole with marshmallows browned to a soft hue, green bean casserole with onions and ginger, and salad with an assortment of dressings. But her pièce de résistance was dessert.

My sister had baked cookies in the shapes of turkeys and stars, and enough different pies to meet everyone's preferences: pumpkin for Lois, pumpkin cheese for my nieces, pecan for Mom, and apple for the rest of us. But no blueberry. Dad's favorite was missing. Just like him.

I was remembering times my father and I had shared blueberry pie when Lois, who must have read my mind, asked, "Do you remember when Daddy used to take us to the Horn & Hardart Automats in New York City?"

"Yeah," Jane chimed in. "He gave us each coins to buy dessert. Remember how we'd drop them into the small slot, open the window, reach in, and pull out what we wanted?"

"I used to get my and Dad's favorite—blueberry pie. Dad called them huckleberry pies, and we'd have extended huckleberry-versus-blueberry debates." I heard the lilt in my voice.

"Those were some great days," Lois added. And while everyone nodded and began reaching for their preferred desserts, I thought back to those carefree days and my conversations with my father.

"Dad, these aren't huckleberries. They're blueberries."

"No, they're huckleberries—because huckleberries taste better than blueberries," he pronounced with the tone of a learned professor.

"You're teasing me. They're both the same. There's no difference," I protested.

"What kind of peasant are you that you can't tell the difference between a huckleberry and a blueberry?" His voice had a glint of merriment in it.

Recalling those days, Jane's delicious sweets now looked less tempting. I, the family member with the biggest sweet tooth, passed on dessert.

—

On Thanksgiving, Jane's synagogue did not hold services—a concept I found unusual. How were mourners or those observing Yahrzeit supposed to pray with others? Sometimes, there's a dissonance between our secular and religious lives.

A member of Jane's synagogue's Caring Committee came to the house after dinner to conduct the evening service, so that we could say Kaddish. She and our clan made up our minyan. We gathered in the family room, facing east toward Jerusalem, recreating those first days after Dad's funeral, when we prayed at home and needed others to recite Kaddish. But unlike those earliest days, when the pressure of ensuring a minyan and caring for our shiva home weighed on me, I could now fully appreciate the graciousness and generosity of spirit that prompted a congregant to leave her home on a holiday to ensure a minyan for another. Her visit reminded us of how profound the gift of a caring person's presence can be.

With the prayers behind us and feast-induced drowsiness upon us, my sisters, our mother, and I left the others vying for possession of the television remote control and trudged upstairs for quiet reminiscences of Dad. Jane, Lois, and I sat on the big bed in Jane's guest room, with Mom on the smaller twin bed. We reminisced about Dad's love of sports—both those he played and those he watched—his lack of fashion sense, and our belief that he wouldn't have stayed single for long if Mom had died first. His imprint on our lives felt vital and meaningful. Looking at my sisters and my mother, I felt blessed to be related to such amazing, accomplished women, all of whom adored the same humble man. When our yawns precluded further speech, we each retired for the evening.

The next morning, after returning from synagogue, I stole away from the others, craving time away from the tumult of eleven people clustered in a house built for four. Opening my journal, a letter to my father poured from my heart onto the page.

November 24, 2000

Dear Dad,

Last night, Jane, Lois, Mom, and I sat up talking about you. Jane read letters you wrote to her when she lived in Santa Cruz. Mom told us you used to say you were the smart one in the family because you picked her. What a wonderful thing to say, Dad. Even though I never heard you say it, I imagined your inflection as the words tumbled around in my brain.

Our time spent reminiscing was the most special part of the day. I know you were smiling as you watched us, Dad. I felt your presence—ironic, on an occasion marred by your absence.

You used to say that all you wanted was for us to cherish one another and have peace between us. If you're watching this weekend, I imagine you're quite proud, Dad. Peace and thoughtfulness have prevailed. If you were here, you'd probably say we were "on our best behavior." And you'd be smiling as you said it.

As I drove to Jane's on Wednesday, I wondered how I could give thanks when you aren't here. But now, I know. I have a remarkable family to be grateful for. I know I'll always miss you, especially at the holidays, but you left a beautiful legacy. I am so proud to be your daughter. I hope you know it now and that you knew it in life.

I love you, Dad.

Your loving daughter,
Sarah

Writing to my father, I felt his presence as if he were beside me. And while I knew that Thanksgiving would feel bittersweet in the future, putting these words on paper loosened grief's stranglehold on my heart. I put my pen and journal in my suitcase, packing some of the grief away with them, and joined the rest of my family with a thankfulness befitting the holiday.

CHAPTER 25

Choose Life

Early in the morning on Thursday, December 14, while sitting in my courthouse office, I was jarred from concentration when the piercing ring of the telephone broke the silence.

"Your daughter was in a serious car accident. Police cut her from her car and brought her to our emergency room." I held my breath while the doctor from Barstow Community Hospital relayed details in a matter-of-fact tone, as if Rachel were just a statistic.

Please, God, let her be all right. Don't take her, too.

Bracing for the worst, I heard my heartbeat pounding in my ears.

"She was unconscious for a while," the doctor stated, as I labored for air. "She has some whiplash and some deep lacerations on her face."

She's alive!

"We're taking her for a CT scan to make sure there's no skull fracture or any bleeding or swelling in her brain."

My daughter had been cut from her car and rushed to a hospital with possible brain injuries . . . while I slept three thousand miles away?

"Can . . . can I . . . speak with her?" I didn't recognize my own voice.

"Only for a moment."

Thank you, God, for keeping her alive.

I stood up to close the door of my office, gripping the corner of the desk, my legs barely holding my weight.

"Rachel . . . ?"

"Mom? I'm so sorry."

Oh my God. It's her voice. She's conscious!

I reached deep inside and made a herculean effort to sound optimistic.

"Don't worry, sweetie. You're okay, and you're in good hands."

"Please . . . don't be angry." Her pleading voice differed strikingly from the rebellious, know-it-all tone she had adopted toward the end of high school.

"Angry? Honey, I'm not angry. I'm just glad you're safe."

"But the car. They told me it's totaled."

"Rachel, it's just a car. It's you I care about. The car can be replaced. Please don't worry about it." I ached to comfort her in person.

"The police assumed I'd been drinking, Mom, but you know I don't drink. I just lost control of the car."

I quieted the questions racing through my mind; I'd have plenty of chances to get answers. Instead, I consoled her.

"Honey, that doesn't matter right now. You are all that matters. I'm on my way."

"But Mom, where would you say Kaddish?"

Did I really hear what I thought I did? Could my daughter, who had disconnected from the entire family after her high school junior year, actually be thinking of my needs—while she's lying in a hospital with possible brain injuries?

A chill went down my spine.

"I don't know, sweetie, but that won't stop me" were the only words I could summon. "Just follow the doctor's orders. I'll be on the next plane."

"Thank you, Mom."

My daughter's voice, tentative yet beautiful, reminded me of the little-girl voice she had relinquished years before.

———

Rachel had been a near-perfect child: a natural childbirth three weeks after her due date, followed by sleeping through the night after only a few weeks, and achieving all the developmental milestones—crawling, walking, talking, feeding herself, counting, and reading—ahead of schedule. She was a voracious reader with an insatiable curiosity, respectful and helpful at school and at home, and kind to others.

Until she began dating Adam. Suddenly, in her junior year of high school, she was violating curfews, developing an uncharacteristic sass, and becoming impertinent. Adam was an older boy who, based on Rachel's secrecy, I suspected of being involved in something unsavory. And because I didn't trust him, my relationship with Rachel deteriorated. During her senior year of high school, I was living with someone I didn't recognize.

———

I hung up the telephone, whispered, "Thank you, God," then grabbed my purse and calendar and raced down the hall of the courthouse without a second's delay. On my way out the door, I tossed my calendar onto the secretary's desk and shouted, "Cancel everything. I'm outta here. Rachel's been in a serious car accident. I'll call you later." I stuffed down my panic as I overheard a colleague say, "That's the nightmare phone call every parent fears."

I flew to my car and raced to Dulles Airport—the closest with non-stop flights to California. I kept the gas pedal pressed to the floor, all the while fighting the sickening sensation rising in my stomach. Desperate to see my daughter, I wanted to hold her and care for her, to let my love enfold her.

At the airport, my eyes scanned the departure board. A United Airlines flight was leaving imminently for Los Angeles. Racing to the ticket counter, panting and distressed, I blurted my story to the ticket agent. In a gesture of compassion, she issued a boarding pass, and I sprinted to the gate like Usain Bolt. True to my word, within forty-five minutes of the call, I was on the very first plane out of Virginia, headed west. Once settled in my seat, I began an internal dialogue with my father.

Dad, you always said, "This is what family is all about." This is what you valued and modeled—unwavering commitment to each other. I trust you want me to be with Rachel.

I could almost hear his reply: "You're absolutely right. Your place is with her, not at home saying Kaddish for me. You made the right decision."

His reassurance calmed me—until reality sank in. All I had with me were my tallit bag, which I kept in my car; my pocketbook; and my journal. It never occurred to me to think about necessities like clothes or toiletries, or details like where I'd sleep. For the second time in less than three months, I was en route to a loved one in a hospital, uncertainty shrouding me in a dense gray fog.

I pulled out my journal and wrote:

> God, I've been feeling sorry for myself because Dad is gone; I've been angry at you for all the killing in the Middle East, all the turmoil over the presidential election, and all the sadness I see everywhere. I'm grateful for your kindness to my father yet furious at you for taking him. I cannot reconcile my conflicted feelings. But if this is your way of reminding me of my many blessings, then you have my attention. Rachel has survived this accident. Thank you, God. I promise you that I'll be more mindful.

My journal steadied me as it had during those protracted Florida days when Dad lay dying.

As the sun began setting over the horizon, I considered asking the flight attendant to announce that a passenger needed a minyan, but I lacked the emotional energy to explain what a minyan was and why I needed one. Jewish passengers would likely understand and volunteer for the mitzvah, but not knowing if nine other Jews were on the plane, or what reactions they might have to a woman reciting Kaddish, I remained silent; I was too fragile to face the potential rejection of another person telling me that "women don't say Kaddish."

Instead, I walked to the galley at the back of the plane while the flight attendants navigated their beverage carts up and down the aisles. With my back against the gray aluminum and stainless-steel equipment, I launched into the prayer. Halfway through the Kaddish, I couldn't remember the rest. My brain stalled and the words stuck in the back of my throat. I restarted it again and again, until I was shaking as if we'd hit turbulence. Finally, I surrendered.

Standing thirty thousand feet above the center of the United States, I prayed that God would recognize my intention rather than my fumbled Kaddish, that my commitment would transcend the words I failed to recollect, and that Rachel would recover. Staring out of the window, I thought back to the day each of my children was born, when my gratitude kindled my faith in God. I returned to my seat, opened my journal, and wrote the words in my heart:

> Thank you, God, for my daughter's life, for saving her and reminding us both of what is most important. My children's lives are your gifts.
>
> You gave me the crimson sunset across the horizon, with its sky-blue and fiery-orange streaks, as I write this prayer; you gave me the transparent, needle-sharp icicles that glistened in the trees as I drove to work this morning; you gave me the deep green of the fir trees set against the bubblegum-colored sky. You created a rainbow of color in today's early dawn.
>
> I've allowed the sadness of these past three months to blur my vision of your many gifts. If today's accident is your wake-up call—a reminder of your presence and of all the blessings I have—I've awakened. I'll carry this gratitude with me beyond my avelah period.

———

By the time I arrived in California, Rachel had been released from the hospital and taken to her dormitory room. No amount of advance warning could have prepared me for what I saw. My beautiful, fair-skinned daughter was almost unrecognizable. Her face was puffy, her left eye swollen shut. The stitches across her left eyelid sealed the place where glass had cut it open, allowing her to see through it with her eye closed. Cuts, scrapes, and bruises, already turning black and blue, covered the left side of her face. Twenty-two stitches stretched from the top of her forehead to her eye. As difficult as it was to look at her, I tried to push aside my anguish and convince myself she would be okay.

Rachel lay across her bed, still in her bloodstained clothes, going in and out of wakefulness. I sat on the edge of her mattress.

"Honey, it's Mom. I'm here."

"I'm . . . so glad . . . you're here," she whispered, beginning to cry.

"You're going to be okay, honey. I'm going to take care of you." It had been years since my daughter wanted anyone, much less me, to take care of her.

"I . . . some . . . rabbi . . . Hillel, Mom . . . morning . . . McAlister Center . . . 8:30. Anyone . . . give . . . directions," she mumbled, dozing off.

For the second time in only hours, I was taken aback by my daughter's sensitivity.

How could she be thinking about me under these circumstances? Had my responsiveness bridged the chasm that had grown between us over these past eighteen months? Could this accident be restoring my daughter's softheartedness?

After Rachel fell asleep, I lay down on the futon mattress next to her. As the stress of the day began to loosen its hold, I slept with one ear open, listening to her breathing, the way I had when I first brought her home as a newborn.

The next morning, I found my way to the McAlister Center for Religious Activities on the Claremont Colleges campus. My mouth flew open in amazement as I counted the fifteen people of all ages waiting for me. Rabbi Leslie Bergson, the Hillel rabbi, had organized enough students and faculty for a minyan with little notice.

The rabbi introduced herself and welcomed me like a longtime friend. A soft-spoken, unassuming-looking woman of about my age, she had short hair, glasses, and a smile that lit the room. She had made this minyan happen.

Imagine . . . a female rabbi! This is one place where I know I won't be told, "Women don't say Kaddish."

"I'm so sorry about your daughter. How is she doing?" she asked.

"I'm not sure yet. It's going to take a while to figure things out. But she's out of the hospital and on a lot of pain meds. I'll know more when she wakes up."

"I've been told you're saying Kaddish for your father. Would you like me to start the service?"

I nodded, unable to find my voice. I just kept staring at all the people who had come to support me, pinching myself to be sure I wasn't dreaming.

"Please say a few words about your father," she urged, about halfway through the service. "This tradition brings him alive to those of us who are here for you and didn't know him." I'd never heard of doing this. Caught completely off guard, my mind began racing.

How could I convey to others the essence of my father, the mensch (person of honor), in a few short sentences—especially on a morning when I was sleep deprived and anxious?

I talked about the good person he was and how he loved life. The interest in the eyes and smiles of the people in the small chapel warmed my soul. When the service ended, I couldn't recall a single word I'd spoken.

As if the beauty of the service and the presence of the minyan weren't enough, the outpouring of support made me feel more like a well-established member of their community than a stranger. One professor had left his classroom while administering an exam to ensure the minyan. Professors offered me and Rachel a place to stay, and one gentleman offered me his car. Another gave me his phone number and told me to call him any time, no matter what I might need. Two people offered me clothes. I was flabbergasted at their generosity.

God reminded me that, as Jews, we never walk alone. People cared. When I expressed my gratitude to Rabbi Bergson, she astonished me by thanking *me*—for showing the students the importance of community and doing mitzvot. The Claremont community lifted my spirit and injected me with the stamina to help my daughter through her ordeal.

For the rest of the day, I focused on Rachel. I drove her to the clinic for a second medical opinion, got her prescriptions filled, bought her a new pair of eyeglasses, completed the paperwork to have her records transferred from the hospital, and stocked her dormitory room with food. I nurtured her in every possible way. Talking was so agonizing for her that I assured her we'd have lots of time to catch up when she recovered. I guessed she must have hit the windshield pretty hard for her face to be so badly bruised and cut, and I fought back my worry that she would be permanently scarred. When she grimaced and moaned in pain, I ached as though her pain were contagious, but I willed myself not to fall apart.

"Thank you so much, Mom," she kept saying, her voice a whisper. She showed her appreciation with gentle hugs throughout the day.

"You're welcome, sweetie. I'm so glad you're letting me help you. I love you."

Two days later, I learned the details of the accident. Her boyfriend had expected her to pick him up at the Las Vegas airport—three and a half hours away from her dorm—at 2:00 a.m. on the night before her final exams. She rolled the car on the return trip, just eighty miles northeast of Claremont, not far from Barstow.

"I was tired before I left to get him, Mom," Rachel confessed. "I don't think I fell asleep at the wheel. I'm not even sure. I just know I couldn't control the car."

I worried that my otherwise independent daughter couldn't say no to him—that she couldn't protect her time and her need for rest. I couldn't understand his hold over her. But this wasn't the time to chide her for those choices. Instead, I bit back the words that wanted to surface. We both knew how lucky she was.

Adam had walked away from the accident without a scratch and had managed to get to Rachel's dorm room to use her computer, rather than go with her to the hospital. Her roommate had retrieved her; Adam didn't have a car. While Rachel's care consumed the day, fighting back my rage consumed my energy.

That first evening, I went to a nearby Reform synagogue that held services only on Friday nights. After the stress of the day, being in a synagogue felt like discovering an oasis. There I put aside my anxieties and chanted the usual prayers, adding my own for Rachel's well-being. I recited the Mourner's Kaddish and cried as I thanked God. As I left, I noticed my feet weren't dragging along the floor the way they had when I'd entered. I was standing taller.

The next morning, I drove to a neighboring Conservative synagogue, where the Shabbat service felt comfortable and familiar. But the closest Saturday evening and Sunday morning services were in Los Angeles, a one-hour drive in each direction. I didn't want to go that far from Rachel, but I had already spent one night without a minyan in the galley of an airplane. I didn't want to miss two more services. My conflict abated with a call to my sister.

"Lois, would you say Kaddish for Dad in my place tonight and tomorrow morning?"

"Absolutely!" Not a moment's hesitation.

My sister reminded me of what I most needed to hear. Jews have an expression, *Baharta b'chaim,* meaning "therefore, choose life." Caring for Rachel was a higher mitzvah, more important at the moment than saying Kaddish, and clearly the choice Dad would have wanted me to make. Lois's affirmation reassured me.

By the third day after the accident, Rachel's recovery was progressing nicely. She was more talkative and beginning to fret about her missed exams.

"I'm doing okay now, Mom. I think I'm on the mend," she said to me.

"Do you want me to stay with you a bit longer?"

"It's okay to go home, Mom. I'm so glad you came when I needed you the most. I'm going to touch base with my professors and see what I have to do to finish my courses."

With Rachel's encouragement, I decided to return home. Relaxing on the homebound flight, I felt a shift. I saw, through a different lens, that when events were beyond my control and I was most vulnerable, God looked after me. I felt blessed and uplifted by the people in Claremont, who had made me feel cared for and less alone, as my father had.

I had inherited my mother's I-must-be-in-control mindset. Hers grew from the powerlessness of watching her mother dying and being unable to help. Mine grew from my powerlessness over her venomous attacks. As I sat by the window, looking out at the sky, I heard God's voice telling me that I could let go of that need to always be in control—that I wasn't alone and could trust that I would be supported.

That had been Dad's message to me when he gave me his Purple Heart . . . that no matter how scared I felt, I would never be alone. Now, in his absence, God was reminding me of it.

CHAPTER 26
A Community of Two

After returning from California, I felt ready to resume my postgraduate program at the Georgetown Family Center. Its founder, Dr. Murray Bowen, created the family systems framework, which conceptualizes the family as an emotional unit. This theory was the foundation for all clinical work at the juvenile and domestic relations court where I worked part-time as a therapist. On September 11, 2000, the day my mother called to tell me my father would be undergoing surgery that afternoon, I had been in class at the Family Center.

Getting back into the postgrad program presented one challenge: I couldn't pray at Beth El in the morning and get to Georgetown in time for my quarterly classes.

Kesher Israel, the Orthodox congregation in Washington, DC, conducts a 7:15 a.m. service. By attending morning services there, I could be on time for my 8:30 a.m. class. Enticed by its early start time, I soon discovered that convenience came with a price. In my own synagogue, praying with my minyaneers was a hallowed experience. Not so at Kesher Israel.

One particular morning at 7:18 a.m., as I sat behind the mechitzah (partition) alone and obscured from view, in a cubicle barely large enough for six folding chairs, only nine men were present. And me. One man announced, "Let's get started. If we don't have a minyan when we get to the Kaddish, we'll keep going." I was the tenth person, but I didn't count. Again.

Even though I understood the purpose of the partition—to separate the genders so that men aren't distracted from prayer by a woman's presence—I was invisible, my voice not mattering: a throwback to my mother's disregard.

"Well, I'm not invisible to you, God." I spoke in an indiscernible whisper, comforting myself. "You see me, don't you?" I felt a warmth on my skin I hadn't noticed earlier.

Everything about the Orthodox synagogue service felt contrary to the beauty of reciting the Kaddish in my own community. Here, the breakneck speed of the worshippers garbling the Hebrew words made the beautiful melodies sound like the gibberish of a toddler who hasn't yet learned to speak. No one announced page numbers or the parts of the service.

After feverishly flipping the pages back and forth, trying to follow the service in the unfamiliar prayer book, I gave up; instead, I started reading the commentaries at the bottom of the pages, learning more about the scripture and Judaism. I felt calmer. I was determined to create a spiritual experience for myself, even if the congregation hadn't.

As I was struggling to find my place in the service, I looked up to see my friend Cheryl in front of me. My momentary surprise dissolved in the embrace of her warm hug. She was a professor at the University of Kansas and a middle-aged former New Yorker, like me, in Washington, DC, for the Georgetown postgraduate program. I had mentioned I was reciting Kaddish and she came to the synagogue solely to support me.

Eventually, a tenth man arrived. As we rose for the Mourner's Kaddish, Cheryl rested her hand on my arm, reinforcing that I was not alone.

In most synagogues, the Kaddish is chanted slowly, each syllable clearly enunciated, so that those unfamiliar with the prayer can follow. It feels respectful. It feels communal. It feels sacred. At Kesher Israel, the words were reeled off as though the worshippers were racing to leave.

I'm grateful to Kesher Israel for the powerful lesson I learned there; while I needed those ten men to recite the Kaddish for my father, I did not need them to create a spiritual experience for me. My connection to God transcended the presence of those men.

"Well, that was uncomfortable," Cheryl echoed my reaction, as we stepped arm in arm into the morning sunshine. "No one even acknowledged us on the way out."

Staring at the ground, I could not shake my guilt at having chosen convenience over spirituality. What would be the repercussions for my father's soul?

"Do you suppose I diminished the significance of saying Kaddish by going to a synagogue where I struggled to pray?" I looked intently at Cheryl. "Do you think I still brought honor to my father?"

"I'm sure God saw your intention, and that's what matters most." Cheryl's assurance massaged my heart. Her word, *intention*, would continue to inspire me.

Throughout that day, Cheryl and I exchanged glances at one another during our classes; a bond had been created between us. Her compassionate spirit reminded me of another time, when a client's graciousness had broken through my solitude.

———

When a client invited me to conduct customer service workshops for a nonprofit organization in Charlotte, North Carolina, I retrieved my worn copy of the *United States Jewish Travel Guide* and researched synagogues in the area. The book's broken binding and dog-eared pages reflected extensive use. Of the four synagogues in Charlotte, only the Chabad center had both a morning and evening minyan.

Although I'd been repudiated by the Chabad center in Ocean City, I squashed my uneasiness and made the phone call.

"You are welcome to recite the Kaddish for your father here," Rabbi Shlomo Cohen assured me.

"Thank you so much." The words sounded feeble compared to my gratitude.

When I arrived at the Chabad center for the morning service, the rabbi was waiting outside to greet me. He ushered me to a separate room, apart from the men. Alone again. I couldn't hear, and even if I'd been able to, I could not have kept up with the pace of the worshippers. Periodically, Rabbi Cohen came in and gave me a page number. Despite his attempts to make me feel comfortable, I was a stranger in a strange land and not at all at ease.

I tried to feel the presence of both God and my father, but I felt isolated and estranged instead—ironic, as a primary reason for saying Kaddish in a minyan is so the mourner does not grieve alone.

After my workshop finished later that afternoon, my client, Lisa, approached me.

"I'd like to come with you this evening," she said. "Is that all right even though I'm not Jewish?"

"It's more than all right. It would be a blessing to me. But I have to warn you: the ultra-Orthodox men will be in one room, and the two of us in another," I added.

"Why is that?"

"Orthodox Jews are committed to the most traditional segment of Judaism and maintain the strictest observance of Jewish laws. Men and women are segregated during worship because Orthodox men believe women can distract them from their focus on their prayers."

"Are you Orthodox?" Lisa asked.

"Oh, no . . . I'm not Orthodox." I chuckled; I'd been asked that question numerous times since I started saying Kaddish. In a synagogue in Scranton, Pennsylvania, a woman actually thought I was a rabbi because I wore a tallit and had chanted the blessings from memory—an accomplishment that, unbeknownst to her, had taken months to achieve.

"I consider myself a Conservative Jew, but I observe some of the traditional practices of Orthodox Jews. For example, I keep a kosher home, which means I keep meat and dairy separate; I have a set of dishes, silverware, and pots for meat meals, and a separate set for dairy meals. I don't eat pork or shellfish at all, or meat and dairy together."

"Wow! You must have a big kitchen."

"Not so big . . . I just have to keep everything organized. Some people think I'm Orthodox because I'm reciting Kaddish twice daily in synagogue, but if I were Orthodox, I wouldn't drive on the Sabbath, I'd wear skirts that come below my knees even when sitting, and after I was married, I'd have had to wear a scarf or a wig, called a *sheitel.* Orthodox women are never seen in slacks and never wear red, which happens to be one of my best colors."

"If you're not Orthodox, why are you going to an Orthodox synagogue?" she asked.

"Good question. . . . There is no Conservative synagogue here with a morning and evening minyan. In a lot of communities, the only place with two services each day is the Orthodox synagogue. At home, I belong to a Conservative synagogue where I'm equal to the men; I pray side by side with them and can have all the same honors that men receive. Praying in an Orthodox community is disconcerting for me. Most of the time, the men pray so quickly that I can't follow the service. And there's no English spoken. It's hard to feel serene and connected to God, like I do in my home synagogue. But I do it so I can recite the Mourner's Kaddish, to honor my father's soul."

"I'm impressed. Isn't there also another branch of Judaism?"

"Yes, there are Reform and Reconstructionist Judaism, which are the most contemporary, modern segments of Judaism." I was thrilled that Lisa wanted to know more and glad for yet another opportunity to educate someone about my religion.

"There are lots of differences, but the biggest is probably that Conservative Judaism abides by Jewish law to a greater extent than Reform Judaism. Conservative synagogues include more Hebrew in their services, while Reform services have more English. The Reform movement allows rabbis to officiate at interfaith weddings, while the Conservative movement does not. And Conservative Judaism considers someone Jewish only if the person's mother is Jewish—it's a religion of matrilineal descent. But the Reform movement considers someone Jewish if either parent is Jewish."

Lisa looked mesmerized as I spoke, taking it all in, which put me in high spirits as we walked into the building. With her presence, I felt like a five-year-old entering kindergarten for the first time, buoyed by having her mother by her side. As we stood next to each other in the empty classroom, I could not follow the service. I listened intently for the words of the Mourner's Kaddish, hoping not to miss it. When the worshippers began the Kaddish, my effort to keep up left me winded.

How do people pray so fast? When the words come out in one big jumble, how can anyone—including God—decipher the message?

"I'm glad I came with you," Lisa said as we left.

"So am I," I replied, as we strolled arm in arm to her car.

I thought back to a passage I'd read in *Gates of Prayer,* a prayer book used in some Reform congregations: "As two walking together in a dark wood feel stronger and braver each for the other's near presence, so too do people find spiritual strength in a common spiritual effort . . ."[ix]

Without the solace of my synagogue, having Cheryl and Lisa—one Jewish and one Christian—join me in my spiritual endeavor made me feel less alone, safer, and stronger—the way I felt when my father was by my side. The presence of these women reminded me that having warmhearted companions in unfamiliar and uncomfortable places can feel as healing as a gentle massage. Cheryl and Lisa ensured I did not mourn alone; this is one of the greatest gifts a mourner can receive.

CHAPTER 27

Grief Squared

One evening, as I hummed to the radio while washing the dinner dishes, the phone's startling ring drowned out the music. Quickly drying my hands, I reached for the handset and sat down at the kitchen table.

"Sarah, I saw an *amazing* sculpture in one of my favorite art galleries today, and I just love it." My mother described the black-and-white swirling circles shaped like an ocean wave, her voice more animated than it had been in months.

"But I don't know if I should buy it. . . . It's really expensive."

My mother was never indecisive about purchases, no matter the price. Her hesitancy was uncharacteristic.

After my twenty-year marriage ended, I felt the stinging loss of a confidant with whom I could brainstorm significant purchasing decisions. I could hear the same anxieties now in my mother's voice.

"I know it's hard to make these big decisions alone, especially after having Dad all these years." I hoped she would hear how clearly I understood her dilemma. "Remember the money Dad gave you when you got your doctorate?"

"Oh, yes. Your father didn't know how to honor the occasion, so he did something he *never* did—he gave me cash."

"Dad was disappointed you never spent it. This sculpture could be your postponed graduation present from Dad," I suggested. "But you know what he would say . . . 'They want *that much* money for a statue that doesn't even have arms!'"

We both giggled. I missed my father's sense of humor—his joviality, which had wrapped us in his warmth.

"Mom, I'm certain Dad would want you to buy it. He'd be thrilled knowing he gave you a gift worthy of your accomplishment."

"Your father *did* want me to get something special . . ." Her voice sounded as if she was considering my words. "I think I'll go back and take another look at the piece."

Before I could affirm her decision, she changed the subject.

"I went to a movie by myself the other night. A first." Her voice dropped off, and I sensed a muffled sniffle.

"That took guts, Mom. I'm sure Dad is proud of you. It's an enormous shift to go from living as a couple to being single, and especially in a place where lots of couples go."

Having been single for the twelve years since my divorce, I knew how loneliness can be magnified when you're alone among pairs of people; the contrast pierces you like the bright lights shattering the darkness after the movie ends.

"You've never lost a spouse of fifty-four years. You have no idea what it's like."

"True. But I've lost my dad. And I'm grieving, too."

I choked back the slow burn rising in my throat. We were both heartbroken over the loss of the same man, and I had hoped that our shared grief would bridge the lifetime of strain between us.

Despite enduring decades of a soul-crushing relationship, I still yearned for a heart-to-heart connection with my mother—even more so, now that my father was gone. But hope dies hard.

Now, on the phone with her, I continued to yearn, wishing she could accept my empathy.

"I know it's hard to shop and cook for one. You wonder whether it's worth the effort. Or you go to a restaurant alone and want to recoil when the hostess says, 'Just one?' I know how hard this is for you, Mom, especially at night, now that Dad's not with you."

At this, my mother's voice began to crack. Never one to be seen or heard crying, she ended the conversation. "I don't . . . want . . . to discuss this . . . any further."

Minutes elapsed before I noticed I was still holding the phone, the dial tone echoing into the silence. I stayed seated at the table, not trusting myself to finish washing the dishes, fearing I'd drop one and have to gather up the broken pieces. My inability to unite my mother and myself around our common grief brought back a flood of childhood memories of feeling invisible. I was startled that those memories could resurge in a flash, in a way that felt truly visceral; little did I realize how close to the surface my emotions really were.

I was grieving not only my father—the source of joy and safety in my life—but also the fantasy of my wished-for mother: the one who would soothe my heartbreak by sharing it. My mother's focus on her own grief, to the exclusion of our shared bereavement, piled more gloom onto my already heavy heart.

"If you were here, Dad, you'd wipe away my tears with one of those white handkerchiefs you always kept folded in a perfect square in your back pocket," I spoke out loud. "Why did you have to die first?"

I hoped that after some thought, my mother would see we were both grieving. I couldn't let go of the notion that a mother's job (even that of a widowed mother) is to console her child when the child is hurting. But it wasn't to be. Over the next two months, our chats remained polite yet superficial. Now I also mourned the death of hope.

Months later, Mom called early one morning as I was dressing for work. Her tone and drawn-out words foretold a serious discussion. I lowered myself onto my bed, bracing for impact.

"I went to the eightieth birthday party of a gentleman in the neighborhood last night," she said. "I was the only single person there. I can't do this. . . . I'm too uncomfortable. It makes me miss your father more."

"I know, Mom. Some things make me miss him more, too. But I'm proud of you for getting out. That took great courage." My effort at empathy miscarried.

"It's not the same. You've never been married to the love of your life for fifty-four years."

Zing! Zapped by my mother again. I winced.

"Okay, Mom." My toneless voice masked my trembling chin.

I knew the loneliness of being single at parties and had enormous compassion for her; but her rejection of my efforts to console her was an exhausting and all-too-familiar emotional tug-of-war.

"I'm crying all the time," she confessed.

My mother equated tears with weakness. Never one to show vulnerability, she always needed to be in control: strong, like steel. Despite wanting to offer her my understanding, I remained silent.

"Now I know how someone can die of a broken heart," she said.

I pictured Fran, the minyaneer who had lost both parents within a year. The thought of losing both my father and my mother left me shaken.

"Please, Mom . . . I hope you're not thinking you're going to die of a broken heart." My voice quivered.

"I can't make you any promises."

When would I learn that turning to my mother for compassion was like returning to a dry well for water?

"I'll pray that you find peacefulness in the life of a widow. Daddy wanted you to go on living and find happiness in the years ahead. That's my wish for you, Mom." I stood up and went on dressing, the phone still in my hand.

"That *is* what your father wanted, so you'd better keep on wishing." Then the familiar click. I returned the phone to its cradle and finished getting ready for work, shadowed by a dark cloud of dejection.

"Dad, I'll pray that Mom finds happiness," I said, putting on my shoes.

Had my father suspected that Mom wouldn't be a source of comfort for me after he died? Had that been in his mind when he gave me his blessing to recite the Kaddish? He certainly knew the fellowship of the minyan would provide solace and be a community where I could be consoled by kindred others.

Before leaving the house, I gave a quick glance at my father's Purple Heart medal.

"You certainly were wise, Dad. Thank you for giving me the gift of your blessing."

CHAPTER 28

God's Love Endures

On Rosh Chodesh, celebrated at the beginning of every month in the Jewish calendar, congregants at Beth El add additional blessings and psalms to their morning worship. One of these is Psalm 118, whose words *Ki l'olam Hasdo* mean "God's love endures forever."

God's love endures forever. Reassuring words. Reminders of something eternal. Reminders to trust in God. My father loved those words, exaggerating the "o" in *olam* as if it were "oy" when he led seders. He believed God's love endures forever; he believed God's love had saved him from death multiple times during his life. As an infantry soldier marching across Germany during World War II, he was a daily target of enemy gunfire. In 1944, a German shell killed everyone else in the circle where he was standing. In 1990, surgical complications from an aneurysm repair caused a major hemorrhage that nearly killed him on the operating table. Each time, he lived.

During those nine excruciating days after Dad's heart surgery when he lay in intensive care, I prayed to God to let him rest in peace. Seeing his arms tied to the bed, restraining him from pulling at the tube in his throat that connected him to a respirator, his systems failing one after another, and his body being maintained in a drug-induced coma . . . I knew he didn't want to live like that. He had made that clear.

"Please, God, bestow your love on my father and eliminate his suffering."

Each time friends and family asked me "What can I do?" while my father showed no signs of life, I said, "Please recite the *mishaberach*, the prayer for healing."

Entreating God's help has a long history in Judaism. The Jewish Bible is filled with stories of petitioners asking God for everything from the simplest material needs to the highest spiritual yearnings. The belief that God hears our prayers is fundamental to Judaism.

When my father's time finally came, God took him mercifully. He did not have to live the compromised life he had so feared and adamantly rejected. Death freed him of the agonies of a protracted life-draining battle with his B-cell lymphoma. God's love for him had endured once again. When my father died, I felt God had answered my prayers and granted Dad his wish. God had shown kindness to a man whose kindheartedness was recognized by all. Knowing Dad's suffering was over, a wave of peace had washed over me.

Until I started to wonder. After doctors confirmed his death, I walked trancelike out of the hospital and began to grapple with countless unanswered questions. *Why, since the surgery succeeded, had his systems failed? Why did he die? What good were all those prayers—the many mishaberachs that were recited—when my father died anyway? And if we believe our futures are predetermined, as many practicing Jews do, why do we ask people to pray?* Blasphemous questions.

I hadn't realized I was talking aloud until my mother's words penetrated my confusion: "If you believe in God, you have to believe it's God's will." It sounded more like a directive than a spiritual response. *It's God's will.*

My father had used those same words just before I left for college, when he gave me his Purple Heart medal and told me about the day he was wounded overseas.

———

"It was November 17, 1944," he began. "I had gotten out of my foxhole and was standing around with eight other guys, just outside Apweiler,

Germany. We were waiting until dawn to attack the town. A German 88 mm shell landed right in the middle of where we stood. When I came to, the medic told me that all the others had died before they hit the ground. I stayed in the hospital for two and a half weeks. When you're nineteen years old and recovering in a hospital bed all alone, four thousand miles from home, you try to find answers: Why am I here when the other eight guys are dead? Why did I survive a round of ammunition that killed eight men instantly but only wounded me? I struggled to cope with it all. My physical injuries didn't torment me nearly as much as the agony of having lived while they didn't.

"I couldn't accept any of the logical explanations of why they died and I lived," he continued. "After much soul-searching and consulting chaplains of different faiths, I finally accepted my mother's philosophy: 'It's God's will.' Your grandmother used to say that all the time. And there is no other answer to the question."

I had been dumbfounded as he spoke. When he finished, I had no words—just a hug for the soldier who survived. Months after he died, I wondered if that near-death experience had shaped his belief in an afterlife, in the destiny of his soul, and in the importance of the Mourner's Kaddish for its fate.

Now I was trying, as my father had, to make sense of something that defies reason. Why had he survived a shell that killed the eight others standing with him? Why had he walked into one of the leading cardiac care hospitals in South Florida for an angiogram, been rushed into emergency double bypass surgery that same afternoon, and then died after we were told the surgery was successful?

Why was this God's will? *Why* had God taken my father now?

I sought explanations for why he died. Doctors could provide none.

"He'll be going home soon," they had repeated for eight consecutive days, like a TV rerun, right up to the day before he died.

———

As I recited Psalm 118 that morning, I remembered attending a bereavement support group in the basement of Temple Shalom one bitterly cold evening in February. The evening's topic was prayer.

I had posed a question to the rabbi. "What if we pray for healing and our prayers aren't answered?"

The rabbi responded, "Judaism teaches us that when our prayers aren't answered, we should pray for the promise of comfort and consolation, to draw us closer to God even in our loss. Prayer anchors us in faith."

"Well, hundreds of people recited the mishaberach for my father and he died anyway, even though the doctors told us he was going to live," I kept on without taking a breath.

"When we recite the mishaberach," the rabbi told me, "we are not only praying for physical healing; we are also praying for spiritual healing."

I was confused. I'd heard the prayer chanted hundreds of times, yet I'd seen only the part that petitioned for the restoration of physical well-being.

"Open your prayer books to the mishaberach," the rabbi instructed the group. Together, we read the words aloud:

> May God, who blessed our ancestors, Abraham, Isaac and Jacob, Sarah, Rebecca, Rachel, and Leah, bring blessing and healing to _____. May the Holy One mercifully restore him to health and vigor, granting him physical and spiritual well-being, together with all others who are ill, and strengthen those who tend to them.[x]

Had all those prayers brought spiritual well-being to my father? Had God comforted his spirit by letting him die peacefully as he'd always wished? I wanted to believe that the flood of pleas sent to God on Dad's behalf had strengthened his soul for eternity. Since he had averted the anguish of future life-sucking cancer treatments, I wanted to believe our prayers had been heard. That is faith.

The rabbi went on.

"The mishaberach also brings us closer to God. When we ask something of God for someone else, our connection to the Almighty deepens."

As my father lay comatose in the ICU, I'd been powerless to help him. Praying for him *had* brought me peace—my defense against being overwhelmed by despair. While I prayed, I was less mired in sorrow; I trusted God was listening.

Could it be that the prayer was as much for *my* spiritual healing as it was for Dad's? Maybe all those who recited the mishaberach for him also felt closer to God. Or at least less helpless.

As the rabbi continued, I pondered what it means to truly pray.

Most of my time spent in synagogue, my eyes inched across the pages of the prayer book, trying to decipher the Hebrew letters the way a first grader reads a school primer. I strained to keep up with the leader rather than trying to comprehend the meanings of the prayers.

Questions bounced in my brain like a pinball. If I chanted the Hebrew words without grasping their meaning and significance, was I praying? If the power of those prayers came from being in community and I lagged behind everyone else, was I still "in community"?

Some days—like the day terrorists bombed the USS *Cole* in Yemen, killing seventeen American sailors; or the day the gruesome lynching of two Israeli reservists in Ramallah was filmed and shown worldwide; or the day 21 Israelis (including 16 teenagers) were killed and 120 more wounded in the Dolphinarium discotheque massacre—I struggled to make sense of how the Almighty allowed such bloodshed.

When I was angry at God, was Adonai listening to me? If I hadn't truly prayed after all these months of being in synagogue every morning and evening, what would happen to my father's soul? I was riddled with doubts. Had my intention been in vain? Did people of other faiths wrestle with these same questions?

I needed to believe that God saw me in synagogue every day bringing fullheartedness and commitment to my efforts. But did God accept this as sufficient?

As if reading my mind, the rabbi said, "Prayer requires *kavanah,* which means not only concentration but intention in expressing ourselves before God. There must be intent in whatever we say, aiming toward closeness to God."

Hmm . . . kavanah means "concentration," I thought. *Concentration is pretty hard to maintain when I'm praying twice daily every day.*

During evening services, my mind wanders: Did David finish his homework? Do I have enough food for his lunch the next day? Did I pay the phone bill? And put the dinner dishes in the dishwasher? During morning services, I think about my clients and my ever-lengthening to-do list, my mind constantly interrupted by worldly matters. Was I praying if my mind strayed elsewhere?

Kavanah also means "intention." I jolted upright at the rabbi's words. If prayer required intention in expressing myself before God, then I was praying very hard. Maybe the commitment to my father that I brought before the Lord each time I entered the synagogue outweighed my ignorance of the prayers, my imperfect pronunciation, my doubts about God's mercy. Suddenly, the set text mattered less. My efforts were sufficient. Praying isn't a pass/fail test.

After his lecture, the rabbi instructed us to write our own prayer expressing what we needed from God and/or our community—one that could help us move on in our lives and find much-needed peace. I opened my journal, my ever-present companion, to a blank page. My prayer flowed from my pen as though the words, thoughts, and feelings were already formed inside, just waiting to tumble out.

Dear God,

Thank you for answering my prayer, and that of my father, that he would not suffer at the end of his days. Thank you for taking him peacefully and saving him from a grueling battle with lymphoma.

I felt your presence in my tranquility and in the warmth of the rays of your sun at his funeral. I felt your presence in the comforting thoughts that Dad was at peace—that he died as he'd wanted and was buried as he'd wanted. I felt you with me when I made all the arrangements for his burial; I felt you in the fortitude I had to take on those tasks, and in my confidence as I made each decision. For your gifts of strength, endurance, and peacefulness, I thank you.

But where have you been since then, and why did you take away my serenity? Why have you allowed these atrocities? I have been feeling alone and abandoned by you.

I pray for you to show yourself to me again. I pray for the strength and tenacity to be able to go through this painful time and feel less alone. I pray for the peacefulness I felt in those hours after Dad died, and for it to bolster me in the difficult months ahead.

I affirm the faith I have in you as I maintain my faith in the sun even on a rainy day, when I cannot see its brightness nor feel its warmth.

Amen.

As I closed my journal that day, the chrysalis around my heart began opening. In freely expressing myself in my own words and allowing myself to be vulnerable, I felt I'd grown closer to God, reaffirmed my faith in the Almighty, and reawakened my elusive inner peace. In writing my prayer, I regained my faith that the light of God's love and protection would shine on my father's soul and let him rest in peace. My spontaneous voice was the most meaningful kind of prayer.

I stopped my reminiscing, and turning back to the cadence of the Rosh Chodesh service, I realized God's love had endured . . . once again. *Ki l'olam Hasdo.* God's love endures forever.

CHAPTER 29

Bigger Isn't Always Better

When a client invited me to make a presentation in Lansing, Michigan, in February, I got excited. But as always, I could only accept if I found a place to say Kaddish.

"Before I can agree to come, I need to be sure there's a synagogue with a morning and evening service where I can recite the Mourner's Kaddish," I told my client. I explained to her the significance of my prayer tradition and my need to find a place to pray in a minyan.

"May I get back to you in a day or two?"

"Absolutely," she responded. "I'm in awe. I've never known of anyone doing this."

I discovered that neither of the two synagogues in Lansing had a weekday minyan, but a Conservative synagogue in Flint, more than an hour's drive from Lansing, had both morning and evening services. My only option: fly into Flint and commute to Lansing.

I could feel my neck muscles tighten as I thought about driving between the two cities. The time between the end of services in Flint and the start of my presentation in Lansing was precariously tight. In twenty years as a consultant, I had never been late, and I didn't want to break my record. I debated: Should I accept the assignment and anticipate a tense commute? (An accident on I-69 would certainly ruin my chances of being on time.) Or should I decline her invitation?

Then came the call that changed everything.

"Hello. I'm Allan Falk, the ritual committee chair of Congregation

Kehillat Israel in Lansing. I heard your voicemail saying you need a minyan. I'd be pleased to organize morning and evening minyanim for you while you're here."

I was so caught off guard, words eluded me. "I . . . I was told your synagogue didn't have morning and evening services."

"We don't, typically. But when someone in our community needs a minyan to say Kaddish, it's our obligation to respond."

I was stunned. I could actually accept my client's invitation and fly directly into Lansing—no worrisome commute. Anxiety floated from my shoulders like dandelion seeds carried off by a gentle wind. I couldn't contain my excitement.

"I'm so grateful." I wanted to say more. I wanted to thank him for embracing my right as a woman to recite the Mourner's Kaddish. I wanted to tell him how his offer had stirred so many simultaneous emotions—happiness, amazement, gratitude, and relief. I wanted to express my appreciation, but the words got tangled in the jumble of emotions.

"We're happy to do this for you. If you let me know where you'll be staying, I'll arrange to pick you up and return you to your hotel."

After exchanging contact information and arranging our next discussion, I called my client and shared the good news.

"Kehillat Israel, a small congregation here in Lansing, is going to organize morning and evening services for me around my work schedule," I said giddily. "I'm delighted to accept your invitation to present to your group."

"Well, while you were connecting with Kehillat Israel, I got a phone call from one of our Jewish members in Flint," my client reported. "She offered to go to services with you there and then bring you here to Lansing, so you don't have to drive in unfamiliar territory. Now you have two options."

Clearly, my best option was to be in Lansing and accept Allan Falk's offer. Before I could respond, she continued.

"I've never seen anything like this commitment Jewish people make to one another. Your dedication to your faith, and the way you respond to one another, is something I've never experienced. You are blessed."

I delighted in being able to introduce Judaism's deepest ideals to someone who knew little or nothing about them—the importance of kindness, community, and *l'dor v'dor* (transmitting values from generation to generation): values epitomized in my reciting Kaddish for my father. Another gift from Dad.

True to his word, Allan Falk and the members of Congregation Kehillat Israel organized a minyan on the evening before my workshop and another the following morning.

I lingered in the hotel lobby until Allan arrived. My first thought, when I saw his affable smile topped with a graying mustache, was *Jolly.* He looked about my age and height, with a receding hairline and graying around his temples. His eyes sparkled through rimless glasses.

"Welcome to Lansing. I'm so glad we could meet, though I'm sorry it's under these circumstances. I'm so sorry for your loss." From his warm handshake and sincere inflection, I felt instantly comfortable.

"Thank you. I'm so grateful for your kindness."

"The synagogue building will be cold, both in terms of temperature and spirit. We only turn on the heat when we're going to use the building, so we thought it would be cozier to conduct the service in someone's home. I hope you don't mind."

"Of course I don't mind. It will be lovely." The minyan in my home after I returned from Florida lingered in my memory as one of the most soothing moments of my Kaddish experience. I anticipated a similarly consoling evening.

We drove a short distance to the home of Bettie Menchik. As I mounted the porch steps, she flung open the door and greeted me with an enormous grin and a warm hug, as if I were a beloved long-lost cousin rather than a total stranger.

"Welcome. Come on in. I'm *so* happy you're here."

Bettie escorted me into her warm living room, where a cushy sofa was arranged across from two comfortable-looking armchairs and a tiny wooden table. The room seemed designed for people to feel comfortable and at ease in this home. And I did. Eight men and women rose to greet me, introducing themselves with earnest smiles that immediately put me at ease. I answered questions about myself, my family, and the reason for my trip to Lansing to attentive expressions and affirming nods.

Folding chairs arranged in a semicircle supplemented the living room furniture, and a pile of prayer books sat on the coffee table. After a few moments, Allan looked at me and suggested, "Shall we begin the service?"

A gentleman offered me the chance to lead the service, but feeling awkward about my limited Hebrew—especially in front of strangers—I declined. One of the women passed out the prayer books, we all turned to face east toward Jerusalem, then one of the men began the service.

When we got to the Mourner's Kaddish, the others sat down, and I recited the prayer alone—gently and slowly enunciating each syllable, a solitary voice among a minyan of people gathered to support me. When I recited the words of the Kaddish at Beth El, other mourners' voices joined mine. Sometimes we had a full minyan of people reciting Kaddish. I had never recited the prayer alone, yet hearing my own voice in the stillness of the room, I felt deeply connected to God. Me. Myself.

Although I stood in the midst of this beautiful group of people, comforted by their presence, I was unaccompanied in my grief: a metaphor for mourning. We can be surrounded by caring others, but ultimately, each of us is alone with our sorrow.

After reciting the Kaddish, someone collected the prayer books, and Bettie invited everyone into her kitchen. Spread out on her counters was enough food to feed thirty people. She had such an array of hot and cold foods, salads, rolls, and desserts that it resembled a holiday feast. I wanted to give her a giant hug, but she was flitting around— ensuring everyone had enough to eat, refreshing the pitchers of lemonade and iced tea, and forbidding anyone from helping her. I filled my plate and carried it into the living room, where everyone lingered for several hours, including me in their conversations and making me feel like a member of the family.

As the evening drew to a close, I felt physically nourished by the delectable meal and spiritually nourished by a deep sense of connectedness to the genuine warmth of the group. I said my goodbyes with handshakes and hugs, and Allan took me back to my hotel.

"I'll pick you up at 7:00 a.m. tomorrow morning. That should give us enough time to get to the synagogue, have a leisurely service, and get you back here in time for your presentation."

"Thank you, Allan. I'll be eternally grateful."

The next morning, he arrived precisely as planned and drove us both to the synagogue. The building was plain, but children's artwork from the religious school decorated the white cinder block walls. Allan told me that the synagogue had been a public school before the congregation purchased it. We walked down a windowless corridor into the room where everyone had gathered. As we entered, my brain did its now-familiar exercise of counting the people: another minyan of ten. Some I recognized from the night before, others were new faces. As we had the previous evening, we faced east toward Jerusalem; one man led the service, and I recited the Kaddish alone. Some lingered to socialize after the service, but I uttered a quick thank-you to everyone, and Allan returned me to my hotel to conduct my workshop.

"I hardly know how to thank you for all you've done for me," I said, getting out of his car.

"I did what any Jew would do. Your father must have been a wonderful man to have a daughter as dedicated as you. It's been a privilege to meet you."

I'd never seen an all-volunteer synagogue where lay leaders ran services; and yet, that small congregation, without clergy, had organized a morning and evening minyan, while the bigger congregation never responded to my phone call, nor to Allan Falk's emails.

To this day, I feel a deep affinity for the people of Kehillat Israel—not only for providing minyanim (and a scrumptious dinner), but for teaching me that saying Kaddish is not only for the mourner and the deceased; it is also for the members of a community.

The Torah commands us to love thy neighbor as thyself. Compassion for others is at the core of Judaism. The members of Kehillat Israel fulfilled the mitzvah of *v'ahavta l'reacha kamocha*—loving thy neighbor as thyself—and embodied the purpose and sanctity of the minyan: supporting the mourner through grief. This small community performed an act of holiness, reminding me that bigger is not always better.

CHAPTER 30

Personal Effects

In early March, five months after my father's death, I flew to Florida to complete my parents' tax returns—a task my father had always handled and which my mother expressed no desire to learn. But I was blindsided by a more onerous task: cleaning out my father's closet.

After I arrived, my mother told me she wanted to change the house from "ours" to "mine" and expected me to empty my father's closet and bureau drawers. As she had during shiva, my mother thrust the most sensitive and difficult tasks upon me. She rejected the idea of working side by side with me, making me wonder, *If she thinks this task too gut wrenching for her to undertake, what does she think it will be for me?* And yet, again, I didn't refuse—an acquiescence that remains a mystery to me to this day.

My father's narrow closet, untouched since his death, reflected his New York and Florida lives: many pairs of khaki pants, Floridian short-sleeved printed shirts, and the polo shirts he wore while playing his beloved golf.

I saw the pink polo shirt that he wore the most, the one my sister Jane had given to him after he moved to Florida. I remembered how he had scrunched up his face when he first saw it.

"Pink? Men don't wear pink!" His inflection revealed his deep-seated views on masculinity.

"But this is Florida, Dad," my sister advised. "Pastel colors are popular here on the golf course. Wait. . . . You'll see."

True to my sister's prediction, this shirt became my father's favorite.

I continued examining his clothes. Two suits in dark colors for formal occasions. Wide-pointed neckties in burgundies and blues, which always ended above his belt. Hmm . . . I wondered what had happened to the gold tie clips that held those in place. Dress shirts: two white and one light blue.

My father hated dressing up. Working in the dusty furniture store, where he was responsible for deliveries, required casual clothing. And when he later began his credit finance company in the basement of that store, no one ever saw him.

Khaki and navy Dockers. One lightweight jacket. There on the one shelf sat the lonely, brown wool hat he wore up north when temperatures dropped. I put it aside for Lois, who had expressed an inexplicable desire for it. And there in the back of the closet hung the long-sleeved plaid flannel shirts that had been his trademark when he lived in New York, before the cancer diagnosis.

My father loved his plaid shirts—too warm for most Florida days. In New York, he wore them whether they matched anything else or not. And mostly, they didn't. But he didn't care. After my grandfather sold the furniture store in 1967, my father ran his credit company from a tiny upstairs office in a run-down New York City building. No one ever visited. And he liked comfort, in keeping with his down-to-earth manner, better than formality.

I pulled the Eddie Bauer navy-and-burgundy plaid flannel shirt— one of Dad's favorites—from its hanger. When he wore it with brown plaid pants, my sisters and I tried, each time unsuccessfully, to endow him with a modicum of style.

"What do you mean, these don't go together?" He sounded utterly bewildered. "They're both plaids."

Nuzzling my face into his shirt, I inhaled the musky fragrance of his Old Spice aftershave. Closing my eyes, I could see him hunched over the bathroom sink, splashing the liquid into his cupped palms and patting it onto his cheeks. To this day, the scent of Old Spice brings back the image of my father dabbing it onto his freshly shaven face.

Wanting to keep something that had belonged to my father, I carried the shirt to my mother's study, where she sat at her desk, completing paperwork.

"Mom, can I have this shirt?" She barely glanced up.

"That won't fit you. It's a large." With that, she looked back down at her papers.

"I don't care about the size. I want one of Daddy's plaid shirts. You're only going to give them away. Please, let me take this one," I begged.

How could I explain to my mother—who lacked any compassion—my need to hold on to a piece of my father, to wear something he wore? How could I explain why I wanted this article of clothing to a woman who would get rid of it anyway?

Later, with hindsight, I wondered why I had even bothered to ask for it; I could have just put it in my suitcase, and she wouldn't have been any the wiser.

Why is it that these types of insights always come after the fact?

"Okay," she sighed. "But I don't see what you need it for." Her perfunctory tone did not diminish my happiness in now owning something he'd loved and worn.

I walked to the guest bedroom and carefully folded the shirt, wrapped it in tissue paper to preserve the scent, and placed it gently into my suitcase. Then I returned to the task of disposing my father's clothes and personal effects.

I emptied the clothes from the closet, carefully laying out everything on the bed and leaving only the hangers behind. Then I turned my attention to his dresser. In the top drawer, my mother's fastidiousness was evident from Dad's perfectly aligned T-shirts and underwear that rested in undeviating 90-degree angles. The remaining drawers reflected his Floridian life: shorts that revealed his toothpick-thin legs, bathing suits, and socks.

The decision to donate his clothes was easy. Packing them wasn't.

I couldn't bring myself to toss them in the bag like garbage, so I took each article and folded it with reverent precision before putting it in the large, black plastic trash bag. The clothes were filled with memories of shared experiences—like dancing together at Jane's wedding, when Dad wore that dark suit, and I marveled at his gracefulness on the dance floor; or playing in the ocean waves together, him in his I-only-wear-beige trunks. Surrounded by his presence, this mournful undertaking felt like another goodbye. I couldn't detach myself from the stories associated with each article of clothing, and I touched each one lovingly because they had belonged to my father.

Finally, I packed his shoes—well-worn beige moccasins, a pair of white Nike sneakers, one pair of black wing-tip shoes—all with metal shoe trees holding their shapes. They had carried his weight and touched the ground he would no longer walk on. Donating them would allow someone else to walk in my father's shoes, but no one could ever fill them as he had.

The next morning, I called AMVETS. As a veteran, my father would have appreciated his clothes and other items going to others who had served.

"Now I'd like you to go through your father's nightstand and empty it," my mother directed me, as if the previous day's task wasn't sorrowful enough. She had moved his toilet articles there, clearing his belongings from "her" bathroom to avoid dealing with them herself.

Her disregard for any emotional toll the task might take on me typified the absence of empathy from her that I had lived with all my life. In retrospect, I wonder why I didn't say, "Let's do it together, Mom. I can't do this alone," especially after the heartrending job of emptying his closet and dresser drawers.

I opened the top drawer, curious to see its contents. On top of all the other miscellaneous items sat his Kent hairbrush. I lifted it as if it were a sleeping baby.

"Kent makes the best hairbrushes in the world," my mother often repeated.

This particular brush, bought when my parents had traveled to England several years earlier, was advertised by Kent as "an absolute work of art." According to their website, its beechwood handle was sanded and drilled by hand, then sprayed with a gloss that made the wood shimmer. Its white bristles, made of the finest natural boar hairs from India, were hand-trimmed and hand-stitched into the brush in the Kent factory. Kent intentionally varied the bristle lengths in order to penetrate the hair and massage the scalp. The soft bristles were ideal for my father, whose hair had thinned and then receded in his midtwenties, after his return from the army.

My father always groused, "I can't believe I have to pay the same amount to that barber as those men with a full head of hair. I should be getting a discount since I don't have any hair on top. Eight dollars is highway robbery!"

Holding the brush in my hand, envisioning my father's fingers curled around that same handle, my skin connected to his fingerprints. Prints on top of prints. The fine wisps of silver hair, almost indiscernible within the bristles, were so thin they could thread a narrow needle.

Was this all that remained of this man I loved—a hairbrush, some clothes, a grieving wife, three daughters, six grandchildren, and the money he had saved? While Dad was alive, I never gave a second thought to this brush—which contained hairs he could barely afford to lose, sparse as they were. How much we overlook and take for granted when someone is alive. After a death, mundane items that we never gave a second glance to before can become powerful talismans.

The hairs in his brush contained my father's DNA. From them, I could get a breakdown of his genetic makeup and perhaps learn some of the history of his family members, who were killed in the Holocaust. Maybe I could learn more about the places his family came from, or even discover unheard-of relatives. This ostensibly commonplace item was a storehouse of information about my father, who died before Ancestry.com and easily accessible DNA testing. It held answers to questions never asked: a touchstone to the past, and maybe to my future.

I relished the idea of extracting my father's DNA from the hairbrush; it represented a way to understand him while guarding against the intrusion of my mother and her DNA.

As I had with my father's shirt, I carefully wrapped his brush in tissue paper and tucked it into my carry-on suitcase, protecting it with the flannel shirt, then returned to clearing my father's nightstand. But this time, I didn't ask permission.

After the folks from AMVETS had collected the large bags of clothing, shoes, and personal effects, and the tax returns were completed, it was time to return home.

As soon as I entered my house, I opened my suitcase and unwrapped my father's hairbrush and shirt. I hung the shirt in my closet and looked for a place sacred enough to keep the hairbrush. I placed it in the top drawer of my own nightstand, where it remains to this day. Every time I see the hairbrush, I'm reminded to be more mindful—to pay better attention to the little things and little moments that make up a life.

CHAPTER 31

Betrayed

I was enjoying a rare social evening at my friend Louise's house, when one of her guests dropped a bombshell on the group.

"So . . . I see your rabbi embezzled money," he said, staring straight at me.

"That's crazy," I chuckled, thinking he was joking.

"Well, it's in today's *Washington Post*."

I bolted from the table, grabbed the paper from the sofa, and read that my revered rabbi had reportedly repaid $300,000 to his discretionary fund, "to avoid the appearance of impropriety and forestall public criticism that might harm the synagogue." The article reported that an internal investigation, begun several months earlier, had been "restricted to a small group."

"I guess you didn't know your rabbi's a crook, did you?" The man's ongoing needling was getting on my nerves, despite my efforts to ignore him.

"No . . . no . . . no . . ." I didn't recognize how vehemently I was protesting until Louise put her arm around my shuddering shoulders.

The word *rabbi* means "teacher" in Hebrew. In addition to presiding over life-cycle events such as bar and bat mitzvahs, weddings, and funerals, the role of the rabbi is to teach Jewish law and to serve as spiritual leader and counselor for the congregation.

In addition to delivering inspirational sermons from the pulpit, my rabbi had been a positive influence on my life. Years before my father's death, he had officiated my get (the Jewish decree that gave me a religious divorce from my husband); his assurance that our congregants were not so narrow-minded as to believe my ex-husband's lies proved true, as did his projection that, over time, after I resumed my maiden name, most members wouldn't realize my former husband and I had ever been married to each other. Now this gentle soul, whom I respected, was being charged with embezzlement, a claim I viewed as unlikely as the idea he would leave his wife for Kim Kardashian.

I especially admired our rabbi for consistently mentoring the young people who attended the synagogue's religious school. The teenagers in Rachel's confirmation class adored him. Rachel and her classmates dubbed him "cool" because he bought pizzas for the kids in their hotel during their class trip to Jewish sites in New York City. This trip was an annual event, led by the rabbi, to further connect the young adults to their Judaism. And I was thrilled that the kids' affection for the rabbi meant the entire group remained together beyond bar and bat mitzvah, furthering their religious studies—my dream for my children since the day Rachel was born.

Rabbi Maltzman stood short in height but tall in stature. He lacked twenty-twenty vision without his round eyeglasses, but he had a clear and far-reaching vision for inclusivity before such a viewpoint became common among Jewish clergy. His oval-shaped face and high, wide forehead made him appear younger than his years.

Focusing on the words in Louise's newspaper, I read that unidentified members of our congregation had divulged confidential information to the *Washington Post*.

"How could someone tell the media before telling our congregation?" I hardly recognized the intensity of my own voice. I looked at the five people seated around the table as though they held the answer. They returned blank stares.

As a child, I was taught that we didn't "air our dirty laundry in public." Keeping family matters private had been hammered into me so deeply that I found it reprehensible for a few congregants to have anonymously leaked private synagogue information to the *Washington Post* without first addressing the board of directors.

A rabbi's discretionary fund is composed of donations, mostly from congregants and people outside the synagogue making contributions in someone's honor or memory. Funds are distributed, at the discretion of the rabbi, to charitable and religious causes, congregants in need and financial distress, and for professional and educational needs, such as the honoraria for guest lecturers. Because congregants who turn to the rabbi for aid go to him in strictest confidence, individual names are concealed.

I was incensed when I learned that people went through the rabbi's office, violating the privacy of our congregants. Their encroachment rekindled memories of my teen years, when my mother went through my drawers and closet as if on a mission to find something nasty, all while telling me, "This isn't your room. . . . It's my house." I knew what it felt like to have a private space violated, and I ached from the breach of congregants' personal and sensitive documents.

It didn't seem coincidental that the article appeared exactly seven months into my mourning period (on April 24, 2001), and on the very day our board of directors was voting on extending the rabbi's tenure as senior rabbi of Congregation Beth El; feelings of betrayal toward those who had brought these allegations stoked the embers of my grief.

I stomped my way to my car, leaving the other guests to enjoy their dessert at Louise's dining room table, and drove to Ohr Kodesh Congregation—the synagogue nearest her home—for their evening service. As soon as I entered the sanctuary, a familiar congregant nudged me with his elbow and asked, "What do I have to do to be eligible for your rabbi's discretionary fund?"

"I guess you have to get on a very long list." The minute the words came out of my mouth, my face flushed with shame.

Had I just implied that I thought the rabbi was guilty, too? How could I have allowed this man to think I accepted the story in the *Washington Post* when, clearly, I didn't?

For me to match one caustic comment with another was completely out of character. But my head was still reeling from the notion that my rabbi might have embezzled the funds of his congregants, and though I couldn't believe it, I was caught off-balance. I wished I had said, "I am here to pray for the memory of my father. Please allow me to pray in peace." Instead, I took my seat, buried my face in the prayer book, and didn't look up until the service ended, when I almost ran from the synagogue.

That same evening, the Beth El Board of Directors approved a three-year extension of our rabbi's contract. Their decision confirmed their confidence in the rabbi's innocence, and it cemented my loyalty to him.

Later that night, I tossed and turned, wrestling with the covers as sleep evaded me. I didn't realize then that my restlessness was a foreboding of the political uproar over the rabbi that lay ahead. I could not foresee the degree to which alignments for or against our rabbi would destroy the sanctity of my house of worship, tear apart my spiritual community, and reopen wounds that I thought had healed long ago.

———

The following morning at Beth El, the serenity of the minyan was shattered. I listened as minyaneers with whom I had shared months of prayer cast a guilty verdict:

"How could he have done something like this?"

"I can't believe he'd use his discretionary fund for personal use."

"Did he really think he'd get away with it?"

I looked at the men who had prayed alongside me during the previous six months; their eyes were narrowed, and their mouths contorted with anger. The women sat in silence. But I couldn't. My father wouldn't have.

"Have you forgotten we're in America? Here, we're innocent until proven guilty." I stood facing the minyaneers, my voice shaking. "This is our rabbi you're disparaging . . . without evidence."

That's when one of the men called me "naïve." I sat back down, my bottom hitting the chair with force, furious that minyaneers were indicting the rabbi only on the basis of scant information.

Overnight, my safe space had transformed into one of hostility, accusations, and alliances. I wondered if this same divisiveness occurred in churches when clergy were charged with crimes. I felt like I was on a roller coaster, accelerating down a steep hill, my stomach in my throat.

Unanswered questions pummeled me. What did these accusers know that the rest of us, including the board, didn't know? And why didn't board members know? My assumption was that if board members knew of any improprieties, they would not have renewed the rabbi's contract. In the absence of evidence to the contrary, I presumed the man's innocence.

Our synagogue's name, Beth El, means "House of God." Judging the rabbi without knowing the content of the investigation belied everything in our prayers. I tried hard to be nonjudgmental, yet I couldn't understand how my fellow minyaneers could condemn our religious leader—in God's house, no less—based on an article in the newspaper. The word *hypocritical* pounded in my brain like a drumbeat.

The oppressive air in the small chapel that April morning was asphyxiating, making concentrating on prayer almost impossible and exacerbating my grief. Seeking serenity in the midst of a tempest of enmity was futile.

—

Two weeks later, as rancor had begun to taper off, another distressing article appeared in the *Washington Post*. County prosecutors had opened an investigation into the way our rabbi had used his discretionary fund and whether funds went to his personal use rather than synagogue use. Some alleged that he had paid for his daughter's bat mitzvah out of the discretionary fund. Rumors were spreading, and no one provided the congregation with any facts.

The journalist who wrote that our members were "deeply divided over how the rabbi . . . managed his so-called discretionary fund" understated the tragic breach between congregants, now split into two sides—either for or against the rabbi. People who'd known each other for years refused to sit side by side or even make eye contact; friends became venomous toward one another, and the ideals of spirituality and community evaporated amidst bitterness. I couldn't understand how people who prayed together every day could be so unkind to one another. *Especially* in a house of worship. The paradox was heart crushing.

What about the passage we read every morning? "My God, keep my tongue from evil. . . . May the words of my mouth and the meditations of my heart be pleasing to you . . ."[xi] Then there's the passage in Proverbs 6:16–19 that lists one of the Lord's aversions as "one who sows discord among brethren."

And what about *lashon hara*—disparaging speech, considered a sin in Judaism? The laws of lashon hara prohibit discrediting or saying negative things about another person, even if those things are true. It is forbidden to listen to lashon hara, and if one has heard the negative talk, Judaism forbids believing it. Psalm 34 reminds us to "guard your tongue from evil and your lips from speaking deceitfully."

Our religion instructs us to always judge one another favorably, a teaching I worked hard to model. I wondered, *What does God think of these behaviors in this house of worship?* I cringed at the thought.

As animosity replaced civility, and chaos permeated my spiritual world, my faith in the steadfastness of the minyaneers eroded. At any other time, I might have admired their ability to express their outrage—something I had grown up too scared to ever do. At the same time, anger frightened me, reminding me of my mother's unjustified, enraged outbursts. I couldn't sleep. I couldn't eat. I was in the middle of a forest fire, with flames blazing out of control and nothing to protect me.

I wanted to believe in the goodness and innocence of the rabbi, a father figure who had guided me through my divorce and had a positive impact on my daughter's life. I had trusted him like I trusted my own father, a man of integrity and character. I couldn't believe he would be like my mother, who violated the sanctity of her role by hurting those she was entrusted to care for, and who lied to protect herself. Was I wearing blinders?

I wondered if this had been my father's experience—needing to believe in the innocence of someone to whom others' lives were entrusted. Had my father worn blinders? Had he, like me, needed to believe that a role model would never abuse their authority?

Where are you, Dad, when I need your shoulder to cry on? I need you to help me navigate this heartlessness. How can I redeem your soul when the discord in the chapel is so thick that it's contaminating my prayers?

I had lost my father, had potentially been betrayed by someone I trusted, and was now losing the community that had supported me. My grief, which had slowly been healing, reopened like an infected wound. How was I supposed to mourn my father and my religious leader simultaneously? How much grief can one person stand and still function? And work? And parent? The old adage "What doesn't kill you only makes you stronger" just wasn't true; sometimes, it brings you to your knees.

"Can we please stop this acrimony and focus on why we came here?" I begged the group. "We're supposed to be united in prayer. We need each other to recite the *Barekhu* [the call to worship at the beginning of morning and evening services] and the Mourner's Kaddish. And some of us need to pray for our parents' souls."

My words were as futile as spitting into the wind.

I recalled a time when, in the synagogue of my youth, my father rose to defend his rabbi. Younger members of the congregation were calling for a more youthful religious leader. My father, who hated public speaking more than a root canal, had spoken on behalf of the rabbi, championing his contributions. I was trying to emulate his courage during Beth El's morning minyan, but unlike my father, whose words saved the rabbi's job, I was failing.

On May 23, the morning of the congregational meeting, Joel, a long-time minyaneer whose presence I treasured, said, "A vote for the rabbi is a vote against me. If he wins tonight, I won't be back here."

My whole body stiffened. I turned and appealed to him one-on-one.

"But Joel, we don't even know for certain what he did with the discretionary fund. He's denied any wrongdoing. What about considering a man innocent until proven guilty?"

"I am the son of a rabbi. To have even allowed himself to get in this position is despicable. I cannot condone it by my presence." His gaze was steady, his timeworn skin showing the wrinkles of age.

"Please don't stop coming," I pleaded. "Hearing you enunciate the words of the prayers helps me hone my Hebrew. And when you call out the page numbers, you keep me on track. Besides, your jokes are much funnier than any of the others. Please stay until all the facts are in. I need you in the minyan to recite Kaddish for my father."

"Thank you for your kind words. I know you need the minyan, but I have to follow my conscience." With that, he turned his head away and lowered his eyes to his prayer book.

Follow my conscience. His words echoed in my brain all day long. What was my conscience telling me? Was my allegiance to the rabbi obscuring the possibility of his guilt?

Having been betrayed by my mother, whose responsibility was the protection of her flock, I couldn't bear the thought that the rabbi, too, could also have betrayed my trust and that of the entire congregation. Thinking that the rabbi might have lied to the congregation—the way my mother lied to my father when she hurt me—triggered a rush of anguish, the way opening a window fuels a raging fire. After Dad's death, my dependence on the minyan for my comfort and healing had made me vulnerable. Only much later did I realize that it was easier for me to focus on the minyaneers' fury than to once again face the pain of broken trust.

"I never betrayed the trust of the congregation or abused my position in any way," the rabbi asserted. He admitted only to poor and insufficient record keeping, a lapse he had already rectified. The facts were about as clear as thick black smoke.

I debated with myself all day: *Go to the meeting? Don't go to the meeting?*

I wondered what my father would do in my place, and I could almost hear his advice whispering in my ear: "I'd stand up for the rabbi at the meeting tonight, as you've been doing at morning services. If you think he could be innocent of any misconduct, then speak in his defense. I taught you to know right from wrong; it's wrong to assume guilt without concrete evidence."

After much internal conflict, I went to synagogue, recited Kaddish, and left before the congregational meeting started. I could not bear any more acrimony. Despite my twenty-year career as a professional public speaker, this time I was afraid of choking on my words if I stood to speak. If a person hears negative speech about another (lashon hara), Judaism requires that individual to reprimand the speaker; but I didn't trust myself to stay composed, nor did I want to mirror the behaviors that I found so offensive. Clinging to the last shreds of my depleted emotional energy, I stayed away—a decision I regret to this day.

That night, in a secret written ballot, the rabbi received a vote of confidence from 407 of the 802 members of the congregation. Despite the win for the rabbi, one thing became clear: the congregation was still very much divided.

The next morning, I waited. True to his word, Joel did not return. As if I'd been punched in the stomach, I hunched down on the bench and dropped my face in my hands. Another loss. I had hoped the discord would diminish after the congregation's vote, but the morning after, it intensified.

Allegations continued. Some called the rabbi a thief. One of my dearest friends said, "I can't turn to the rabbi as my moral guidepost any longer." Hateful signs posted in the synagogue parking lot were visible from the street; more inflammatory information was passed to the press.

The rabbi's supporters accused those involved in the investigation of having a long-standing vendetta against the rabbi and using the discretionary fund to discredit him. I wondered if it could be true. Could his accusers be homophobes who opposed the rabbi's acceptance of LGBTQ couples as members of our synagogue? Or could they be people who disagreed with his outreach to interfaith couples? The idea that some might retaliate against the rabbi's acceptance of nontraditional Jews brought me even lower. I couldn't bear to think about it.

Praying for my father's soul depended on being part of a community. But rather than a community, we were now a group of alienated individuals, the air around us so polluted with bitterness that I could hardly breathe. What would happen to my father's soul if I couldn't pray for him in peace?

"I'm losing sleep at night over this whole situation," Rick confessed one morning.

"Me too," said Jonathan. "I don't even feel like eating at the morning breakfasts, but I don't want to leave you three."

"I'm glad to hear you say that," I said. "I thought I was the only one of the four of us who was struggling. I'm not sleeping well either, and looking at food makes me nauseous. Most days, I feel like I've lost my footing on a very long staircase."

"I can't imagine what the rabbi's life must be like now." Jonathan's remark awakened a sensitivity in me that I hadn't felt in a while. "Even if he is innocent, some people will always judge him. If he is forced to leave Beth El, he'll never get another pulpit."

"I guess we just have to ride this thing out. At least we have each other for consolation," whispered Rick, testifying to the solidity of our bond.

"I'm going to try to stick it out to stay with the three of you," I responded. But I wasn't sure I could, especially since no one knew how much longer the malevolence would go on.

My father counted on my prayers; I wasn't about to let him down. That's when I decided to make the twenty-mile round trip to attend evening services at Adas Israel Congregation in Washington, DC—a distance that had been off-putting until praying at Beth El became too painful. Even though my father had remained at the synagogue he helped to found for almost thirty-five years, I trusted he would have supported my decision to pray in a more conducive setting.

During the service at Adas Israel, when we got to the Mourner's Kaddish, the prayer leader invited each of us to say aloud the name of the person for whom we were reciting the prayer. Some voiced the English names of their loved ones; others spoke the Hebrew names, as I did: "*Moshe Israel ben Yoseph Tzvi v Roisa.*" Speaking Dad's name aloud, in public, was a salve on my torn heart. The beauty of this practice, combined with the acrimony at Beth El, made the decision to keep going to evening services at Adas Israel an easy one.

Finally, at a congregational meeting on July 25, three months after the first article appeared in the *Washington Post,* the board of directors accepted the rabbi's resignation. To this day, no one knows unequivocally of his innocence or guilt. He consistently refuted the allegations and wrote in his resignation letter, "The ideal of *shalom*—peace and harmony—must take precedence over everything else. . . . To heal the fissures within our congregation, I have chosen to resign."

I had lost my spiritual leader and my second trusted male in less than a year. Gone. One more farewell. How was I to mourn this loss while also grieving for my father? The rabbi hadn't died, but my agony at what had happened to him felt almost as intense.

Gone too were many of the longtime members who had comprised the congregation for decades. People I had known since 1981, when my husband and I joined Beth El, left in protest. I held my future with the synagogue in abeyance, at least until I finished my avelut.

The ongoing friendship and support of the other three musketeers grew deeper over the course of our ordeal. Jonathan's words helped me to surrender my anger at the so-called "small group" and rediscover my empathy for *all* who were hurting, including the accusers, the rabbi and his family, and those who had left Beth El in anger.

I came to respect—and even envy—the minyaneers' ability to express anger and open hostility. Had I spoken in front of my mother the way the minyaneers had aired their grievances, she would have dragged me to the bathroom and shoved a wet bar of Ivory soap into my mouth—oblivious to my gagging—to wash out the "bad words," as she had when I told my sister to "shut up." Belatedly, I realized that underneath the minyaneers' acrimony lay the same hurt I felt at being betrayed by someone whose role was supposed to ensure trustworthiness.

I slowly recognized that all of us in the congregation had experienced a crushing loss, whether we believed in the rabbi's guilt or innocence. Everyone's distress was as real as my own. Tenderness began to unfold in my heart like a budding flower. After I emerged on the other side of pain, this became one of the many hard-learned lessons that I carry with me to this day.

CHAPTER 32
What Matters Most

In the midst of the dark turmoil over the rabbi, a beacon of light shone on my spirit.

"Mom, can you come and help me pack? I want to move back home when the semester is over."

Rachel's words on the telephone left me feeling as elated as if she had said, "I love you, Mom"—something I hadn't heard in years. Her call reminded me of the times she had reached out to me as a little girl, needing to hold my hand to cross the street, or for me to retrieve something for her from a high shelf, and I felt the same parental contentment in being needed.

"Sure, honey. When do you want me to come?" I couldn't respond fast enough.

"I have to be out of the dorm by May 15, so maybe the week before?" Her voice ended in an almost-question. Rachel's recovery from her December car accident had been slow but steady. Her only issue now was homesickness.

"Well . . . if I say Kaddish at Beth El before flying out, I can take a late-night flight, but I'd land during the wee hours of the morning." I didn't realize I'd been thinking out loud.

"I'll meet your plane regardless of the time, Mom." I didn't ask her how she would meet me, or if she had a car; her previous vehicle had been totaled. I knew better than to pry and bring up memories of that accident.

219

This trip promised to be vastly different from my December visit.

True to her word, Rachel met me at the airport. When we got to her dorm room, I was surprised to see Sabbath prayer books stacked on her bookcase.

"What are these?" I asked.

"I went to the Hillel to borrow prayer books. They only had the ones for Shabbat and the High Holidays, so I signed out the Shabbat prayer books. I figured they're better than nothing."

"Good thinking, kiddo."

"You can say Kaddish here in the dorm. I emailed kids in this dorm and the neighboring ones asking them to be part of a minyan."

I reached out and hugged her, grateful for her support and afraid to even hope she might be finding her way back to Judaism. At least she was honoring my religious practice, and her genuine hug in return reassured me that we were okay.

"And I promised food so that we'd definitely get kids to come."

"More good thinking." I chuckled at the idea of using food as bait for worshippers.

I thumbed through the Sabbath prayer book, picked out prayers common to weekday services, and composed an improvised service. We woke after only a few hours of sleep and bought bagels, donuts, and juice for the students who were coming. We met in the living room of the dorm, with its torn-up furniture and musty odor of beer and sweat.

Students wandered in slowly, in singles and in pairs. It didn't matter that some straggled in with sleep in their eyes or that some arrived still wearing their pajamas, or that loud rap music thumped in from a nearby open window. This kaleidoscopic gathering testified to the cohesiveness of the Jewish family and the importance we place on being present for others in their time of need. Not to mention the quest of college students for a decent free breakfast.

Only a few students came at first, but they roamed the dorm and woke others. When I began the service, we had eleven. And I had a full heart.

After the service, Rachel and I had a breakfast filled with cheery talk and shared laughter. When she left for her part-time job, I started packing; books, her principal treasures and a passion we shared, filled six boxes. I worked without stopping until the time came for Shabbat services and dinner, leaving only what she needed for her remaining time in California.

When I arrived at the Hillel, Rabbi Bergson greeted me as warmly as she had in December; later, she honored my father again by inviting me to say a few words about him before reciting the Mourner's Kaddish. This time, I was ready, and I shared the story about Dad's selfless pride in others' accomplishments told by his golf buddy during shiva.

About forty young people attended the service and twenty-five or so stayed for dinner. The enticing aroma of pasta primavera wafted from the Hillel kitchen as I entered the dining room, reminding me that it had been hours since I'd eaten. The students served me as though I were a princess, and their food rebuilt the energy that the day's physical labor had depleted.

Singing followed dinner. Sweet and gentle voices filled the room and stirred my soul. I sang along with the familiar Jewish tunes, enjoying the sight of young people embracing Judaism and appreciating how they had welcomed me into their midst. How different from my own college experience when I had abandoned Judaism.

I was helping with the cleanup when Rachel arrived from her part-time job. The students immediately prepared a dinner for her. We stayed for the Grace After Meals blessing (known as *Birkat Hamazon*), sang more songs, and laughed with the group, before eventually strolling back to the dorm arm in arm. I felt the same euphoria I'd experienced when, as an infant, Rachel first wrapped her tiny fist around my finger. A perfect Shabbat evening.

With the exception of Friday night, Rachel voluntarily joined me for every Kaddish, lifting my spirits and fulfilling the Fifth Commandment to "honor thy mother." We attended Shabbat services at Beth Sholom on Saturday morning, and we returned to the Hillel for the evening service. On Sunday morning, she organized another minyan of students in the dorm, complete with a continental breakfast, and at night, we returned again to the Hillel.

On Monday, the morning of my departure, I had planned to recite the Mourner's Kaddish at the Chabad center near the Los Angeles airport. When we arrived, a sign on the door showed directions to a shiva home nearby.

"Uh-oh. I hope we're going to be able to say Kaddish this morning." I voiced my apprehension to Rachel as we walked the few blocks to the mourner's home. "What if they don't want a woman praying with them?" Her gentle squeeze on my arm was only slightly reassuring.

We arrived and knocked on the door, and beads of sweat dripped inside my shirt as I realized I lacked a backup plan. But I had worried for naught; when I said, "I'm saying Kaddish. May we come in?" we were warmly welcomed.

Once inside, I saw no other women or girls. A man handed each of us a prayer book and ushered us up a flight of stairs. The loft of the house created a balcony from which Rachel and I could see the men in the living room below. But unless they looked up, we were out of their view.

About sixteen men were draping their tallit over their shoulders and donning their tefillin. As the service proceeded, one man took the Torah from an ark that sat near the bookcase, and three men received aliyot (honors). The home had a glass jar for *tzedakah* (charitable donations), and after praying, each man made a donation. They had recreated a synagogue. I stared, unable to avert my eyes, as mesmerized as when I beheld Monet's original *Water Lilies* paintings in the Musée de l'Orangerie in Paris.

It had never occurred to me to have these ritual items in our shiva home. We didn't have a tzedakah box, even though it is a moral obligation to perform charity when we pray; and no one from my parents' synagogue brought a Torah for the Monday or Thursday morning minyanim—the days when the Torah is read aloud in synagogue.

Seeing their makeshift synagogue rekindled the longing I'd had for more traditional observances in our house of mourning. I belatedly wondered why, instead of following my mother's directive to call friends to make the minyan, I didn't just call my parents' synagogue and ask them to send congregants to make a minyan, as many synagogues do when a congregant is sitting shiva. But complying with my mother's expectations had become my modus operandi.

The mourner's graciousness was a blessing, as he periodically announced page numbers so that Rachel and I could follow along; but the men mumbled the prayers so quickly that I couldn't find my place in the service, and I sat and stood at all the wrong times. They chanted the Mourner's Kaddish so fast that my words jammed together in my mouth. By the time the prayer ended, I was out of breath.

I remembered this passage from Wieseltier's *Kaddish*: ". . . her voice should not be heard. Otherwise, the man who hears her may be aroused to an evil thought . . ."[xii] Being in this all-male Orthodox home, I felt a heavy weight of responsibility on my shoulders. On the balcony, Rachel and I had no partition (mechitzah) to shield us from the men. I kept my eyes focused on my siddur, committed to preventing any perception of disrespect.

A gentleman asked if I wanted him to recite the *El Malei Rachamim*. The question caught me completely off guard. Why I said yes, I'll never know; the El Malei blessing is recited only at funerals and on the Yahrzeit (anniversary of the date of death) of the deceased. My answer confirmed their assumption that I was there for my father's Yahrzeit, but I was still in my avelut (mourning period). One man asked my father's Hebrew name. As he chanted the prayer for my father's soul, I took my daughter's hand in mine, her tender grip a handclasp across the generations.

Our host invited Rachel and me to stay for coffee after the service, but we declined because I had to catch my homebound flight. I wish I had stayed longer, shown my appreciation for his hospitality, and expressed my condolences. Instead, we returned to the car, and Rachel drove us to the airport.

I have regretted our quick departure since that day. Without thinking, I left this man's home without learning his name and without keeping his address. My determined efforts to find and thank the man who blessed us with his kindness have been in vain.

"Thank you for joining me, honey. It means a lot to me." I voiced my gratitude as Rachel focused on the road.

"Well, I really appreciate you coming, Mom, and helping me. I'll be home toward the end of the month, and if you need someone to make a minyan, you can call me."

I leaned my head back onto the headrest, feeling the embrace of my daughter and my faith community. Rachel's caring renewed a closeness we hadn't shared in a long time. I closed my eyes and imagined my father blessing the bond linking mother and daughter once again.

CHAPTER 33

The First Father's Day

June had hardly begun, and relentless ads for Father's Day already dominated the radio. No matter where I turned, reminders followed me like a stalker: Father's Day television commercials for sporting goods, clothing, and aftershave showed fathers with their sons and daughters; newspaper ads urged consumers to buy shirts, ties, and toiletries; pictures of fathers and their children filled store windows. Each one plucked at my heart as if aggravating a scab-covered wound.

The only way to escape the bombardment was to cut myself off from the world. I stopped listening to the radio and watching television. I ignored the ads in the *Washington Post.*

I wanted to celebrate my father. I wanted to pore over cards in the Hallmark store until I found just the right one—humorous yet appropriate. I wanted to go shopping for golf balls or a golf glove or a gift card for that steak place Mom disapproved of. I wanted to look forward to talking and joking with him on Father's Day. But I couldn't.

As kids, my sisters and I always gave him socks for lack of other ideas. Really, he wanted for nothing; anything he desired, he could and did buy for himself. We'd put the socks in a box and gift wrap it, then put that into another box that we wrapped and put into another box, until we had five or six gift-wrapped boxes inside one another, disguising the contents.

"Oh, I love these socks!" or "How did you know these are just what

I need this year?" he'd exclaim, reacting as if he'd been given the most unique gift a man could receive. Dad always followed these exclamations with big hugs, and we would gleefully dance around the living room hand in hand, polka style.

I expressed my dread of the impending holiday to Judi, the fellow mourner whose mother had died before my father.

"What did you do for Mother's Day?" I asked.

"A few weeks beforehand, I sent a letter to Mom's friends asking for memories of her. I got more responses than I ever anticipated. Some had funny stories, some were poignant," she told me, tiny pools filling her eyes. "I learned things about my mother I hadn't known. Waiting for those responses gave me something to look forward to."

Judi talked so passionately that I became inspired to do the same thing. I decided to write to my father's friends and extended family members asking for their recollections of Dad, as an antidote for the longing I anticipated on Father's Day.

I wanted a picture of my father and me at the top of the letter, like a masthead. I spread out all my photo albums and loose photos, then sifted through fifty-plus years of pictures. Some made me chuckle, like the ones of him at the beach in the 1950s, when he was so skinny that his ribs showed when he inhaled. Some made me misty-eyed, like the one of us dancing together at my college sorority formal.

I finally found the perfect photo: Dad and me dancing at Jane's wedding. His black suit, white dress shirt, and red tie coincidentally matched my red-and-black dress. He wore a boutonniere on his lapel, and his white yarmulke (kippah) still graced his head. We're dancing cheek to cheek, Dad's left hand holding my right hand, both of us wearing broad grins. I gazed at the snapshot so long, the image lingered the way light spots stay in our eyes long after the flash has gone off.

I spent days writing, rewriting, and editing the letter, until it did justice to my sentiments. I was as giddy as a kid eagerly awaiting a birthday present as I put twenty copies of the letter into the mailbox.

Dear _____,

I'm looking ahead to Father's Day with misgivings, and as we approach his birthday and the dedication of his gravestone, I've been wondering how I can best honor Dad's memory. I'm writing to you to help me assemble a permanent memory book of Dad . . . something I can pass on to Rachel, David, and my nieces, so that future generations will know him, and he will never be forgotten.

Please share your memories of Dad with me. Stories, pictures, poems, jokes—anything that conveys what was special about your relationship with him. Please be as creative, sentimental, silly, or even outrageous as you'd like. Through these stories, I hope to learn more about him, as well as the impact he had on your life.

I'm hoping you can send your recollections to me by Father's Day. I'll devote that day to compiling them. Thank you in advance for giving me yet another gift. My best wishes for peace and health to you and those you love.

Love,
Sarah

Each time a letter arrived, I held it as if it were a fragile butterfly wing, examining the return address and trying to imagine its contents. I bought a beautifully decorated box that resembled a treasure chest and put each letter aside to read on that third Sunday in June.

On Father's Day morning, after the conclusion of the prayer service, Jonathan, one of the Four Musketeers, motioned to me. He reached into his tallit bag and pulled out a copy of *Wait Till Next Year*, Doris Kearns Goodwin's story of a girl and her father, who loved the Brooklyn Dodgers.

"I had the idea to get this for you after you talked about your father's love of baseball," he said.

I looked back and forth between the book and Jonathan's eager face. The lump in my throat blocked me from speaking—the only sound that came out was "Aww . . ." He and I had shared so much sorrow that words were unnecessary. He saw the gratitude in my eyes and felt the warmth of my hug. He knew I was deeply moved.

Later that day, as I read the back cover, I laughed out loud; the Brooklyn Dodgers were archrivals to my dad's revered New York Yankees.

My sister Jane decided to visit Dad's grave that day. The words *Dad's grave* were still incongruous to me. Even though nine months had passed, I didn't want to picture my father lying in a box in the ground. . . . I wanted to imagine him picking a golf ball from the bottom of the cup on the eighteenth hole.

I decided to spend the day outdoors at my beloved home at Beeler's Mill. I hadn't been able to move in as the area lacked synagogues, but some days, I visited the house between morning and evening services.

I dragged a heavy wooden Adirondack chair from my car to the edge of the stream above the front waterfall. By the time I settled down, the day had warmed to 80 degrees. Drawing in the fresh air, feeling the sun caress my skin, and listening to the gentle trickling of the water, God's handiwork cradled me.

I opened the box of letters full of anticipation and excitement, like a kid who peeks inside a closet and finds brightly wrapped presents. My hands trembled as I opened the first envelope.

The letters were little vignettes of Dad. Some made me choke up and miss him even more. Some made me chuckle. Some contained stories I already knew; others were new to me.

Two of the men who had played racquetball with my father wrote about their games and the conversations that took place as they played, how a point was played, and what great workouts they had. One shared that they didn't tell their wives much of what happened during the games because the women would say they were crazy to continue abusing their bodies. He called it "A MAN THING!" My father loved playing racquetball and was as competitive as any professional athlete.

My father's closest and dearest friend, a man named Jack Brown, also wrote about racquetball, using Judaism as a metaphor:

> As you well know, in our religion we have three divisions of Judaism: Reform, Conservative, and Orthodox. When it came to Wednesday night, we were orthodox observers: We were devout Wednesday-night racquetball players, and nothing could sway our faith in racquetball. We went from one place to another, starting at the YMHA at 92nd Street and then the YMCA on 62nd Street. . . . The gym was our place of worship.

After Dad died, Jack Brown called him a "man's man." I didn't know exactly what that meant, but after reading these letters, I got a peek into the part of my father's life that I never saw growing up. I hadn't realized how important these relationships with other men were, and how those friendships played out through sports.

Another longtime friend of my father's, from high school, wrote about inviting Dad to play baseball together one Sunday morning in 1952:

> Marvin really enjoyed that day and was up bright and early the next Sunday to join the team again. By the time our summer vacation came to an end, Marvin was already bitten by the baseball bug, and he joined our winter team at Van Cortlandt Park in the Bronx. I have to say, your dad enjoyed playing immensely every Sunday. All troubles were forgotten on the ball field; it gave us all a few hours of relaxation away from thinking about anything but hitting and catching that ball.

My father played with that team for years—until younger men joined, and he could no longer get to first base before the ball. On many of those Sunday mornings, I joined him for the ride to Van Cortlandt Park, delighting in having Dad all to myself. Often, I watched the teams play. Other times, I wandered the 1,000-plus acres of parks and trails, delighting in nature within one of the country's largest metropolitan cities.

Some of Dad's golf buddies also shared stories. One wrote: "Marvin spent many hours trying to teach me how to get out of the sand traps. He somehow did a pretty good job, even though he usually ended up with all of the sand in his hair." I laughed, considering how little hair my father had. He also wrote that "nobody could keep track of the scoring better than Marvin," and included a photo of him and my dad wearing huge smiles on the day they won their golf tournament.

Another friend shared a story that, as he put it, characterized "Marvin's philosophy of life." The man had complained to my father about a problem with a landscaper who wasn't completing his job the way it was supposed to be done. He was ready to hire a lawyer to sue the man. "Marvin said I should get rid of that guy and hire someone new. Hiring a lawyer to sue would only prolong the aggravation and cost me more money in the long run. Nothing positive was to be gained. His advice was absolutely correct: *doing something negative is going backwards.*"

I imagined my father speaking those words. One of the most powerful lessons he ever taught me was that we don't make mistakes; we make decisions and choices based on the best information available to us at the time. If the outcome isn't what we wanted or expected, that means we have a learning opportunity, not a mistake, and we move on from there. Dad didn't spend time looking in life's rearview mirror.

Two of my cousins shared the same story about the day of my aunt Ruth's funeral. As the funeral procession was about to enter the cemetery, the cemetery director came to the window of the limousine and insisted that my uncle pay the balance due before he would permit the graveside service. My father, my uncle Norton, and my two cousins got out and went into the office. Before my uncle could pay the balance, my father intervened. From this point, the two stories differ slightly. One cousin reported that my father yelled, "You'll get the check when the funeral is over and not one minute sooner, you disgusting, ugly, fat little man!" The other reported that my father said, "Why, you miserable, fat son of a bitch! For this amount of money, you're bothering us at this time?"

I burst out laughing as I read the two letters. Neither cousin had ever seen my father get angry. Neither had I, for that matter. Imagining my father calling the cemetery director an "ugly, fat little man" was hilarious; I could more easily believe he'd called the man a son of a bitch. But Dad didn't tolerate injustice, and he thought stopping a funeral procession at the cemetery for payment was just plain wrong. Family loyalty was of paramount value for my father. He wasn't about to allow his brother to be humiliated minutes before burying his wife.

The letter that most closely reflected my own feelings about my father came from my cousin Ritasue, born a few months after me, who saw my father only a handful of times each year.

> Uncle Marvie was my favorite because he had that uncanny way of always making me feel so special. What I did mattered to him, what I said mattered to him, and mostly, how I felt mattered to him. I loved being in his company, even as a little girl, because it felt so easy. One never knew if Uncle Marvie had lots on his mind, or if he was feeling sad, or pained. He wanted those around him to feel sunshine, his sunshine, and it was genuine and came from deep within. . . . His gentle manner somehow always made me feel safe and comforted.

Safe and comforted. Those words brought on tears. My father had been the source of safety and comfort in my home life. And like my cousin's experience, he had always made me feel special. I could have written those same words describing my relationship with my father, for he truly was the light in my life, and his death brought the end of his sunshine.

Throughout all the letters, my father's essence rang loud and clear. He was described as "good-natured, "making the best of any situation," having "a mathematical mind that made the most difficult and complicated situation simple, "a very good sport," "a great guy," "a good friend," and a man whose "warmth was contagious."

After I'd read each letter several times, I folded and returned it to its original envelope, gently placing it back in the box as if I were returning a baby bird to its nest. The letters were a balm for my wound; my father came alive on those pages. They made me feel as close to my dad as I did when he lived—an irony on my first fatherless Father's Day.

Through the letters, three things became clear: my father was deeply loved; he had a profound impact on those whose lives he touched; and I could continue to learn about him even after he was gone.

CHAPTER 34

The Tenth Man

Mom had decided to hold the unveiling of my father's gravestone on July 27, the day that would have been Dad's seventy-seventh birthday. Visiting the place where his body lay in the ground to dedicate his gravestone wasn't my idea of a celebration.

This ritual originates in the biblical story of Jacob, who constructed a memorial for his wife, Rachel, after her death. In the past, it was customary to have a ceremony called *hakamat hamatzevah* (installation of the monument) when a tombstone was placed at the burial site. The unveiling ceremony, however, is a modern custom. Because the gravestone is often in place before the official dedication, a cloth, veil, or handkerchief is placed over it. At the ceremony, the cloth is lifted and the inscription is "unveiled" for the first time.

While there is no prescribed time for dedicating the grave marker, it is typically done between the end of shiva and before the first anniversary of death.

Driving to the cemetery in New York, I felt relieved to have silence; Rachel was reading *Harry Potter and the Goblet of Fire* in the back seat, and David was asleep next to me. In the days leading up to Dad's birthday, I woke most mornings with a clenched jaw and tight neck muscles—physical symptoms of the anticipated emotional agony of saying goodbye to him again. This goodbye felt more real.

Immediately after Dad died, my time filled up with so many arrangements, details, and activities that I couldn't fully absorb the magnitude of my loss. I moved through the hours and days after his death in a zombielike trance. I hadn't yet heard the silence of his absence.

Before the service, as our small group of family and friends congregated in the main building at Mount Ararat Cemetery, I walked the short distance to Dad's grave to spend a few minutes alone. I passed the grave markers of people—fathers and husbands who had died in wars; mothers, wives, and children buried too soon—whose names were etched in stone, ensuring their presence in perpetuity.

The air was warm, the sky clear. "Another perfect golf day," Dad would have said.

It's easy to find our family plot. Just go past the American flag and turn right. Our family graves are on the right side of the narrow road where hearses pull up. The grass had grown back over the grave, disguising the place where the open earth had swallowed my father's coffin. The smooth, gray granite bearing my father's name and his birth and death dates revealed itself through the gauzelike white veil. I shuddered as my hand flew over my mouth, muffling my gasp. This was real. There lay my father.

"I miss you, Daddy. Living without you has left a hole in my life."

I was grateful to talk to him . . . just me, alone, with no one else present.

"I hadn't really accepted you were going to die, Daddy. I knew you had terminal cancer. I know we all die. But nothing prepared me for what life without you would feel like."

Can we ever visualize our lives without our loved ones, even when we know they will die? If I had been able to conceive of my future without him, what would I have done? Savored the moments more? Asked more questions or had more long talks with him? Why is it that we don't value the blessing of what we have until we lose it?

"Happy birthday, Daddy." I dried my cheeks with the back of my hand as I turned from his grave.

Ambling back to the main building, luxuriating in the solitude, I wanted to believe I would have visited Dad more often, talked more about important subjects, and relished our time together more deeply if I had foreseen the black void of loss. I'd had seven years after his cancer diagnosis. Why hadn't I asked him the many questions I now wished I could ask? Questions like "How did your war experience change you?" or "What do you know about your grandparents and great-grandparents?"

Then I remembered. My father hadn't wanted to talk as if he were dying. He had refused to live as a cancer victim and insisted we treat him as though he had never received the diagnosis. This recollection relieved me, but only slightly.

As soon as I rejoined my family and friends, we led the walk back to the gravesite. Rabbi Arzt officiated, as he had at Dad's funeral.

"The unveiling comes toward the end of the mourning period," the rabbi began. "It marks the transition between two periods: the first is marked by grief and sadness; the second is marked by remembering what the deceased brought to the world and how he touched our lives. After the unveiling, it is time to begin to move on."

Wise counsel. But difficult to do.

"The unveiling also comes at the time when we truly begin to internalize the loss. Before this, reality hasn't quite settled in. Now, we know it's real."

The rabbi gave Mom a nod, and she leaned over and lifted the veil from the stone. I gasped, my throat tightening as if someone were strangling me. My father was gone, along with any remaining shreds of disbelief.

The stone read:

Here rests Moshe Israel son of Yoseph Tzvi
Passed on 20th day of Elul 5760
Marvin E. Birnbach
A Man of Honor
July 27, 1924 – Sept. 20, 2000
May his soul be bonded to eternal life

A man of honor. That was my father.

I thought back to the letters I'd read on Father's Day only weeks before, in which friends and family members had given written testimony to this epitaph. He was seen as a good person by those around him; he gave of himself to benefit others; he was loyal to his family, his friends, his faith, and his country; and he lived his life in keeping with his values. My mother had chosen the perfect inscription.

I wondered how my children and nieces would remember him. What would they tell their children about him? Would his great-grandchildren have any concept of what "A Man of Honor" means? Or how it so perfectly characterized our father? Would they be curious about the man buried in that grave? Would they even visit it?

The real death is being forgotten.

As if to ease my anguish, God reminded me that Rachel knows much about my paternal grandmother, a woman she never met and whose Hebrew name she carries, because of the collective memories that have been shared with her.

She knows about the spindly legs that carried my grandmother's large, stout body, about her marvelous cooking, about her commitment to family and Judaism, and about the many awards she'd won for being the most outstanding saleswoman at Macy's on 34th Street in New York City, before she left to run the family furniture store. She knew that my grandmother opened her home to feed strangers and always gave to the poor no matter how little she had, and that she had an uncanny ability to obtain extremely scarce rationed items to send to my father on the front lines during World War II. I had told Rachel about the annual trips to Radio City Music Hall during every winter break from school, when my grandmother and I waited for hours in the cold to buy tickets to see the Rockettes' *Christmas Spectacular* (before ticketing companies like Fandango); and about her final torturous months, when she clung to life beyond everyone's expectations, before she finally died in my parents' home, in the arms of my mother.

The Jewish tradition of giving a newborn the same Hebrew name as a deceased loved one—typically a parent or grandparent—means that the living carry the names and stories of the beloved into future generations. My grandma Rose lives on through the recollections I and others have passed to my daughter—links in the chain of continuity between my grandmother's past and my children's and grandchildren's futures. The Jewish naming tradition connects time and eternity, keeping the past alive.

I spoke a silent prayer. *Please, God, may one of my children someday name a child for my father and carry his memory forward.*

Before leaving the gravesite, the rabbi reminded us of the tradition of placing a small rock or pebble on the headstone when visiting a grave. My paternal grandmother had purchased a family plot back in the 1950s with a simple granite headstone displaying a Jewish star and the name BIRNBACH.

In biblical days, Jews marked graves by putting stones on the gravesite to demonstrate that their loved one wasn't forgotten. Because we believe that both stones and souls endure forever, the tradition continues. I had brought a few small rocks from the Mill House, which I took from the pocket of my skirt and gently placed on top of the family headstone. My sister Jane, in a tribute to my father's love of golf, added a golf ball to the pile.

Extended family and friends slowly drifted away until only my immediate family remained, each face reflecting the same forlorn look of grief.

———

The trip home from the unveiling illuminated the old Yiddish expression *A mentsch tracht und Gott lacht*: "A man plans, and God laughs."

We left the cemetery in two cars, intending to get home in time to say Kaddish in our own synagogues. Jane, Stuart, and their daughters, along with Lois, were returning to Philadelphia. Mom, Rachel, David, and I were heading back to Maryland.

What had we been thinking? We had lived in New York long enough to anticipate Friday night rush-hour traffic during the warm days of summer. Cars were lined up at a standstill. We sat on the Belt Parkway, going nowhere, for hours. As we watched the time tick away, moving only inches at a time, the red brake lights of the cars in front of us signaled the news: we were not going to make it home in time to say Kaddish. We speculated. Could we get across Staten Island before sundown? With each successive fifteen-minute increment, my anxiety intensified, leaving my stomach jolting like the Mexican jumping beans we played with as kids.

Since it was Shabbat, most synagogues had evening services. With Mom driving, I pulled out my trusty *United States Jewish Travel Guide*, glad that I'd had the sense to put it in the car. Rachel and I pulled out our cell phones and started calling various synagogues in Brooklyn and Staten Island to find an evening minyan. I looked at my watch: 5:30 p.m. Most evening services on Staten Island began at 8:00 p.m. Should we spend those hours waiting on Staten Island? We decided to keep going.

We had four cell phones between the two cars, all calling one synagogue after another, trying to find a place to pray. Humor overcame the tension when we belatedly recognized that we had, in our two cars, nine people. We didn't need to find a synagogue with a minyan—we only needed one more Jewish person.

As we sat in bumper-to-bumper traffic in one of the most rundown neighborhoods of Brooklyn, Jane called me on my cell phone.

"Hey, let's watch for pedestrians. Maybe we can spot one who looks Jewish. Then we could conduct our own service on the side of the road."

Of course, when one is stuck in the center lane on the thirty-mile stretch of the Southern State and Belt Parkways, it's hard to even get to the side of the road.

A few moments later, my phone rang again. "Look, quick! There's our man!" Jane's excitement was contagious.

I strained to see. "Where?"

"Over there, on the sidewalk."

I saw a disheveled man in ragged clothes wheeling a grocery cart stuffed with trash bags.

"Jane, he doesn't look Jewish to me." I chuckled for the first time in days.

Jane's humor, so reminiscent of Dad's, immediately smashed through the tension and lightened the mood. Dad would be laughing, too.

"Well, let's have a contest. Let's see who can find our tenth man first?" The tenth man—the last person to complete a minyan—is considered honored.

Soon, Jane called back. "I'm the winner! See that blue sedan up there in the distance? It has a bumper sticker with Hebrew letters!"

Sure enough, about eight cars ahead of us in the right-hand lane, a blue sedan had Hebrew words on its bumper that I couldn't translate.

"Jane, you might have found the tenth man, but if we can't get to that car, you don't win the contest. Besides, just because the car has a bumper sticker, doesn't mean its occupants are Jewish."

"Well, at the rate we're traveling, I could get out of the car, walk over to it, and find out."

"I hope you're not going to do something that crazy." The admonition of the eldest sister worked. Everyone remained in their seats.

The shared laughter released some of the heaviness of the day, the stress of the traffic, and the anxiety about finding a minyan. My sister's merriment lightened grief's burden, just as it had during shiva when my sisters and I frolicked in our mother's bedroom. And like that day ten months earlier, I could almost feel Dad's delight in our combined hilarity, knowing he would have gotten in on the jesting.

Creeping forward at a snail's pace, we finally identified a synagogue in Northern New Jersey with an 8:00 p.m. Shabbat service. After painstakingly meandering through the state, we arrived at the synagogue tired, hungry, and emotionally drained. Entering the sanctuary, I did my customary head count to make sure we had a minyan. I saw more than enough people, let out a sigh of relief, and then remembered: we only needed one. We settled into seats at the back of the sanctuary.

As weary as I was, I felt renewed energy listening to the voices of my family members—mostly off-key—joined together in prayer, the hot summer day's sweat drifting off each of us. I smiled at seeing David, who had rarely been in a synagogue since his bar mitzvah, discreetly glancing over his shoulders at his aunts and me to figure out the correct page in the prayer book, just as I had done on my first day in the Beth El morning minyan. And I looked over at Rachel, taller now than I. I imagined Dad smiling down on us as we recited the Mourner's Kaddish for the second time that day, the entire family gathered together, joined in a common goal, sharing both tears and laughter. I felt my heart opening like a morning glory at dawn.

CHAPTER 35
Sacred Community

Every challenge comes with rainbows to conquer it.
AMIT RAY

In the midst of life's storms, a ray of sunshine can produce a rainbow. That's what happened at the end of July, only six days after the unveiling.

In an act of utter desperation, I hung my note on the message board in the continuing education building at the University of Delaware, among job postings, requests for rideshares, and an offer of concert tickets:

WANTED:
People to be part of a morning minyan
7:15 a.m.—Clayton Hall, Room 123

I felt awkward putting a personal religious appeal in a place with such a mishmash of advertisements. But I was at the university to teach leadership and management courses to nonprofit executives, and I couldn't find a minyan.

Prior to accepting the contract four months earlier, I had, as always, done my research to find a place to recite Kaddish in the area. The campus had both Hillel and Chabad houses, and the nearby Conservative and Orthodox synagogues all reported daily minyanim, so I accepted the teaching commitment.

Once on-site, I called the ultra-Orthodox Chabad house, hoping my gender would not be an issue.

"I'm calling to find out the times of your morning and evening services."

"I'm sorry, but we don't have services during the summer. Not enough people to make a minyan."

"Do you know where I can find a morning and an evening minyan? I'm at the university in Newark this entire week, and I'm reciting Kaddish for my father."

"I'm truly sorry. I don't know. Many people go south for the summer or are on vacation. And the kids go home during the summer recess. I wish I could help you."

"Thank you." What else could I say? I hadn't anticipated that prayer in an ultra-Orthodox congregation would be season dependent.

When I called the campus Hillel, I heard a similar story. And again from the Conservative synagogue in Wilmington.

As my search for a minyan became more futile, the drumbeat of worst-case scenarios got louder. I felt like a lost child who couldn't find her way home. Life trumpeted its lesson that no matter how much effort I expended, and no matter how strong my conviction, some things remained out of my control. But with my father's soul in abeyance, I didn't want to listen.

Forever hopeful, I launched into plan B: I called the university Chabad and Hillel and the Newark Reform synagogue, almost begging them to send congregants to the campus to serve in a minyan. No one responded.

My faith held strong. God had not let me down this far, and I had only ten more days until the end of my avelut (the eleven-month mourning period).

Over lunch, I shared my concern with another longtime faculty member and colleague. She was unfamiliar with Jewish customs and had never met anyone who'd chosen my prayer practice. Her questions signaled her eagerness to learn more: "What does the Kaddish mean?

Do you say the Kaddish for all relatives? Do the other people in the minyan say the prayer with you?"

I gleefully explained our rituals as she listened attentively and with nonjudgmental grace, wanting to learn, and I felt a bridge being built across religious backgrounds in real time. I left lunch grateful—that she wanted to know more about Judaism and my value system, that I had deepened her understanding of this Jewish tradition, and for having shared the kind of exchange that builds tolerance of differences.

Her sincerity was real. She announced to her class that I needed ten Jewish people to pray and explained the significance. Her students posed questions, and some expressed admiration for the unfamiliar. One man volunteered to come.

Ironically, I hadn't made such an appeal to my own class, considering it too private to disclose in a professional environment. I had always assumed that sharing personal information would undermine my credibility. Now I realized that I had created a distance contrary to my own teachings. This experience taught me that when I allow myself to be vulnerable, my interactions are more honest. Since then, I have been more open and have gotten more positive feedback from workshop participants, who have said that I am more authentic.

Before retiring for the evening, I ambled back to the message board, hoping for responses to my request. As I approached, I saw a yellow Post-it Note on the bottom of my message, and the words: "I will be there. Arthur Gordon."

"Oh my gosh!" I couldn't believe my eyes.

I grabbed hold of the message board to steady myself while I absorbed his message. Arthur Gordon had been my uncle's name; even more significant, A. Gordon was the alias my father had used when sending collection letters to delinquent customers from his credit company (and when making dinner reservations, since many found the name Birnbach difficult to grasp).

Now A. Gordon, a man with my family name, had volunteered to give his "Amen" to my prayer. I heard God whisper, "It's okay. I see your intention. Your father's soul will be in my care."

Afraid someone might see me trembling, I hurried back to my room with my most upright posture.

The next morning, I got to my classroom in Clayton Hall at 7:00 a.m. I readied the room for my class, unpacked the borrowed prayer books, and waited, hardly taking my eyes off the door. A gentleman arrived and introduced himself. A second man entered a few minutes later and said, "I hope it's okay I'm here. I'm not Jewish, but my wife is, and I know a lot about the rituals and customs. I came to be in your minyan."

"I'm grateful that you're here. Thank you for coming."

When Arthur Gordon entered, I couldn't contain my exuberance. He introduced himself, and despite my desire to give him a big embrace, we shook hands.

"I appreciated your Post-it Note on the bulletin board last night."

"Of course. When someone needs a minyan, especially in this kind of environment, I'm privileged to respond."

"Your name is the same as that of my late uncle. I felt an immediate connection as soon as I saw your note." I didn't tell him that meeting the man who carried my uncle's name, and my father's assumed name, felt symbolic and spiritual.

By 7:15 a.m., only three men had come to my classroom. I made polite conversation while shifting my eyes from their faces to the door, then to the clock.

At 7:17 the clock seemed to stand still.

Optimism faded one minute at a time; by 7:20 a.m., no one else had come. I did not have a minyan. My brain was racing. Should I hold a service anyway? Ignore the requirement for a community of ten? Or should I thank these men and send them on their way?

Remembering the primacy of kavanah (intention), I decided to run a condensed service. The four of us, after a bit of jovial debate, determined which direction was east, and the men's voices joined mine in most of the prayers. Despite the lack of a minyan, I recited the Kaddish anyway. At the end, they gave their "Amen," filling the room with the spirit of more than ten.

"Will you need us tomorrow as well?" asked Arthur.

"I'd be grateful if you could come again tomorrow."

"Fine, we'll be here," responded another, as the three men left to go to their classes.

In the evening, I made the twenty-five-minute drive to the Orthodox synagogue in Wilmington. Seven men were present.

"I'm so sorry," said the cantor. "There's nothing we can do. Many of our regulars have died recently, and others are away for the summer. The secretary left early, and the list of nearby people is locked in her office. I'm new here and don't know who I could call."

"Well, I appreciate those of you who came. Thank you for being here. My condolences on the loss of your members." I put my hand over my heart, hoping to show my sincerity. With that, they dispersed with barely a word.

I returned to my car, shoulders slumped. Once again, expecting other congregations to operate as Beth El did was as foolhardy as expecting to win the Powerball jackpot.

This first full day with no minyan, I felt I'd fought an invisible enemy and lost. To have come so far, to be so close to the end . . .

Driving back to the campus, my spirits were sinking like an anchor dropping into the ocean. I voiced my wonderings aloud, as I had when I left the Chabad center in Raleigh months before.

"How stringent are you, God? Will you view my kavanah as more important than reciting the prayer in a minyan? Please see my effort as worthy and show your grace to my father's soul."

Night had fallen by the time I got back to the university. I bumped into a dear colleague and fellow instructor, Ed McMillan, who was taking an evening jog.

"Why do you look so down?" he asked.

I told him about my inability to find a minyan.

"Do you know the Serenity Prayer?" he asked.

"Yes," I responded. "God, grant me the serenity to accept the things I cannot change, the courage to change the things I can, and the wisdom to know the difference."

"Well, you need to heed those words," he chided with a smile. "You can't control everything, as much as you might want to. I'm sure God knows your love for your father, and this one day without a minyan won't overshadow your many months of devotion."

"I hope you're right. But if I can't pray with a minyan in a synagogue, I'll go pray in God's other house—nature." I tilted my head toward the wooded area behind the dormitories.

"I'm coming with you," he asserted, taking my arm in his. "I don't want you going out into those woods alone at night." That solidified my decision.

"Thanks, Ed. That's an offer I can't refuse."

We walked past the dormitories with the moon lighting our way, the tall birch and oak trees creating a sanctuary with their canopy of leaves, through which stars flickered like glitter in the sky.

I sat on the ground and took in the earthy smell of the forest floor before reciting a few short prayers and a psalm. Then I painstakingly enunciated the words of the Mourner's Kaddish, making sure God heard them clearly. Ed sat alongside me, silently giving witness to my prayers. When I finished, he helped me up, and we strolled back to the dormitory where visitors were housed.

As Tuesday melted into Wednesday, still without a minyan, I tried to draw comfort from Ed's words.

On Thursday morning, the three men who had joined me each previous morning arrived again. I began praying, facing east toward Jerusalem with the door behind me. To this day, I don't know how it happened, but while we were praying, seven people noiselessly slipped into the room as though on cat's paws. I sensed a quiet movement over my shoulder and turned to see ten people, all with kippot on their heads.

I couldn't breathe. I could hardly see the words in the prayer book. Then Arthur Gordon spoke.

"We'll follow your lead, whenever you're ready."

I filled my lungs, blinking to clear my vision. I improvised and did much of the service in English so the others could follow. When I recited the Kaddish, the chorus of "Amen" resounded through that small classroom with the richness of the National Cathedral choir.

Worries about my father's soul evaporated like the steam from my morning cup of tea. The tender hugs of these men and women reminded me of my father's gentle embrace. When Arthur Gordon approached me, I felt off-balance. I leaned against him and whispered, "How can I ever thank you?"

"Not necessary," he whispered back. "It was a privilege."

We mingled for a few moments as I acknowledged their kindness before people moved on to their classes. As I prepared to teach my class, I whispered a prayer to God.

"Thank you for the gift of this community. The intention of these men and women is yet another assurance that you have embraced my father's soul."

The holiness of their deed lingered, as if a light shone from within me, while I taught my final class of the week.

At lunch, one of the men from the morning group asked, "Was it acceptable? Was it all right?"

How should I tell him that these men and women had created the most inspirational moment of these past ten months? How could I let him know that he and the others had given me a most sacred experience—one I would never forget?

I wanted to say something poignant, but my emotions choked the words. So I put my hand over my heart, tilted my head, and gave a slow nod and a heartfelt smile, which crinkled the crow's-feet around my eyes.

The word had spread that I needed ten people to recite Kaddish. In the absence of ten Jews to make a minyan, these Christian men and women had stood with me and provided a community in which to pray. They gave the minyan its ultimate significance: to stand with the mourner, to show her she is not alone, and to praise God.

As my eleven months of saying Kaddish drew to a close, I experienced one of the most profound and hallowed events of the entire period— the ultimate expression of a true *kehilah kedoshah* (holy community): people supporting and lending strength to one another in the face of sadness and need.

What did it matter if they didn't know Jewish rituals and prayers, if they prayed in different institutions, or if they didn't pray at all? They had performed a sacred act. After three consecutive days without a minyan, God reminded me of three very important lessons: that when I am open to serendipity, I will be graced with blessings; that I still needed to learn acceptance for things outside my control; and, most importantly, that although we have diverse religious views, our common humanity binds us.

CHAPTER 36

The Final Kaddish

Every ending is a new beginning.
PROVERBS

As the calendar turned from July to August, my final day as an avelah approached, and peacefulness returned among those of us who remained at Beth El. I remembered Judi's words: "There is no prescribed custom to signify the ending."

In our Jewish-American culture, we note time's passage in many ways: we watch the ball drop in Times Square on New Year's Eve, set off fireworks on the Fourth of July, and blow out candles on birthdays. At the Passover seder, we eat bitter herbs and dip vegetables in salt water, representing the bitterness of slavery and the tears of the slaves. And we mark the end of the Sabbath, transitioning from the holy day to the rest of the week, with the Havdalah service—a multisensory experience that includes a candle, spices, and wine.

I needed a rite of passage, some sort of ritual: something to make my eleven-month journey tangible, to ground me as I anticipated my farewell to the community that had bolstered me for months, and to signify my transition from one stage of grief to another. Rituals had always sustained me. August 9, 2001, my last day as an avelah, warranted a ritual.

I decided to lead the service that morning, as doing so is believed to bring more holiness to the soul of the departed. Even though I knew that my kavanah (intention) was more important than impeccable Hebrew, I was anxious about standing up in front of the congregation and leading the prayers. I remembered my first day at the Beth El minyan, when I couldn't even follow the service and had to watch Fran to know when to turn the page. I had come a long way. I could now read along with the leader. Still, my Hebrew reading remained as slow as that of a first grader.

I caught sight of my father's Purple Heart medal out of the corner of my eye, still on the table near my journaling sofa, reminding me of my father's courage. I chuckled. "Okay, Dad. If you could conquer the fear of being shot at daily for two years, I can certainly survive the fear of shepherding the minyaneers through one morning service."

I practiced the prayers for weeks, listening to recordings of the service in the car so I could discern nuances in tone and inflection. Every Monday morning, I met with one of the congregants who was fluent in Hebrew, who listened to and corrected my mispronunciations. I wrote out English transliterations for every Hebrew blessing.

On August 9, I arrived at Beth El early, donned my tallit, and stood on the bimah (raised platform) behind the lectern, signaling to the minyaneers that I planned to lead the service. No raising of hands like in grade school—just get to the bimah first.

As I waited for the precise moment of 7:30 a.m. to say, "Open to page one," I felt relieved that no one noticed my knees knocking or saw the transliterations I'd written in my prayer book to help me correctly pronounce the Hebrew words. Unlike many of the other minyaneers, who chanted as though in a race to finish, I enunciated every syllable of every word. Reading the prayers aloud in front of those with Hebrew fluency, I understood the trepidation of a young bat mitzvah girl. How vastly different from reading it silently in my seat, where I could skim over words I couldn't pronounce.

My snail's pace extended the service beyond its normal ending time, but no one watched the clock or stole a glance at their watches. No one read ahead of me. And the nods of approval made me feel more relaxed.

When I said, "Those in mourning or honoring a Yahrzeit, please rise for the Mourner's Kaddish," my voice cracked ever so slightly. I led the Kaddish and then gave the honor of reading the daily psalm to the other three of our Four Musketeers—Jonathan, Rick, and Roz—as a gift to treasured friends.

After the psalm came the final Mourner's Kaddish of my avelah period. I took a deep breath. *This is it. This is the last one.* I tried to look composed, masking my tight shoulders and pounding heart. I gave myself a silent talking-to.

You have come this far. You can finish this service with the same poise with which you started it. Remember your goal: to bring honor to your father.

I chuckled to myself, realizing I sounded like my mother had at Dad's funeral.

I gave the instruction to rise again. This time, I grabbed the sides of the lectern, took several more deep breaths, and repeated the Mourner's Kaddish. I stood on firm ground now. I knew this prayer.

"Yitgadal v'yitkadash sh'mei raba . . ."

Glorified and sanctified be God's great name . . .

Instead of reading, I watched the people who had supported me for the past months, trying to etch their faces into my memory, knowing I wasn't coming back the next morning. At the end of the Mourner's Kaddish, I took the customary three steps back, then bowed left, right, and center, to signify taking leave of God as one would leave a king. While the congregation gave its final "Amen" to the last words of the Kaddish, I saw Jonathan, Rick, and Roz beaming at me, mirroring my pride. I had done it. I had led the service. They knew what a challenge it had been for me to learn to read Hebrew aloud, and to learn the tunes of the prayers. I had brought the maximum honor to my father. Now his soul could rest in peace. Serenity washed over me.

My heart slowed as I closed my prayer book, removed my tallit, and placed them both in my tallit bag. Together with my journals, that bag had been my constant companion for eleven months. I had carried it in suitcases, beside me in my car, stuffed in the backs of synagogue seats, and under my arm. Like a child's well-loved blanket, it had been scrunched, tossed, shoved, and squashed—a well-traveled, worn, and stained symbol of my journey.

I stepped down from the bimah as if floating and walked down the aisle of the small chapel to smiles, extended hands, and wishes of "*Yasher Koach*" (May you grow in strength), exhilarated by my sense of accomplishment. I felt my father sharing my pride. I had transformed, through daily prayer and hard work, from being unable to follow the service to leading it by myself.

A few weeks earlier, as I felt my final day drawing closer, I composed an earnest letter to the minyaneers. For several nights, I had curled up with my journal, pouring my gratitude onto the pages, scratching out words and paragraphs until I had conveyed everything in my heart.

Before leading the service that morning, I had hung my letter on the bulletin board in the chapel for the minyaneers to read.

Dear Minyaneers,

I have fulfilled my commitment to my father and his soul. I owe a debt of gratitude to each of you, for I couldn't have done this without you.

Other than my love and respect, my father asked little of me. This is the only gift my father could not give himself. Being a self-sufficient and very independent woman, I found it hard to fathom that I had to depend on others to achieve this goal.

You have sustained me through my most difficult days. You have laughed, schmoozed, and reminded me of the importance of laughter even in my darkest moments. You have supported me when I cried, asked about me, and cared about my and my family's well-being. You've reminded me of the most important function of the minyan: to assure the mourner that she is not alone. We are a spiritual community bound to each other by the principles of our faith.

I remember a passage from one of our prayer books that reads, "To attain a degree of spiritual security, one . . . needs an atmosphere where the concern for the spirit is shared by a community." Thank you for allowing me to draw my strength from you, and for enabling me to honor my father and his memory in accordance with our shared beliefs.

Shalom,
Sarah

That might have been sufficient, but I wanted to do more. So I wrote a personal note to each minyaneer, expressing gratitude for the unique contribution they each had made to my Kaddish experience. Many of these were little things, like making sure I had a prayer book (and knew the correct page), enunciating Hebrew words so I could improve my pronunciation, hugging me when I felt sad, or simply being a quiet presence helping to make up ten people. Writing those notes had been easy—you get to know people when you share the same space every day for months, and the small acts of kindness of the various minyaneers had enhanced my life.

As people exited the chapel after the service, I gave the hand-written, personalized note to each minyaneer, and most looked astonished.

Some asked, "What is this?"

"It's my thank-you."

I sponsored a full breakfast that morning in my father's memory, with platters of lox, whitefish, kugel, cream cheese, blintzes, and a variety of pastries. To top it off, we had fresh bagels instead of the usual once-frozen-then-warmed-in-the-microwave ones. Minyaneers loved it when someone sponsored breakfast, a welcome change from the usual fare.

I donated a bottle of Johnnie Walker Black Label (only the best for the minyaneers) to be used for the blessing at the morning kiddush. It had become a tradition at Beth El for many of the minyaneers to have a nip of Scotch before eating. Not caring for the taste, however, I never participated.

When I handed the iconic bottle to Ralph, who typically provided the Scotch, his eyes flew wide open.

"This isn't necessary."

"I know, but I wanted to show my appreciation."

Ralph held up the bottle for everyone to see, the morning light illuminating the amber liquid.

"Today is Sarah's final day saying Kaddish. Let's drink to her and the memory of her father."

Ralph filled each person's jigger-size plastic cup and raised his drink in the air as he recited the blessing, the others following suit. For the first time, I joined them.

—

According to the Hebrew calendar, August 9, 2001—corresponding to the twentieth day of the Hebrew month of *Av*—fell exactly eleven months after Dad's death. At 9:00 a.m., after sharing breakfast with Roz, Rick, and Jonathan, I walked out of my synagogue. Now the Four Musketeers would be three. We stood together on the curb by the parking lot, feeling the warmth of the morning sun, and exchanged hugs.

"How does it feel?" Roz asked.

"It's like letting go of the process of letting go. I have so many mixed emotions. I'm glad to have the time back in my life, but I'm going to miss you and the other minyaneers."

"You can keep coming, you know," Rick reminded me.

"I know. But my avelut is over. My obligation to recite Kaddish is complete."

"You can still come by to support your friends," he winked.

I winked back and nodded. Then I gave them each another embrace, lingering to postpone the departure. These three had become as much a part of my life as daily prayer. They had been present with me almost every day, eased my pain, comforted me in my grief, and enabled me to stand stronger.

Walking toward my car, I knew that without the minyan, I would have mourned alone—and not as well.

I was a different woman than the one who had entered Beth El's morning minyan eleven months earlier. I had undertaken a sacred journey with no expectation of reward and received countless unanticipated blessings. I had forged my own path through Jewish practice, becoming more convinced that I could integrate traditional Judaism with my feminist outlook in a meaningful way that honored both. In dedicating my entire being to a commitment, I learned that I could devote unswerving energy to any undertaking I set my mind to, no matter the obstacles to success. I had deepened my relationship with God. I felt more peaceful, more spiritual, more compassionate, and more confident. I now understood the importance of quiet, reflective time to restore my soul. I had evolved, the way an infant progresses to a toddler, then to an adolescent, and, ultimately, to a mature adult.

That night, for the first time in eleven months, I had no place to be at 8:00 p.m. No more hurried dinners, no more racing to synagogue or orchestrating my life around the time of services. I expected to feel relieved.

Instead, I felt like I had after Dad removed the training wheels from my bicycle. I guess I had been about eight or nine years old, because we had already moved out of the city to Long Island. Our neighbors on the south side of our house had a huge tree at the front of their yard, whose roots buckled the sidewalk. To avoid this, Dad always pointed me north.

Holding on to the rear of my bike with his back bent, he ran alongside me, keeping me safe and secure as I teetered from side to side down the street. Only after I stopped wobbling and swerving did he let go, leaving me to ride alone—balanced but slightly fearful. The minyan had steadied me through a shaky time in the same way; in both situations, I felt proud of my accomplishment but anxious about my ability to continue without support. Moving on without the minyan was like riding my two-wheeler without my father.

At 7:35 p.m., I looked at the kitchen clock and had a momentary scare. *I'm late for synagogue.* Then I remembered: no need tonight.

I wandered aimlessly around the house, washed the dinner dishes, sorted through the day's mail, and checked on David, who was doing his homework.

7:55 p.m.

Were there enough people to recite the Kaddish tonight?

I didn't know what to do with myself. I made a cup of tea and carried it to my favorite sofa. I nestled in, picked up my journal and pen, and wrote.

I have fulfilled my deepest desire: to bring the maximum honor to Dad and his name, and to assure his soul's ascent to Gan Eden.

Had my father's soul been elevated to Gan Eden? While no one could know for certain, I had faith that it had. I was certain of my father's pride in me. He knew what it took to recite Kaddish in the traditional way for eleven months. I was equally sure that God had witnessed my act of love and smiled upon it. And if paradise does exist after life, then I can only imagine that God admitted my father's soul and gave him the best tee time on its golf course.

The framed photos of my father and his Purple Heart medal smiled at me from the coffee table, where I had put them before the October open houses. I leaned my head back against the cushions, a gentle smile on my lips. I don't know whether I dozed off, but I felt my father sitting next to me, as if we were on the mustard-yellow sofa of my childhood living room.

"I'm so proud of you, sweetie," he said. "You did good."

"I'm so happy I could do this one final thing for you, Dad. After taking time to mourn you and think about you every day, I feel closer to you now than I ever did. If there is a Gan Eden, Dad, I hope your soul flourishes there and God's eternal light shines upon you."

"God bless you." He repeated the same words his mother had used to end every letter and every conversation.

"I love you, Dad. Thank you for giving me your blessing, and for all the gifts I received from saying Kaddish."

"Well, you didn't need my blessing, but I'm sure glad I gave it to you, sweetie. I love you, too." The words faded away softly.

I felt the softness of his kiss on my cheek, and a deep, quiet contentment radiated through me.

"Goodbye, Dad," I whispered, as I closed my journal and headed off to sleep.

The Gifts

In school, you are taught a lesson and then given a test.
In life, you are given a test that teaches you a lesson.
MALCOLM X

At the outset of my journey, I had a singular focus: to show God that my father's soul was worthy of being elevated to Gan Eden and to give my father the gift of an eternal life spent there.

While grieving my father's death and struggling through eleven months of reciting Kaddish, I hadn't anticipated the gifts and immeasurable blessings I would reap, transforming me into a recipient as well as the giver.

My religion became a stabilizing force in my life. Walking in the footsteps of my ancestors, the continuity of Jewish mourning practices linked me to my father and the generations before him, inspiring my healing. When I walk into my synagogue now, I have an invincible bond with my spiritual community. I am part of a larger whole. I belong. Inclusion was a huge gift from my father.

I remain grateful for the fluidity of Conservative Judaism, which gave me the freedom to choose where to reside along the continuum of traditional and modern practices. While some of the differences in religious practice that I witnessed during those eleven months hindered and frustrated me, I now recognize them as the multicolored threads that make up the tapestry of our religion and of our universal humanity.

Throughout the eleven months, whenever events were beyond my control, others came through for me. In Lansing, Michigan, in Claremont, California, and in Newark, Delaware, people came forward so that I didn't have to stand alone. I learned to have faith—to trust in God that I would be okay and could relinquish my lifelong need for control.

Depending on nine others to fulfill God's commandments meant surrendering my typical I-can-do-this-alone attitude. Forced dependence humbled me. Needing others to rise to my highest self became life changing. Rather than a sign of weakness, I came to see that reaching out gives others the opportunity for compassion and acts of kindness.

In reflecting on this journey, I see I exercised more discipline than I ever thought possible. Redeeming my father's soul was my priority, and I attended synagogue religiously. Not when convenient. Not when it fit my schedule. But every day, twice a day. I maintained a steadfastness unfathomable to me before my father's death. I have a new self-confidence that will remain a part of me.

I have learned the value of taking time to slow the busyness of my life, to decide who and what is truly important, to still my mind, and to connect with that which is larger than myself. I am conscious, in a new way, of the need for serenity and the importance of protecting that time.

Taking the time to be in synagogue twice each day and using my journal for daily reflective writing gave me structured time to think about my father and his values, deepening my love for him. Reading and listening to others' stories of him, I learned more about the man. At the end of my avelut, I felt as close, if not closer, to him as when he lived.

My bond with my father wasn't the only one that deepened. No one, not even my father, could have prepared me for the way my relationship with God grew stronger. My twice-daily connection cemented it. I trusted God would care for my father's soul. And I realized belatedly that when I felt alone and abandoned by God, it was I who had lost faith in the Almighty. In praising and thanking Adonai daily, I focused more on my many blessings than I ever had before. Over the eleven months, I had been able to get angry—an emotion that had always frightened me—and to express my anger at God, knowing I was safe and loved unconditionally. I learned not only how to talk with the Almighty but how to hear God's voice, too. I learned that my personal prayers are as important as the traditional prayers for connecting with God. Prayer heals.

Many Jewish prayers contain the words "Our God and God of our ancestors . . ." Over the eleven months, those words took on new meaning; while Adonai is the God of my father and his father before him, the Almighty is now also *my God*.

My sisters and I are now closer to one another from having shared grief. Our bond is a testimony to our shared love for our father, and I know he's beaming at us.

I learned how to comfort mourners. I now know that it is enough to show up and be present, that words are sometimes superfluous, and that holding a mourner's hand can speak louder than a thousand words.

I remember having read, "To attain a degree of spiritual security, one cannot rely upon one's own resources. One needs an atmosphere where the concern for the spirit is shared by a community." The minyaneers created that atmosphere, wrapping me in the cocoon of caring I needed after losing my father. The Beth El morning minyan was, and continues to be, my spiritual community.

———

After my avelut, life continued to offer opportunities and abundant blessings. On my father's first Yahrzeit—the anniversary of his death according to the Jewish calendar—I stood in front of the Torah, and my entire congregation, and honored my dad by reading from the sacred scroll. I stumbled over words and the *gabbai* (the one who ensures the Torah is being read correctly) corrected my mispronunciations. But I made it through the reading, even though I continued shaking long after I left the bimah.

In Judaism, honoring the anniversary of death is more important than marking the day of birth. When a child enters the world, no one knows how the newborn will develop. But when a person leaves this world, we know the nature of their deeds and what they have achieved.

Jonathan, Rick, and I continue to attend the morning minyan on the Yahrzeits of each other's parents, standing shoulder to shoulder, and give our "Amen" to each other's Kaddish—though the recent pandemic has made those meetings virtual. Even though Roz and her family now live in Omaha, we other three musketeers attend the morning minyan on the Yahrzeit of each of her parents, too, joining her in spirit. We have cried together and laughed together. We have celebrated each other's joys, simchas (happy occasions), and sorrows. We met in sadness; our friendship brought us peace; we sustained one another. We are friends for life.

Three years after Dad's death, my mother sold the house in the golf community Dad had so loved and she moved to a continuing care retirement community in Florida. In 2018, she moved to a similar facility in Maryland that was just two blocks from our home, and I became her primary caretaker. She died just as I submitted this manuscript to my publisher. Until the day she died, she remained as married to my father as when he lived, proving that their love endured forever.

Through my postgraduate work at the Georgetown Family Center (now the Bowen Center for the Study of the Family), I came to see that my mother's behaviors stemmed from her childhood trauma and the absence of much-needed attention and nurturing after her mother's death. After learning more about the transmission of anxiety in families, I realized that my mother's anxiety heightened predictably as I neared age ten—the age she'd been when her own mother died. That year I suffered the worst of my mother's abuse. While this new understanding didn't erase the pain of my upbringing, I could finally accept that I wasn't responsible for her beatings, and I saw my mother and her suffering in a different, more compassionate light.

While my mother never acknowledged nor apologized for her

brutality and the degree to which it traumatized me, she mellowed in the last two years of her life, even going so far as to thank me for all I had done and continued to do for her. The more needy and dependent she became, the more empathic and compassionate I was able to be, enabling me to care for her in her final years, months, and days, and to find peace after her death.

For the six years following my avelut, I lived in the house at Beeler's Mill, where my attachment to the water, the trees, and the stars felt even more powerful for having first fulfilled my spiritual journey. Waiting to move into the Mill House taught me patience—increasingly elusive in our same-day-delivery world—and that waiting can make an outcome even more precious. I have since sold the Beeler's Mill property to a couple who are marvelous stewards of this historic property, and although I miss it, I have new blessings in my life.

In 2003, I met my current husband, Jake, on a dating site. On our first date, he presented me with two dozen red roses in the parking lot outside the agreed-upon restaurant. When we went inside to eat dinner, the maître d' asked, "Is it your anniversary?" I was about to say, "No, we just met in the parking lot." But before I could open my mouth, Jake said, "Yes, it is." The maître d' comped us a bottle of champagne. I fell in love at first sight.

Jake embodies the values my father held dear. He is a generous, kindhearted man whose commitment to family never wavers. Like my father, he is honest, hardworking, patient, and supportive. I'm convinced that my loss and the lessons learned during my avelut opened me to this relationship, which has enriched my life and that of my entire family. Five years after my father's first Yahrzeit, Jake and I married in my synagogue. And as we stood under the *chuppah* (marriage canopy), I felt my father witnessing our love and blessing our union.

My granddaughter, Dahlia, born the year after my father died, carries the feminine equivalent of his Hebrew name. Being a part of my children's lives—and now my seven grandchildren's lives—reminds me that life goes on, and that we can experience happiness even after intense sorrow. Dad would delight in his great-grandchildren, but even more so in our remembering him and moving beyond our grief to embrace life's joys.

In the years since my avelut, Beth El has implemented many changes to help facilitate the mourner's experience. The cantor initiated a class to teach people how to lead the evening service. More women lead the morning minyan, and some say they have been inspired to do so as a result of both my example and the support of other minyaneers. All meetings in the synagogue now adjourn at the time of the evening service and reconvene after it in order to guarantee the minyan, ensuring that minyan duty takes precedence over synagogue meetings. And our synagogue adopted a new, more egalitarian prayer book with extensive transliterations and explanatory notes. I can't help but think that if I'd had that when I began saying Kaddish, I could have participated earlier and more often.

Just prior to the publication of this memoir, Congregation Beth El hired its first female rabbi, a decision I wholeheartedly endorsed, as her beliefs about faith and religion mirror my own. Rabbi Deborah Megdal has already enhanced my life with her inspiring and uplifting words, as well as her guidance in our one-on-one conversations.

In September 2001, the Montgomery County State's Attorney ruled that his office had "insufficient evidence" to establish that Rabbi Maltzman had committed any criminal offense. No charges were brought against the rabbi, who, along with a number of families from Beth El, created a new congregation that fall. Kol Shalom, meaning "a voice of peace," is today a thriving Jewish synagogue in Rockville, Maryland, where Rabbi Maltzman remained the senior rabbi until his retirement in the summer of 2019.

———

The role of women in Orthodox Judaism has undergone an evolution in recent years, with more opportunities opening up for Orthodox women to study rabbinic texts. In 2013, the glass ceiling of leadership in Orthodox Judaism shattered when the first group of female rabbinical students graduated from Yeshivat Maharat, a New York seminary. Today, almost fifty Orthodox women have been ordained as rabbis. In addition, women who have studied Jewish legal texts on family-related topics have become "advisers" and "guides," providing an alternative source for answers on Jewish law, sometimes preempting ordained rabbis. In recent years, the role of the rabbi's wife (known as *rebbetzin*) has gained more institutional authority. While some of the distressing, invalidating situations I experienced still occur, this expansion of women's roles in Orthodox Judaism is, in my mind, a step in the right direction.

I recently discovered it is now possible to hire a Kaddish on the Internet! The Holy City Prayer Society will recite Kaddish for the full year of mourning for only $500—plus $18 per year for Yahrzeits. An impersonal, detached business arrangement. Acts of love should not be delegated, nor should they require payment. And even if using the services of the Holy City Prayer Society had been an option in 2000, the society's members could never have fulfilled the obligation with the same devotion as mine.

While compiling this manuscript, it dawned on me that I could have hired a Kaddish, as my father had originally requested, *and* recited Kaddish myself, giving my father's soul a double assurance of ascent to Gan Eden. But I couldn't see that option when my father announced his terminal cancer diagnosis.

My tattered copy of Israelowitz's *United States Jewish Travel Guide*, with its broken binding, notations of service times, and Post-It Notes with driving directions, sits on my shelf as testimony to my efforts to find a minyan everywhere I travelled. That aspect of my year has receded into the back corners of my memory, the way recollections of labor pains diminish as the joys of parenthood multiply. Now I have only to use Google and my GPS to find a synagogue anywhere in the world.

When I began reciting Kaddish for my father, I did not anticipate the degree to which the practice would become a lesson in how to live.

I had seven years between my father's cancer diagnosis and his death—seven years to visit more, develop a closer relationship, and ask more questions. Many people never get such a warning. But I squandered it. His death always seemed so far away, and he never wanted to live as if he were dying. My father's death gave me a greater appreciation for the brevity of life, the preciousness of every minute, and the importance of using each day wisely. Now I never miss a chance to share my feelings with the people in my life on a regular basis.

Thinking back to the day my father beseeched me to hire a Kaddish, I realize that if I had done as he originally requested, I would not have gained a community, enjoyed the support and embrace of others when I most needed it, deepened my faith and relationship with God, or attained the confidence that spiritual discipline has given me. In giving me his blessing, he gave me the gift of a life-altering transformation.

Did my father know the abundant treasures I would have missed if I'd hired a Kaddish? I doubt he thought about that. To this day, I remain grateful that I didn't hire one.

When I began my eleven-month journey to redeem my father's soul, I saw my path as my final gift to my father. But it wasn't. The final gift is living a life worthy of the man. I continue to live the values we shared and to honor the memory of my father, who remains a part of me—and who will remain, all the days of my life, a source of blessing.

GLOSSARY

Adonai   Lord, Supreme Being, or Creator. As the divine name has power, Adonai is a substitute for the divine name.

Afikomen   "That which comes after" or "dessert." A half-piece of matzoh that is broken during the seder and set aside to be eaten as a dessert after the meal, reminding us that everyone must always put something aside for the next meal. Recovering the hidden afikomen is essential for continuing the seder.

Aleinu   "It is our duty." This prayer has been recited at the end of every service since the twelfth or thirteenth centuries. It praises God's rule, emphasizes the special relationship between Israel and God, and expresses hope for the speedy arrival of God's Messiah.

Aliyah   "Ascent." An honor involving being called to ascend to the Torah (as the scroll is read on a raised platform; see *bimah*). This could apply to reading the blessings before the reading of the Torah, the reading of the Torah scroll, or the re-dressing of the Torah scroll.

Aliyot   Plural of *aliyah*.

Ark   Ornamental closet in which the Torah scrolls are housed. It is typically located on the synagogue wall that faces Jerusalem.

Ashkenazim   Jews originating from Germany and Eastern Europe, and their descendants.

Av   Month of the Hebrew calendar corresponding to July–August on the Gregorian calendar. The saddest month of the Jewish year, as the destruction of both temples took place during Av.

Avel/Avelah   Man/woman in mourning.

Avelut   Period of mourning.

Bar/Bat mitzvah	"Son/Daughter of the commandment." At the age of thirteen and one day, a boy attains legal maturity and responsibility; for girls, this occurs at age twelve and one day. At the bar/bat mitzvah, the person becomes a responsible member of the Jewish community.
Barekhu	"Let us bless." The opening word of the invitation to pray. This prayer opens the morning and evening services and introduces the reading of the Torah.
Bimah	"Elevated place." The elevated platform at the front of the synagogue where the reading desk stands and on which the Torah is placed for reading. In the US, it is generally located on the east side of the building since Jews in the west face east toward Jerusalem when praying.
Birkat Hamazon	Grace After Meals. This prayer teaches us to be humble and to recognize and show our appreciation for God's blessings. The prayer is made up of four smaller blessings: blessings for food, land, Jerusalem, and God's kindness. The practice of thanking God after our bellies are full, in addition to when we are hungry, is considered a truer sense of appreciation.
Bris	Short for *brit milah*, which means "covenant of circumcision." This religious ceremony welcomes Jewish infant boys into a covenant with God through a ritual circumcision performed by a mohel (circumciser). It derives from Genesis 17:1–4 and Leviticus 12:3. The bris happens on the eighth day of the child's life, in the presence of family and friends, and is followed by a celebratory meal.
Cantor	Also called *hazzan*. This is a trained singer who leads prayers, assists the rabbi with conducting services, and is knowledgeable about Jewish prayer.
Chabad	An Orthodox religious and social movement established by Lubavitch Chassidim, a subgroup of the Chassidic Movement founded in eighteenth-century Russia. Chassidim means "pious ones."
Chanukah	"Dedication." Chanukah celebrates the victory of the Jews over King Antiochus in the year 165 BCE, after he banned Jewish practices such as the observance of Shabbat.
Chanukiah	Special candelabra lit on each of the eight nights of Chanukah. Unlike the traditional menorah, the chanukiah has nine candles—one, the shammash, is used for lighting the others.

Charoset	A sweet, dark-colored paste placed on the seder table during Passover. (There are many variations, but our family uses apples, walnuts, and red wine.) Its color and texture are meant to recall the mortar that the Israelites used to make bricks while they were slaves in Egypt. The word *charoset* comes from the Hebrew word for "clay."
Chuppah	Canopy under which a Jewish couple stands during their wedding ceremony. It symbolizes the home that the couple will build together.
Daven	"To pray."
El Malei Rachamim	"God, full of compassion." A memorial prayer, asking God to guard the souls of the deceased. It is recited at funerals, on the yahrzeits of the deceased, and during Yizkor.
Elul	Month of the Hebrew calendar, usually coinciding with parts of August and September on the Gregorian calendar, which immediately precedes Rosh Hashanah. The month is a time of repentance to draw close to God in preparation for the coming Days of Awe. My father died during Elul.
Erev	"Entering." Erev means "evening" in Hebrew. In the Jewish calendar, days begin when daylight leaves, as opposed to other systems wherein a day begins at midnight.
Gabbai	Nonclergy synagogue member who assists with the reading of the Torah and ensures the religious service runs smoothly. It is considered an honor and a great responsibility to be the gabbai. (See also *shammos*.)
Gan Eden	Garden of Eden. Paradise in the afterlife.
Gehinnom	Purgatory; place for the wicked after death.
Get	Jewish document that effects a divorce between a Jewish couple. Required to be presented by a husband to his wife. Without a get, a Jewish woman is considered anchored to her husband and cannot have future religious marriages.
Hachnasat orchim	"Hospitality." Value learned from Abraham, whose tent had four doors so people could enter from any direction.

Hadassah   Women's Zionist Organization of America. The largest Zionist organization in the world and one of the largest women's volunteer organizations in the United States, founded by Henrietta Szold in 1912.

Haggadah   "Telling." Derived from Exodus 13:8, which prescribes that "thou shalt tell thy son." The Haggadah contains the story of Passover and is used during the seder to teach the story of Jewish liberation from slavery in Egypt and its implications for our lives today.

Halakhah   "The way; the path to go." Collective body of Jewish law comprising the rules of Jewish religious and civil practice; the Oral and Written Law. Along with customs, it defines every aspect of a traditional Jew's life.

Hallel   "The Praising." Selection of songs of praise from the book of Psalms that are recited on major holidays, when sacrifices were historically made in the Temple, and on Chanukah and Rosh Chodesh; specifically Psalms 113–118 (special joyous poems).

Halvayat hamet   "Escorting the dead." Considered one of the greatest acts of piety.

Havdalah   "Distinction" or "separation." Ceremony over wine and spices marking the closing of the Sabbath. Blessings are made over the distinction between the holy and the profane, between light and darkness, between Israel and the nations, between the seventh day and the six days of work.

Havurah   A small, informal group of Jews who study and celebrate Judaism together. I started a havurah of divorced and separated Jewish men and women in 1994.

Havurot   Plural of *havurah*.

Hillel   Largest Jewish campus organization in the world, located on more than five hundred college and university campuses. Consists of a global network of regional centers, campus foundations, and Hillel student organizations. Its mission is to enrich the lives of Jewish undergraduate and graduate students.

Kaddish	"Sanctification." Various versions of this prayer are recited to mark divisions in the service. The central theme is the sanctification of God's name. It has become the prayer for the departed; for a deceased parent, it is recited for eleven months from the date of burial. "Saying Kaddish" is often used to refer to the recitation of the Mourner's Kaddish.
Kashering	To make proper or ritually pure, according to Jewish law.
Kavanah	"Intention" and "sincere feeling." In its simplest meaning, it refers to concentrating the mind on the performance of a religious act to ensure that it doesn't become rote mechanical action. The Bible and rabbinic literature stress that observances and prayer must be conducted with inner devotion and steadfast intent. Many Jews believe that the intent of the individual is more important than the words of the prayers.
Kehilah kedoshah	"Holy community."
Keriah	Rending (tearing) of a garment, an expression of grief following the loss of a relative. Jacob tore his garment when his sons told him that Joseph was killed (Genesis 37:34); David tore his clothes when he learned of the death of King Saul; Job tore his clothing when he mourned the death of his children (book of Job 1:20). In modern times, in some denominations, a black ribbon is torn and worn over the heart in lieu of tearing a garment.
Ki l'olam Hasdo	"God's love endures forever." Passage is found in the Hallel prayers and the prayers in the Passover seder.
Kiddush	"Sanctification." Blessing spoken over wine and the cups that hold the wine. Often used interchangeably with *oneg* to indicate the social gathering of people following services.
Kippah	"Dome." Hebrew word for skullcap. Traditional Jews believe it is a mitzvah to pray with heads covered to show respect for God. Also referred to in Yiddish as a yarmulke.
Kippot	Plural of *kippah*.
Kittel	White robe that serves as a burial shroud, providing equality for all in death. It is also worn on special occasions such as the Passover seder and under the chuppah (wedding canopy) at a wedding. It is worn during High Holiday services to represent the purity we hope to achieve through our prayers on these holy days.

L'dor v'dor	Concept of keeping values alive from generation to generation. The process of honoring one's deceased parents by fulfilling their values is the embodiment of l'dor v'dor.
Lashon hara	Negative speech about a person that emotionally or financially damages them or lowers them in the estimation of others. Lashon hara is prohibited, even if those things are true. It is forbidden to listen to lashon hara, and if one has heard the negative talk, Judaism forbids believing it.
Matzoh	Unleavened bread made from flour and water, baked under supervision and eaten during Passover. It represents the "bread of affliction" eaten by our forefathers and the "bread of liberation" eaten as the Jews fled Egypt.
Mechitzah	Partition separating men and women in Orthodox and traditional synagogues.
Mensch	Person of character who possesses a sense of what is right; someone who is honorable and to be admired.
Mezuzah	"Doorpost." A parchment scroll with the Hebrew words of the Shema encased in a decorative container and attached to the doorpost of a Jewish home. It denotes a home as Jewish and reminds occupants of their connection to God and their heritage. The commandment to attach the mezuzah originates in Deuteronomy 6:4–9: "inscribe them [these words] on the doorposts of your home and on your gates."
Minyan	"Number" or "count." A quorum of at least ten Jewish people (traditionally only males) over the age of thirteen, required to recite prayers that are connected with public worship (the Mourner's Kaddish, the Barekhu, and the Amidah). The sanctification of God's name is considered a public matter rather than a private one.
	There is contemporary controversy between liberal and traditional Jews concerning who is to be counted in the minyan. Some liberal Jews count women, but each synagogue establishes its own rules regarding the counting of women in the minyan. A secondary contemporary meaning refers to a prayer service.
Minyaneers	A term used by the author to refer to people who regularly attend the weekday morning service at Congregation Beth El, and who served as part of the requisite quorum so that she could recite the Mourner's Kaddish.

Minyanim	Plural of *minyan*.
Mishaberach	Prayer invoking God's blessing on an individual or community; its focus is the welfare of the individual or community, and it is often recited to bless the sick.
Mishnah	"Repetition," "study," "teaching." The early rabbinic legal codification of Jewish law, originally compiled in the second century, it contains basic Oral Law that was transmitted throughout generations.
Mitzvah	"Commandment." Often refers to a good deed or act of kindness.
Mitzvot	Plural of *mitzvah*.
Ner daluk	"Burning light." Refers to the large shiva candle that burns for seven days and nights during the shiva period. It is placed in a prominent place and lit without reciting a blessing.
Ner tamid	"Eternal light." Lamp that hangs in front of and above the ark in every synagogue, symbolizing the light of truth and God's eternal presence in our lives. Where the ner tamid was once an oil lamp, today, most are fueled by gas or electric light. The eternal lights are never extinguished or turned off.
Passover	One of three pilgrimage festivals (with Sukkot and Shavuot), when Jews recount the story of the Exodus from Egypt and relive God's rescue of the ancient Israelites from slavery under the hand of the Pharaoh.
Payot	Sidelocks worn by some ultra-Orthodox men. The hair-cutting restriction comes from biblical scripture, which states that a man should not "round the corner of his head." The boundaries of the prohibited zone are on each side of the face, roughly between the middle of the ear and the eye, below the bone which runs horizontally across.
Rabbi	Traditionally, judge and arbiter. Currently, teacher of the Torah. As the religious head of the community, he/she officiates at life events, leads services, delivers sermons, offers comfort and consolation, counsels, conducts outreach, and represents the synagogue in the community.

Rebbetzin	Wife of a rabbi. Term is sometimes also used to refer to a female Torah scholar or teacher. In some congregations, the rebbetzin is considered the "first lady" of the community, performing social roles and ceremonial tasks. With the growth of independent leadership roles among Orthodox women, some women have received the title irrespective of their husbands.
Rosh Chodesh	"Head of the month." Marks the beginning of every month on the Jewish calendar. It is recognized by the birth of the new moon.
Rosh Hashanah	First day of the seventh month (on the Jewish calendar), Tishri, considered the New Year. It is the beginning of the Days of Awe—the period between Rosh Hashanah and Yom Kippur— and the beginning of the Jewish calendar year.
Schmooze	"To talk, chat, converse, in a friendly way." A gossipy, heart-to-heart talk, or to have such a talk; chitchat.
Seder	"Order." Ceremony conducted in most Jewish homes on Passover, which recounts the telling of the story of the Exodus from Egypt.
Seudat havra'ah	First meal after the funeral, considered the meal of condolence and healing. Traditionally includes eggs or other round foods symbolizing the cycles of life, death, and eternity. Because the primary obligation of the mourner is to do nothing for him/ herself (to be free to focus on grieving), it is considered a mitzvah (commandment) for people to provide the mourners with food, reminding them that others care.
Shabbat (Sabbath)	Seventh day of the week, the day of rest, lasting from sundown on Friday to sundown on Saturday.
Shacharit	Daily morning service.
Shammos	"Helper" or "servant." Caretaker of the synagogue. In the old country, the shammos kept the synagogue clean, called members to prayer, announced sunset and Sabbath times, collected dues, and organized the minyan. Today, it is synonymous with *gabbai*. The term also refers to the candle that is lit first and then used to light the other candles in the chanukiah.
Shavuot	"Weeks." One of three pilgrimage festivals (with Sukkot and Passover); originally an agricultural festival representing the harvest of the wheat, Shavuot is the final day of the forty-nine-day period called the Counting of the Omer. It is also the anniversary of Moses receiving the Torah on Mount Sinai.

Sheitel	"Wig." Hair on a married woman is considered comparable to exposure, and in some Orthodox marriages, women wear a wig to cover their natural hair.
Shiva	"Seven." Period following burial when mourners withdraw from the world. "Sitting shiva" lasts for a week because the world was created in seven days, and each person is considered as a world. Customs for shiva include covering mirrors, sitting on low stools or benches (symbolizing the mourner's lowered emotional state), reducing personal grooming, burning a seven-day candle, and focusing on the deceased.
Shul	Yiddish term for the Jewish house of worship and study. It originates from the German word for "school" (*schule*)—one of the three primary roles of a synagogue. The others being prayer and assembly. This word is often used synonymously with the word *synagogue*.
Siddur	"Order." From the same root as *seder*. A prayer book for weekdays and Sabbath.
Siddurim	Plural of *siddur*.
Simcha	"Rejoicing." A happy occasion; a celebration.
Sukkah	Temporary dwelling made to provide shelter for farmers gathering the harvest so they could remain in the fields. It is a mitzvah to build a temporary dwelling in which to eat and sleep during Sukkot, to remind us of those built by our forefathers during the harvest period.
Sukkot	"Feast of booths." Sukkot, the fruit harvest, occurs five days after Yom Kippur and is the last of the three pilgrimage festivals (with Passover and Shavuot). Its significance is mentioned in Exodus 34:22 and Leviticus 23:42–43.
Synagogue	Jewish house of worship. Also called a shul or temple, it holds consecrated spaces for prayer, study, and assembly.

Tallit	Rectangular prayer shawl with a fringe (tzitzit) or tassel on each of the four corners, worn during morning prayers and on Kol Nidre (the eve of Yom Kippur). It is a tradition to bury a Jewish person with his or her tallit. Wrapping ourselves in the tallit aids in attaining a mood of reverence for God and a prayerful spirit during worship. It is written: "The Lord spoke to Moses, saying: Speak to the children of Israel and bid them to make for themselves fringes [tzitzit] on the corners of their garments throughout the generations . . . look at them and recall all the commandments of the Lord and observe them." (Numbers 15:37–40.)
Talmud	Rabbinic commentary that explains and interprets the teachings of the Torah, compiled between 200 BCE and 500 CE. It provides guidelines by which a Jewish person should live.
Tefillin	Small black leather cases containing passages from the Bible, fixed to the head and arms with black leather straps, worn during weekday morning services as a reminder of God's presence and commandments. Instructions for donning tefillin are found twice in Exodus and twice in Deuteronomy.
Tikkun olam	Refers to acts of kindness performed to perfect or repair the world.
Torah	First five books of the Jewish Bible; also considered the body of Jewish teaching.
Tzedakah	"Compassionate justice." Refers to the mitzvah of giving assistance and money to the needy; considered acts of equity. It is often considered synonymous with *charity*. The Torah legislates tzedakah in numerous places.
Tzitzit	"Fringe." Refers to the fringes on the four corners of the tallit. The tzitzit typically consists of five knots and thirty-nine wrappings and must be made of wool (or the same fabric as the tallit). The white of the tzitzit represents purity. "Make . . . fringes on the corners of your garments throughout the ages . . ." (Numbers 15:38.)
Unveiling	Historically, a ceremony when tombstones were placed at the burial site. In contemporary times, the gravestone is often in place before its official dedication, and a cloth, veil, or handkerchief is placed over the stone. At the ceremony, the cloth is removed, symbolizing the erection of the tombstone, and the inscription is "unveiled."
	The ceremony at a cemetery to dedicate the grave marker is customarily held between the end of shiva and the first Yahrzeit.

Yahrzeit	Anniversary of the date of death (according to the Jewish calendar). The day is marked by burning a memorial candle and reciting Kaddish.
Yahrzeit candle	Memorial candle lit in memory of the deceased. It is lit on the Yahrzeit and on the four holidays that include a Yizkor service—Yom Kippur and the last days of Passover, Shavuot, and Sukkot.
Yarmulke	See *kippah*.
Yasher Koach	"May you grow in strength." Expression given to a worshipper who has received a Torah honor. Performing an aliyah requires knowledge and understanding. The mental concentration expended is perceived as robbing an individual of his/her strength. Following the performance of an aliyah, the individual is wished continued and increased strength so he/she can perform additional mitzvot in the future.
Yizkor	"Remember." Memorial service held on Yom Kippur and on the final days of Passover, Shavuot, and Sukkot. Its primary purpose is to remember the deceased by giving tzedakah (charity) and performing good deeds to elevate the souls of the departed. As the Torah reading on the last day of each of the pilgrimage festivals mentions the importance of giving charity, Yizkor was added to these holiday services.
Yom Kippur	"Day of Atonement." Coming ten days after Rosh Hashanah, it is the second of the High Holidays and the holiest day of the Jewish year.

NOTES

i Jack Riemer, ed., *Jewish Reflections on Death* [New York: Shocken Books, 1974], 178.

ii The biblical source for the requirement of ten men to complete a minyan is Numbers 14:27. Moses sent spies to scout the land of Canaan. Ten of them returned and issued a negative report. God referred to the ten men as an "assembly." From here it is deduced that an assembly is composed of ten men. In Leviticus 22:32, God says, "I shall be sanctified amidst the children of Israel." This verse, in combination with another verse, Numbers 16:21, teaches that an "assembly" must be present when God is being sanctified.

iii Leon Wieseltier, *Kaddish* [New York: Avon Books, 1982], 178.

iv Ibid., 185.

v Ibid., 187.

vi Ibid., 189–90.

vii Jules Harlow, ed., *Siddur Sim Shalom: A Prayerbook for Shabbat, Festivals and Weekdays* [New York: United Synagogue of America, 1985], 25.

viii Ibid., 789.

ix Central Conference of American Rabbis, *Gates of Prayer* [New York: CCAR Press, 1993], 7.

x The Rabbinical Assembly, *Siddur Sim Shalom for Weekdays* [New York: United Synagogue of Conservative Judaism, 2002], 69.

xi Harlow, *Siddur Sim Shalom*, 121.

xii Wieseltier, *Kaddish*, 187.

ACKNOWLEDGMENTS

I have been blessed by the support of many people on my long and winding path to this memoir. Much gratitude goes to my agent, Barbara Krasner, for believing in the importance of my story when few others did.

To my brilliant and patient editor, Allison Serrell, and copy editor, Sydney Radclyffe, goes my endless appreciation for strengthening my story and showing me how much I needed them. When I describe to friends the ways in which Allison has enhanced this memoir, they say, "She sounds like the perfect editor for you." To which I always answer, "She is." To Maggie Langrick and the entire staff of Wonderwell: for getting this book to market, I am eternally grateful.

Through the years that I worked on this memoir, several writing coaches offered me sage critiques, for which I am much obliged. I take my hat off to Victoria Barrett, Nancy Evans, Thomas Larson, Tanya Martin, Jordan Rosenfeld, and David Taylor.

Since I started writing this memoir, I've attended workshops, classes, writing retreats, and conferences too numerous to mention. To the many instructors and participants who offered feedback and taught me to "show, not tell," I send my gratitude.

It is my good fortune to live in close proximity to The Writer's Center in Bethesda, Maryland, where the faculty and staff are dedicated to encouraging and developing writers of all genres. I am a better writer thanks to the many instructors I had through the center. Two of my earliest instructors—Ellen Herbert and Dave Singleton—made me believe that I had a story worth writing. Their masterful and soft-handed feedback made this a stronger manuscript. I am indebted to two additional instructors from The Writer's Center—Lynn Auld Schwartz and Laura Oliver—who provided detailed developmental edits to my "I-think-it's-finally-finished" manuscript.

One of the greatest gifts to come out of The Writer's Center has been the ongoing writers' group that I've now been part of for more than a decade. This memoir would never have come to fruition if it hadn't been for the group members, both past and present. Jean Campbell, David Goodrich, Andrea Hansell, Darci Glass-Royal, Sherlyn Goldstein-Askwith, Leslie Lewis, and Silvia Spring never complained about seeing the same chapter again and again (with revisions based on their feedback, of course). Other earlier group members include Janna Bialek, Arch Campbell, Paul Carlson, Jane Oakley (of blessed memory), Bonnie Rich, and Molly Zemek. And a toast to Andy and Dave for keeping us together for so many years, even through COVID.

To my early beta readers, Sherry Askwith, Patricia Braun, Lisa Dailey, Chaim Lauer, Reeva Shaffer, and Lois Wolf—my heartfelt thanks. Your early support motivated and inspired me. Special shout-outs go to my sister Lois and my longtime friend, Chaim, for always making themselves available to clarify specific details, brainstorm wordings, and reread passages . . . multiple times.

Every writer needs cheerleaders—people that share the writer's excitement for their work and provide encouragement. I am blessed to have a number of such cheerleaders—particularly Deborah Bloch, Louise Davidson, and Carolyn Finney. Members of my book group who willingly read an early version of this memoir in 2010 and offered their insights include Sherry Askwith, Deborah Bloch, Louise Davidson, Darlene Levenson, Judy Tyson, and Marilyn Witkowski. And more recent book group members have joined the ranks of cheerleaders: Jean Campbell, Debby Goldberg, Judi Portugal, Barbara Schaffer, and Jo Shifrin. My life would be less fulfilled without my Heart Writer

Sisters—Kathi Gowsell, Dotty Joslyn, and Janine VanderWhitte—who have cheered me from afar.

I am grateful for the prepandemic Montgomery County Public Library system. I often wrote in the quiet rooms in my county libraries— particularly the recently remodeled Gaithersburg library, with its excellent lighting and free parking. I derived a powerful energy from being around others also engrossed in concentration, but having to close my computer and put away my notes and papers each time the library closed became a hassle. That's when I sought quiet retreats, away from the distractions of home, where I had unlimited space to spread out my notes and papers, and where I could work and sleep according to the timetable of the muse.

I have sequestered myself in three peaceful and tranquil places over the past decade, and three wonderful women have played a role in this part of my progress. I am thankful to Ginger Hankins, whose Cottage at Rockymarsh in Shepherdstown, West Virginia, was the best of every world. I had the entire secluded cottage to myself, including a kitchen and a writing room with a huge desk, and Ginger's accommodating hospitality was endearing. I spent many weeks writing and editing at the Loudoun Valley Manor in Waterford, Virginia, where the remarkable owner, Olga Cataldi, delighted me by calling me her "distinguished guest." During the pandemic, I was grateful to have the peace and quiet of an empty classroom at Glen Echo Park in Bethesda, Maryland, thanks to the generosity and openheartedness of Laura Doyle.

I encourage writers to find a quiet, remote location where you can leave all your materials out overnight, where you don't have to worry about cluttering your dining room table, and where peacefulness and tranquility can birth the muse. As an aside, Maya Angelou kept a hotel room in her town that she paid for by the month. She would arrive there at 6:30 a.m. and leave by about 2:00 p.m., never sleeping there.

The members of the Washington, DC, chapter of the Women's National Book Association has offered a community of stimulating women writers whose support and warmth have inspired me. High praise to Tabitha Whissemore for her ongoing leadership of the group.

I'm indebted to the editors of *Talking Writing* magazine and the *JOFA Journal,* a publication of the Jewish Orthodox Feminist Alliance, for publishing excerpts of this manuscript, and to the judges of the Soul-Making Keats Literary Competition, an outreach program of the National League of American Pen Women, for bestowing awards on five excerpted chapters of this memoir.

I could never have written this memoir without referring to my recorded experiences in the four journals I filled during my avelut (mourning period). Søren Kierkegaard wrote that life must be "lived forwards but understood backwards." My journals have given me that opportunity.

I would have been lost without the ongoing support, friendship, and creativity of Wendy Francis. If ever there was a woman with a can-do attitude, you are her. The words *thank you* can never suffice for all you have added to my life.

To my husband, Jake: you have my gratitude for your patience, understanding, and unyielding support of the time and space I needed to finish this manuscript. And for all the household chores, errands, and grandparent duties you undertook so I could write. I couldn't have done this without you. I love you as much today as I did the day you met me with two dozen roses in the parking lot of that Chinese restaurant.

Last but not least, I am grateful to the Almighty for the many blessings in my life and for always loving me, even when I couldn't give love in return.

ABOUT THE AUTHOR

Sarah Birnbach began her encore career as a nonfiction writer in 2016 after successful careers as a human resources management consultant and family therapist in a juvenile court. She was a sought-after motivational speaker at numerous industry conferences and has delivered more than five hundred presentations and workshops. Throughout her professional life, she dedicated herself to enabling individuals to become their best selves.

She has been journaling since she was a teen and her decades-long love of journaling led her to become one of the country's first certified journal facilitators—a designation from the Center for Journal Therapy. She has taught numerous journaling workshops and introduced journaling into her therapeutic work with families.

She is a six-time award winner in the Soul-Making Keats Literary Competition and a two-time award winner of *Bethesda Magazine*'s annual essay contest. Her articles have appeared in *Talking Writing, Bookwoman, JOFA Journal* (Jewish Orthodox Feminist Alliance), *Intima: A Journal of Narrative Medicine*, the *Michigan Jewish History Journal*, and *Pen in Hand*.

Her education includes a bachelor's degree in sociology from George Washington University, a master's degree in human resources from American University, and a master's degree in social work from the University of Maryland.

Sarah is a member of the Chevra Kadisha (Holy Fellowship)—women who perform the holy ritual of preparing a body for burial, midwifing the soul of the deceased from this world to the next.

Sarah recently retraced her father's footsteps on the front lines of World War II Germany and is at work on her next book, *In My Father's Footsteps*.

She lives outside Washington, DC, with her husband. In addition to indulging in chocolate, her passions include frequenting local bookstores, traveling, dancing, and being an active grandma to her seven grandchildren.